T

MW00680849

Shopping

Online

There are more than two hundred
Rough Guide travel, phrasebook and music titles,
covering destinations from Amsterdam to Zimbabwe,
languages from Czech to Vietnamese,
and musics from World to Opera and Jazz

www.roughguides.com

ROUGH
GUIDES

Credits

Text editor: Paul Simpson
Contributors: Victoria Williams, Helen Rodiss, Sue Weekes

Production: Sarah Carter, Ian Cranna, Caroline Hunt, Ann Oliver

Thanks to: Simon Kanter, Mark Ellingham,
Bob from US Customs, Elvis Presley's 1960s box set

Photographs: Tony Stone/Photonica

Publishing Information

This first edition published September 2001 was prepared by
Haymarket Customer Publishing for Rough Guides Ltd,
62–70 Shorts Gardens, London WC2H 9AH

Distributed by the Penguin Group

Penguin Books Ltd, 27 Wrights Lane, London W8 5TZ

Typeset in Adobe Clarendon and Helvetica
to an original design by Sarah Jane Voyce, Martin Tullett.
Printed in Spain by Graphy Cems.

A catalogue record for this book is available
from the British Library. ISBN 1-85828-767-7

The publishers and authors have done their best to ensure the
accuracy and currency of all the information in *The Rough Guide
to Shopping Online*, however, they can accept no responsibility
for any loss, injury or inconvenience sustained as a result of
information or advice contained in the guide.

CONTENTS

Part One: Basics

Part Two: The Directory

Contents

A few words to the wise...

Remember when using this guide that the Internet being the fast-moving, unpredictable and sometimes downright frustrating beast that it is, some of the sites, addresses and prices which are quoted here will have changed by the time you peruse it. As this book went to press (on one of the tightest schedules known to mankind) all the web addresses here actually worked and the recommendations made were accurate.

If the site you like has changed or, worse, died, we're sorry but there is nothing much we can do about it except to say that even so, with well over 1700 web addresses quoted and with specific guidance on where you can buy works of art made of old fruit crates, Napoleon XIV's seminal single *They're Coming To Take Me Away Ha Ha Hee hee!* and diet pet food for the too portly pooch you should still find this guide seriously useful.

Online shopping has a a reputation for being dodgier than Florida's old voting system but it doesn't entirely deserve the bad press as this book will show. Anyway, let us know how you get on by e-mailing the editor at paul.simpson@haynet.com.

Part one

The secrets of successful (and safe)
shopping over the World Wide Web

THE BASICS

Save money, save time, save your blushes...

ONLINE SHOPPING

Don't believe what you read in the papers. The Internet isn't about to revolutionise the way we have sex, but it is already revolutionising the way we shop, whether we're looking for a car, ordering groceries or just buying some new fridge magnets

Is the Internet shopping revolution all hype?

Not at all. Evidence suggests that of the 300 million total Net users, 120 million are buying stuff online, and more than half of all transactions were made in the good ol' US of A. And by "stuff" we mean anything from solar panels (***www.solar-panels-for-energy.com***) to a 10-acre island off Florida (***www.islandforsale.com***) or a classic car (through ***www.cars-on-line.com***). And in many cases – ie with the notable exception of that aforementioned Floridian paradise – it is now more than possible to save yourself money if you opt to buy over the Internet.

So how does online shopping work? Economically, it's supposed to be a very simple model. Traditional retailers invest millions in malls and countless sales staff in the belief, sadly not always vindicated, that you will drop in and buy something. **Freed from such financial shackles,** e-tailers, as they like to refer to themselves, only have to worry about taking your order on their website, ensuring they've got the item you want stored somewhere, and then organizing its delivery.

Some of the money saved by not having a bricks-and-mortar presence at the local mall can be passed on to you, the buyer. This is why so many online stores offer **savings of at least 20 per cent** over street prices. The added bonus for them is that people buying online spend more.

There is, of course, a catch to all this. For a start,

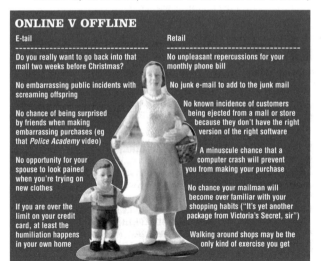

ONLINE V OFFLINE

E-tail	Retail
Do you really want to go back into that mall two weeks before Christmas?	No unpleasant repercussions for your monthly phone bill
No embarrassing public incidents with screaming offspring	No junk e-mail to add to the junk mail
No chance of being surprised by friends when making embarrassing purchases (eg that *Police Academy* video)	No known incidence of customers being ejected from a mall or store because they don't have the right version of the right software
No opportunity for your spouse to look pained when you're trying on new clothes	A minuscule chance that a computer crash will prevent you from making your purchase
If you are over the limit on your credit card, at least the humiliation happens in your own home	No chance your mailman will become over familiar with your shopping habits ("It's yet another package from Victoria's Secret, sir")
	Walking around shops may be the only kind of exercise you get

many online businesses soon realised that there was rather more to the mundane business of delivering a product than met the eye.

Online shops also discovered that, although they were making savings on logistics and staffing, they needed to invest between 60 per cent and 83 per cent of their earnings in marketing themselves, a level of spending which would prove ruinous in the long term. There is also evidence that online shoppers are even less loyal than regular shoppers although, once again, no one can say if this will still be true in 5 years' time.

125 million Americans now have Internet access

So is the online shopping revolution stuffed? No, because even the most pessimistic forecasters predict that 5 per cent of our shopping will be done via the Net by the end of this decade. About **125 million Americans now have Internet access**, and 80 per cent of those have already shopped online with **annual spending between $30 billion and $45 billion**, depending on which survey you believe.

Sadly for those who prefer to see the Internet through the eyes of the *Weekly World News* ("Click here to **buy an autographed JFK photo** – signed seven years after he faked his down death!") it is actually very hard to buy ballistic missiles, human kidneys or illegal drugs over the Net. It is, alas, all too easy to buy the greatest hits of Brotherhood of Man. And that ultimately is what online shopping is all about: giving you **freedom of choice**, which is one of the things capitalism was supposed to guarantee but, in an increasingly monopolistic age, has found it too often uneconomic to do so.

Welcome to a world where you can...

SHOP TILL YOU DROP

Online shopping needn't be technically arduous, financially hazardous or even unduly time-consuming as long as you abide by a few simple principles. This chapter is designed to explain the ins and outs, dos and don'ts, ifs and buts, etc, for beginners

How to buy over the Internet

Let's assume, for the sake of argument, that you want to buy a copy of Leonard Nimoy's seminal album *Highly Illogical*, a must-have for every connoisseur of truly bad singing. Composed, in unequal parts, of songs sung in character as the first science officer of the USS Enterprise and his own versions of such standards as *If I Had A Hammer*, these recordings explain why his post-Enterprise career as a cabaret artiste was so shortlived.

There are two ways to proceed. You can key Leonard Nimoy into the shopping part of a general search engine like Yahoo and see what comes up, or you can go straight to a specific site like Amazon which you suspect may stock the goods you're after. The advantage of going to a

The basics

specific site is that you might feel much safer dealing with a company known to you, or recommended by a friend, or by one of the multitude of Internet magazines, or indeed by a convenient little guide like this.

Log on to your online shop

For the purposes of illustration, log on to your favourite browser and key ***www.amazon.com*** into the address bar. In the time it takes to say "Live long and prosper" your screen should fill up with a page which says **"Welcome to Amazon.com"**. Like most such pages, Amazon bombards you with a bewildering array of apparent bargains designed to tempt the online shopper who wants to buy something but isn't sure what. Be single-minded and go to the box next to the search button (top left) and key in **Leonard Nimoy**. As you know you want a CD, not one of his vulcanised volumes of memoirs, you can change the **"all products"** strap to **"music"** to save time and click on **"Go"**.

You are then presented with a choice of four items, only one of which is the real thing and two of which are inferior versions with the "bonus" of including even more

If it's an entrée into the world of online shopping you're after, you could do a lot worse than start at the Amazon.com homepage

Searching under Leonard Nimoy means you could find a gem or two other than the one you're after – like Nimoy and William Shatner in tandem...

embarrassing performances by William Shatner, plus a collaborative effort with, er, whales. The price, $25.99, does not include shipping (that comes later). The delivery time, between 1 and 2 weeks, is not bad for such an obscure artefact of popular culture. More mainstream stuff should arrive within 3-7 days.

Often a product will be accompanied by a customer's review but you should bear in mind that these may well be written by true devotees, people with an axe to grind or people for whom penning reviews on such sites is their nearest brush with fame.

So now you've found what you want...

Sometimes you can inspect the product in closer detail (by seeing a track listing or a larger photo of the cover). If you're buying a book, you will usually get a paragraph-long synopsis. To buy Nimoy's finest hour, click on the **"add to shopping cart"** button which will say you have one item in your cart, costing $25.99, and gives you a chance to order more than one copy.

Click on **"proceed to checkout"** and you will then be

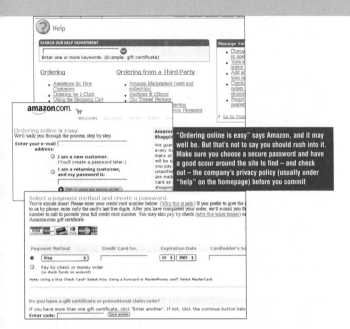

"Ordering online is easy" says Amazon, and it may well be. But that's not to say you should rush into it. Make sure you choose a secure password and have a good scour around the site to find – and check out – the company's privacy policy (usually under "help" on the homepage) before you commit

asked whether you're a new customer or not. If you are, clicking on the right button takes you to a form which asks for the usual details (name, address, e-mail, etc).

It's at this point that new online shoppers may have a few qualms about handing over this information, wondering just what else this personal data might be used for. Most reputable online stores have a button at the foot of the page marked something like **"Privacy notice"**. If you click on this you should find a statement which will explain what information they need, why, what they use it for, how they protect this data, and whether this information will be given to anyone else. (For more detailed info on these issues see chapter 3.) But if a site does not have such a policy then you should only buy an item if it really is not available anywhere else.

What happens if things go wrong?

While you're checking out the online store it's probably worth examining their policies on returns, refunds and delivery. Some, like Amazon, have a "no quibble" guarantee which states that if you are unhappy for any reason and can be bothered to wrap up the goods that you've bought and send them back, they'll refund the purchase price. These policies may be buried beneath a **"help"** button situated on the homepage but too often a casual browse will fail to reveal any obvious policy on these mundane but vital issues, in which case e-mail or phone the company concerned for the lowdown.

After filling in all the correct fields you will be invited to enter a password and re-enter it. Best practise is to use a unique word which has personal significance so your memory won't need jogging, throw in a couple of numbers if you can be bothered, and use this all the time.

Having read the privacy policy (and chapter 5 of this guide) you should feel confident enough to enter your credit or debit card details and click **"continue"**. Most online stores let you key in your details on what is known as a **"secure server"**. With the almost daily reports of hackers pillaging the Pentagon's database, you may be wondering if "secure server" is an oxymoron. Suffice to say these services wrap an extra layer of code around your confidential details to protect them (for more on this see chapter 3).

You can pay by check, but Amazon says this delays orders by 7-10 days. Alternatively you can just enter the last five digits of your card number and the

Only buy from a site with no privacy policy if you can't go anywhere else

expiry date, on the site, and phone up to give the rest of your number. Some companies have experimented with a separate pin number so financial details do not have to be given out over the Net.

Let's assume you go for the full online shopping experience and hit that **"continue"** button. You are then invited to confirm your address and delivery method. Many online shoppers like to have stuff delivered to work rather than find a card telling them they have a parcel at a local sorting office which can't be found without the purchase of a local map, but it depends on how much trust you place in your company's mailroom.

You're only a few clicks away now

If you order more than one item you will be offered the choice to have them all delivered at once (cheaper, but can you wait that long?) or have them delivered individually (more expensive but faster and you help the mailman's campaign to save his back). Another click and you get to confirm your debit or credit card number and then you are presented with the electronic

Your order is not complete until you click here: ▶ Place Your Order

Purchase Summary

Invoice Address: To be paid by Credit or Debit Card
paul simpson   Details: £330
41 gaston way   Expiry Date: 04/?00?
shepperton middlesex TW17 8EZ   [edit]
United Kingdom
[edit]

Purchase Details

Order #1: paul simpson

1 paul simpson   Subtotal of Items   £15.76
41 gaston way   Gift wrap   £0.00
shepperton middlesex TW17 8EZ Postage & Packing   £3.54
United Kingdom   Promotional Gift Certificates -£0.00

                              Total Before VAT   £19.10
Dispatch method: First Class Vat   £0.00
Dispatch Preference: Dispatch this order when complete
[edit]   Total   £19.10
                              Gift Certificate: -£0.00
Order Items
                              Total for this Address: £19.10

Just time for a last-minute count-up – hoping that you haven't busted your budget – before setting the whole process in motion

"invoice" which tells you how much you have to pay for shipping. (Some sites deliver for free but you usually find "free shipping" is reflected in the purchase price.)

You are now just a click away from doing something which will mean dollars and cents disappear from your account. Time to take stock and decide if you are that keen on Nimoy. If you are and click on **"place your order"** a "mean that most sincerely" thank you page will pop up.

You may want to print out a copy of what you have ordered. Some online stores (and Amazon does this) e-mail confirmation of your order and tell you when they've got around to sticking the item(s) in the mail. Within 2 weeks, you should hear that soon-to-be-familiar scraping noise as the mailman tries to squeeze the cardboard-wrapped CD through your spatially challenged mailbox.

If not, most reputable online sellers have some kind of button (usually marked **"Your account"**) which you can click on to check what's happening to your order. On some sites, however, **"Your account"** buttons simply tell you, on inspection, that your order is in progress.

Buying on the Internet really is (almost) that easy and, despite all the scare stories, only a tiny percentage of online shoppers find that, having disclosed their financial information to a respectable online store, their bank accounts are mysteriously depleted of large sums which are subsequently traced to international drug syndicates.

Sometimes it's not as easy as it looks...

So why is Internet shopping only "almost" that simple? Partly because many online stores have very different user interfaces. The late, unlamented (except by people who worked there or invested in it) **Boo.com** had the kind of user interface which gave visitors a headache and feelings of deep technological inferiority. Even mainstream sites demand you download a certain software package to make the most of their virtual shelves.

First-time shoppers can get lost in the process. While buying a CD from Amazon is pretty straightforward, buying your week's groceries can take up to an hour the first time and that's if your computer doesn't crash. Even on well-tried sites like Amazon, if you click **"back"** to look at the preceding page, you sometimes get a page popping up with the intriguing headline **"Browser bug?"** Usually it's easy to get back on track but nervous buyers might get lost.

SO WHAT ARE PEOPLE BUYING ONLINE?

Don't believe all you read in the press. Online shopping is still growing despite the "dot bomb" hype. Those c onsummate pollsters Harris and Nielsen reckon more than 100 million Americans have now bought online, so 4 out of every 5 web users have bought something off the Net.

Time was, that people mostly bought safe items like books and CDs but last March $368 million was spent online on clothes and $1 billion spent on travel.

...especially the delivery part

Then there's the delivery, which is where online shopping too often goes wrong. Last Christmas the press was full of sob stories about online shoppers who didn't get what they'd ordered when they'd been promised they would. Indeed, the US government went so far as to fine seven US e-tailers for late delivery and several irate customers even took out a class action suit against Toys R Us for spoiling their Christmas.

When Mick Jagger famously belted out "you can't always get what you want", he almost certainly wasn't thinking of online shopping, but that sentiment is certainly applicable.

Even apparently reputable e-tailers have been known to send the wrong CD in a box with a fat "postage due" sticker planted erroneously on it. And yet surveys continue to show that 7 out of every 10 online shoppers are satisfied with the service they get, the most conclusive result since Whiskas first consulted cats.

The right product, the right price

For simplicity's sake, the purchase of Leonard Nimoy's CD was followed through just one site. In reality, once you'd found Amazon had the product and the price ($25.99) you might be tempted to see if you could find it cheaper elsewhere. So let's type in **www.yahoo.com** and click on the word **"shopping"** just below the slit where you normally type whatever you're trying to find.

Up comes a natty little page snappily captioned **"Welcome, Guest"** and, in the search box just below, you type in those mesmerising words **leonard+nimoy** and, lo and behold, you discover there are 199 products associated with the pointy-eared personage, available from 15 stores.

One of them is another collection of Nimoy's greatest hits which may only cost $15-16. Upon further inspection you see that you can buy it from a company called **cd world**, which has a full array of delivery rates, along with the warning that they are having problems with first and fourth class mail, so either you spend almost half as much as the price of the CD for UPS or Federal Express, or wait until your next trip downtown.

This experience has not been totally in vain, however. New though you are, you have realised that although online shopping is usually an intensely exhilarating experience, it can also be as frustrating as those January sales where you spend hours flicking through racks of CDs marked down to $9.99 only to discover that they have cut the price of every **Talking Heads** album apart from the one you haven't got.

And finally, a few words of advice...

Be organized. If you just surf hopefully in the belief that you'll stumble onto the right present for dad's birthday, you could drown in cyberspace. Generally the more specific you are about what you want to buy, the faster, and more pleasurable, shopping online will be.

Set a budget. Virtual shopping still uses real money but somehow it doesn't feel as financially painful when you just click a button on your computer screen. Sticking to a budget is particularly vital if you are buying through an online auction (see chapter 4).

Consider using your credit card. If you do use a credit card your consumer rights will be protected, as Visa points out in its round-up of handy hints (***www.visa. com/nt/ecomm/consumer/main.html#tips***), although obviously it could work out being more expensive if you don't instantly pay off the $600 you lavished on that rare F Scott Fitzgerald book *The Vegetable: Or, From President to Postman*.

Don't rush. Online shopping still takes time, especially if you're looking for something rare, so check delivery times and don't leave it to the last possible minute.

Trust your instincts. If you don't feel comfortable buying, back off. According to The Internet Fraud Watch (***www.fraud.org/internet/intset.htm***), high-pressure sales tactics are often a sign that there is something fishy going on.

You may find these sites of help:

http://uk.kelkoo.com helps you compare prices before you buy.

www.bizrate.com rates companies in the online shopping business, comparing different sites' price/delivery details on the same product.

www.consumerworld.org is big and brash and has everything from product reviews to the news that 76 per cent of e-mail response systems at 1,000 e-commerce operators failed to, er, respond to e-mails.

www.zdnet.com/pcmag/features/e-comm_sites/sb2.htm "Shop safely in unknown corners" is this site's boast and it almost lives up to that promise with tips for online shopping and a selection of "legitimate" sites.

**How to shop online
and not feel paranoid**

SAFE AS HOUSES

"'d like to go shopping online but..." The "but" in that sentence invariably refers to a fear that shopping over the Internet is likely to expose you to all sorts of frauds, scams and cybercrimes, many of which you may not even be aware of. With online bank accounts appearing to be about as private as the post-gym lesson shower in your schooldays, and daily headlines about a global epidemic of cyberfraud, shopping over the Internet seems fraught with unacceptable risk. In truth, there's no conclusive proof that online shoppers are more likely to be the victim of fraud than those who do their shopping offline

If it's so safe why do I read so many scare stories?

The Federal Trade Commission says: "There's a general public concern about transmitting credit card numbers over the Internet which is not well-founded. All in all, it's much riskier to give your credit card to a waiter or waitress than it is to send it over the Internet." Many reports of online credit fraud actually relate to breaches of security in offline databases. That said, there is a risk, but you can reduce your chances of becoming a victim.

What are firewalls?

At its simplest, a firewall is a cyberforce which protects corporate IT networks from external communications systems such as the Internet. Often the firewall will be a physical computer with a couple of network interface cards: it will check every packet of data going between the internal and external network and reject those it is programmed to consider inappropriate. You need to be aware of this if you're buying from work, because some **corporate firewalls can actually prevent your order** from being processed without you realising.

If a site has US in its address, can I assume that it is an American company?

No. Which is why you're better off checking their physical location (or "snail mail" address) to be sure.

Any other general advice?

Beware of sites/e-mail offers which use too many exclamation marks and capital letters for NO APPARENT REASON, promise "secrets of success", have ludicrous testimonials from customers defined only as "Mrs S, Canada" and start their sales pitch with the protest-too-much headline "This is not a scam!" Also, guard your **"shopping carts"**. Some sites stick stuff in them when you click for more info while others wouldn't let you pull items at the last minute.

Some sites now greet you by name if you have ordered from them before. If you do place an order, and you share your terminal or use a public one, be sure to **"log out"** of that site after you have completed the transaction. Otherwise the next user of that terminal could mistakenly order items with your credit card details (though at least the items will be sent to you).

Security guards

www.ftc.gov/bcp/conline/pubs/online/sitesee/index.html is the Janet-and-John guide to surfing for the ultimate newbie from those nice folks in the federal government. Also check out ***www.safeshopping.org*** from the American Bar Association.

www.scambusters.com does exactly what it says on the web address but be warned – it may make you paranoid. ***http://privacy.net*** covers similar territory – and will leave you even more paranoid.

www.web-police.org is Interpol's electronic arm, which comes complete with a comedy western sheriff's badge, a string of Java error messages and, 7 out of 10 times, a crash to your terminal.

The government takes would-be surfers gently by the hand and leads them into the vastness of cyberspace

You can take precautions...

1 **When you visit a site, check how secure it is**. Sites which are encrypted may have an address which begins **"https"** (the extra "s" indicates the site is using a bit of technical know-how called Secure Sockets Layer to encode your data).

If you're using either Internet Explorer or Netscape Communicator, a secure site should have a little golden padlock at the bottom of your screen. (But remember that this lock may only appear when you enter the part of the site where you actually buy something.) In Netscape version 4.6 onwards, there is a security button on the toolbar next to **"Print"** which, if you click on it, will tell you whether the site you're on uses encryption.

If you're still uncertain, check their web address with a service like **_www.enonymous.com_** which will tell you, for instance, if the online store you're visiting will give out your data to other companies.

2 **Don't use a simple password** when registering on a site. Dates of birth, mothers' maiden names, etc, can easily be guessed. Try something more obscure (mixing letters and numbers is one idea) which you can still easily remember. If you're really worried about still being too obvious, use complex passwords and store them in a software program like Password Keeper (**_www. gregorybraun.com/PassKeep.html_**) which will cost you $20. Or you could surf the Web anonymously with free trial software from **_www.anonymizer.com_**.

3 **Don't buy anything you hear about in junk e-mail**. According to those awfully vigilant people at Internet ScamBusters (**_www.scambusters.com_**), your chances of getting anything at all from such a source are less than 45 per cent and your chances of actually getting what you ordered are a statistically unimpressive 1 in 20. Also, take care if a seller is using a free e-mail service. While most people using these services are as honest as the 21st of June is long, these services make it easier for a seller to hide their real identity.

4 **Use a credit card**. It limits your liability if you're ripped off. Visa, for example, guarantees you against any fraudulent use of your card providing you haven't done anything seriously daft like send your card number and expiry date to all your e-mail contacts. For teenage shoppers, check out the CobaltCard and Visa Buxx, which help to limit spending.

5 **Don't buy anything from a website which doesn't have a physical location**. If that physical address begins and end with a PO Box number, consider moving on. Similarly, if a person you're buying from at an auction won't give you their real name, address and phone number, take your business elsewhere.

6 **Buy branded names from known sources**. One estimate suggests that between 10 per cent and 20 per cent of luxury goods sites are selling fakes. Sites such as **_www.epublic eye.com_** are useful in such cases because they offer online shopping with "reliable" companies only.

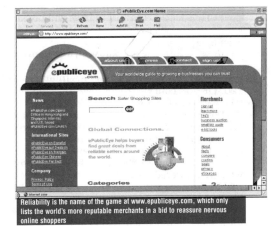

Reliability is the name of the game at www.epubliceye.com, which only lists the world's more reputable merchants in a bid to reassure nervous online shoppers

7 **Save copies of every e-mail** and document related to your purchase. It might just help you get some redress if you're ripped off.

8 **Check every little detail**. Bargain headline prices may be offset by ludicrous shipping costs, especially if you want the item delivered yesterday. On the plus side, some e-tailers will have goodwill policies which mean they'll refund your shipping fees if you're not happy for any reason.

9 **Be careful with personal info**. We're probably all just about smart enough not to stick a Post-It with our passwords onto our keyboard, but don't give out any other info about yourself (addresses etc) unless on a secure site.

10 **Remember: if you do decide to buy from an individual**, your rights of redress will probably not be as good as if you had bought the item from a company.

11 **Know your software**. Both Explorer and Communicator have devices which can help you to shop more safely. For example, in the way most Internet users have their browsers set up, their name and e-mail address are available to every website they happen to visit.

12 **Look out for cyber-wallet** and other similar systems which ease the process of buying and paying online. iPIN at ***www.ipin.com***, for instance, allows you to buy at an iPIN-supported site and the goods can be put on your monthly ISP bill.

Auctions are for everybody, not just Noel Barrett or Lovejoy

GOING
GOING, GONE

Auctions are no longer the preserve of art collectors or dealers in dodgy motors. The current glut of auction sites allows folk all over the world to recycle their stuff. That is not to say that online auctions are problem-free but the more way-out rumours about desperate people selling their kidneys for transplant or buying nuclear weapons from the former USSR are unfounded

Know the ground rules

Even if someone were trying to offload their internal organs to the highest bidder, reputable auction sites are pretty strict about what they will accept as a lot. They are subject to the same laws as any offline retailer about what they can sell, although individuals who sell through the sites are not governed by consumer laws, which can lead to problems for the buyer (see *How Not To Get Conned*, p29). But sellers who try to break the rules will find their auction accounts terminated and very possibly replaced by an intimate tête-à-tête with the local law enforcers.

That's not to say that you won't still find some bizarre and compelling items. If you missed your chance in 1981, you can now pick up a Charles & Diana Commemorative Wedding Coin for a very reasonable price. Others may decide they must have a 1914 edition of *Golf Monthly*. Where caution is required is the urge to possess any number of strange items that will end up collecting dust until you finally get around to auctioning them yourself.

How auctions work

Most online auction sites, whether they offer general or specialist merchandise, work the same way. On general sites, like ***www.aaands.com*** or ***www. auctionus.com***, the offerings are broken down first into rough categories such as computer hardware or household goods, with further sub-categories appearing as you progress through the site. There are usually featured auctions on the home page, as well as on the main page for each category, but these are not necessarily the best bargains on the site – the sellers probably paid for their lots in order to get some extra publicity.

Auction sites are free to buyers. They make their money by charging sellers small fees to list an item, and another fee if a sale is successful. On specialist auction sites it helps to know exactly what you are looking for, or to be very careful in assessing what's on offer.

A computer package may seem like an extraordinary deal, but look closely and you may find that it comes minus small details, like a monitor. This may not worry you, but if you were looking for a ready-to-plug-in PC, it's not the deal for you.

If you are just surfing auction sites to see if anything appeals to you, you don't need to register on most sites. But once you decide to buy or sell, you will have to register to show that you are a real person and can be contacted if there's a subsequent dispute.

Private sellers usually have to provide more information on themselves than the buyers do, including credit card details. And after a number of online shouting matches and disputes about

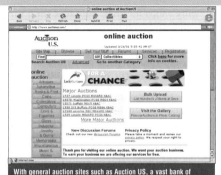

With general auction sites such as Auction US, a vast bank of categories provide a starting point whatever you're looking for

deals that didn't go through or goods that never turned up, some sites now insist that you provide an e-mail address that is registered either at your home or place of work (a Hotmail address that can be run from a cyber café is much too worryingly anonymous).

The art of selling

Once you have decided which site will benefit from the contents of your attic, you need to list your item as a lot on the site. The first things you will be asked for are fairly obvious – a title for your lot, a brief, accurate but attention-grabbing description, and a starting price.

After that it can get a little more complicated. You will have the option to upload a picture of your item, and to put a reserve amount on your lot. So if your rollerblades cost you $150 and a broken wrist, and you don't want to sell them for less than half of what you paid, a good trick is to make the starting price very low to attract attention, but then place a reserve price of $75 on them.

Some sites discourage reserve prices, which they say make a sale less likely. This is true, but their concern is really more for their sale fees than for your profit. Other decisions to make include: the duration of the auction, who pays for shipping (almost always the buyer), and what forms of payment you will accept. It is also vital to let potential buyers know a little bit about yourself in order to allay fears that you might be a criminal.

If someone wins your auction and is now looking forward to breaking bones of their own, you are legally obliged to sell the rollerblades to them. The auction site will forward you details of who has won the bidding and it is up to you to arrange payment and delivery.

The art of buying

Before you do anything, remind yourself that any bid you place is a binding contract and if you win the lot, you cannot change your mind – so don't bid for anything just for a laugh or that stuffed badger could be yours.

Make all the checks you want (see *How Not To Get Conned* opposite) and if everything looks good, the best and most efficient way to proceed is to decide the most you are prepared to pay, and then ask the site to bid on your behalf up to that amount. If no one bids above you, and the reserve has been met, the blades are yours, hopefully below your top price. If someone outbids your maximum, the site will notify you to see if you want to bid again. This is when auction fever can set in. Don't fall into the "oh, it's only another 20 bucks" trap. Go and make a cup of coffee. Then rush back, throw caution to the wind and bid like crazy until they're yours. You know you're going to, at least once.

Don't make a bid just for a laugh or that stuffed badger could be yours

Once you have fought off the other contenders, the seller will contact you to let you know the final price of the rollerblades, including their shipping cost. Think about this extra expense before you make your final bid.

HOW NOT TO GET CONNED

According to The National Fraud Information Center *(www.fraud.com)*, 87 per cent of Internet fraud last year was on auction sites. This is no surprise. Auctions are like tag sales with the added thrill of not knowing if the goods will even turn up. Placing a lot for sale, or bidding, is in theory a binding contract but in practice is unlikely to be worth the effort and cost to enforce it. The big sites have introduced tighter security, but you can reduce the risks.

Start small. It's not the end of the world if you lose $10 on something that turns out to be dodgy.

Try to buy only from rated sellers. You can check out other buyers' experiences with sellers in the feedback section of the site. See if the seller is a regular on the site's message boards and is open about what they're selling.

Buying from the auction site or a registered company using the site as a sales tool is a lot safer than buying from an individual. Most consumer protection laws don't deal with private sales, so disputes could be hard to settle.

If you do buy from an individual get an address and other identifying information before sending money. If buying from a company or the auction site, check details of returns, warranties and service if the product is faulty. Ask that higher priced items are insured in transit.

Be aware that some sellers get friends (shills) to bid on items to raise the price artificially. Don't always rush to bid back on an item you want (unless the auction is about to close). This will reveal how keen you are to win the lot.

Pay by the safest way you can. If possible, pay by credit card (more and more sites are offering individuals a way to accept credit card payments); then you can dispute the charges if the goods are misrepresented or never arrive.

Tell the auction site if you come across dodgy dealings, as the site can (and will) investigate on your behalf.

Remember the golden rule of auctions – if it sounds too good to be true, it probably is.

General auctions Something for everyone

Auction One

www.auction1online.com

Not one of the big boys but Auction One remains a competent auction site. Search by category, covering everything from gourmet coffee to Beanie Babies, to view detailed descriptions and images. Thankfully less complicated to participate in than the more seasoned sites, there are no charges for buying and only 1 per cent will be deducted from your account if you're a seller, on the provision that the sale is successful.

Auction Warehouse

www.auction-warehouse.com

Though the Auction Warehouse does appear to be branching out into more household and personal items, it is still one of the better options for computer goods and peripherals. All auctions end on either a Monday or a Thursday, making it easier to keep track, and there are multiple numbers of many of the smaller items so there's less chance you'll be pipped to the post.

Boxlot

www.boxlot.com

This comprehensive site offers all the usual categories, but can be slightly tiresome to search with no sub-categories to narrow down your search. Registration and listing an item is free, although a prime spot on the homepage as a featured lot will set you back $12.95. Pictures and additional information about each lot is limited but top bargains include worldwide airline tickets – bidding starting at $29.99 – and a desktop PC for less than $300.

Ebay

www.ebay.com

The first (and still one of the biggest) auction sites with items ranging from N-Sync concert tickets to Palm Springs timeshares. The homepage looks hectic but there is lots of info about each lot and lively message boards. It's free to buyers but for sellers there is a complex fee structure – check before deciding what to list. On each sale there's an insertion fee (between 30 cents and $3.30) plus a final value fee based on a percentage of the sale price. There's also a fee to put a reserve on your item (refundable if it doesn't sell).

First Auction

www.firstauction.com

The homepage, complete with spring flowers, could be deemed quite cutesy but First Auction is perfect for first-timers as most lots are goods you'd inevitably end up buying from somewhere, so why not make it all a bit more fun. If your wife-to-be can hang on for a few days, you may not have to spend an entire month's wages on that diamond she had her

Ebay was one of the first and is still one of the biggest: great for buyers, a bit more complicated for sellers

eye on. And for you, how about a steak dinner party pack, bids from $9?

Popula

www.popula.com

The price of kitsch items can vary wildly but at Popula you can set your own price for those must-have Betty Boop and Mr T nodder toys, and vintage evening gowns for a true slice of Hollywood glamour. Prices start low, and the handy hints and tips are useful to get you started.

Yahoo Auctions

auctions.yahoo.com

Plenty to browse through and easy to find your way around. It's free to place bids and list lots on this site, though they do insist on holding any seller's credit card details for security purposes. Buyers are only allowed to bid on a few items at a time until they have some positive feedback from a seller. The better their rating, the more lots they can bid on.

321 Gone

www.321Gone.com

Bright and inviting, particularly to the auction novice, and items are generally cheap. Categories include household goods, toys and books. Descriptions and images are available but the product pages can be confusing with multiple key codes. The best and most unusual selections include the Dot-com name "DVDGiveaways.com" for $100 and a Coke glass for $2.

Specialist auctions — Something in particular

Art
www.sothebys.com
Get ready to add a lot of noughts to your usual auction maximum. See also
www.phillips-auctions.com and www.christies.com or, for something a
little less highbrow, www.posterauction.com.

Business Equipment
www.salvagesale.com
Outstanding site for surplus and salvaged business goods for buyers and
sellers. Bidding is simple and speedy. See also www.equipmentstore.com.

Cars
www.paradia.com
Search according to price or simply for your favourite Dodge or Ford model.
Images, descriptions, reasons for sale and spec sheets are all available.

Collectibles
www.goldnage.com
Quality antiques, art and jewelry, from Santa and Mrs Claus salt and pepper
shakers to *Six Million Dollar Man* dolls.

Computers
www.cnet.com
A review and auction site for computer hardware and software, especially
good if you need a little guidance about products and this auctioning lark.

Sports Memorabilia
www.SportsAuction.com
Plenty of unique sporting items such as boxing gloves signed by Muhammad
Ali and 1950s baseball trading cards featuring Bowman Hank Aaron.

Stamps
www.stamphall.com
Stamp collectors' paradise covering a vast range of countries. Register your
details and they can send reports covering particular categories and auctions.

A bite from every sale

SALES TAX

Taxes on goods are essential to every state's income but the collection of such taxes from online sales is currently in limbo, leaving shoppers reaping the benefits

A taxing question

Sales tax is a tax on the buyer of goods and services. If you buy from a retail store, the retailer collects the tax at the point of sale and then pays it on to the state. If you are buying from an out-of-state retailer, this is technically called a use tax, though it is commonly known as a sales tax. If a **vendor does not charge a sales tax** and one is due, then the buyer is **obliged to remit this tax** to the state. Both these taxes are used by the state to pay for its infrastructure, essential services and education – the concern is that, as e-commerce increases, confusion over who should pay and how they should pay will eventually erode the revenues collected and needed by the state.

At the moment, **Internet sales are taxed similarly to mail order.** The retailer must have a physical presence (a nexus) or agents in the state where the purchase is being made, or sent to, in order to be required to charge a sales tax. What constitutes a physical presence is currently under debate. It did mean a store or warehouse, but may be expanded to mean another type of presence – for example if the online retailer's ISP is in another state, this may be considered a nexus.

Each state has different tariffs... some states have no tax at all

The Internet Tax Freedom Act (1998), in effect until October 2001 and likely to be extended, prohibits states from charging a tax on Internet access fees. Some states were already charging a tax when this came into force and they can continue to do so. The Act also prevents the imposition of any new taxes, but existing sales taxes may be enforced. **An Advisory Commission on Electronic Commerce has been set up** to look into the future of taxation on the Internet.

As tax-free saving is a big draw to purchasing online, some major retailers that have branches in just about every state have legally separated their offline and online businesses. The chain store you buy a product from at the mall is a different company than the same named one on the Internet. However, a connection may still be there – some stores separated this way still allow you to return purchases made tax-free online to the offline shop. Kind of like having the best of both worlds, but ultimately it is the smaller independent retailer and other taxpayers that have to make up the shortfall from "lost" tax revenue.

We all know that each state has different tariffs on different products, and **some states have no sales tax** at all. This difference and the confusion of who and how and if a consumer pays a use tax means that the laws are very difficult to enforce. For example, Georgia has a tax on goods purchased out-of-state, but has no method for collecting this tax. **Some states will only chase the bigger items purchased online**, like cars and boats, while some states have included a line in tax return forms requiring a payment for out-of-state purchases.

Local government and retailers are obviously fiercely in favor of some kind of tax to be put on e-commerce. The states are in favor because of lost revenue; the stores are in favor because of the unfair competition. It should also be remembered that the majority of purchases made online are either business-to-business, travel, financial services or food and drugs that are exempt from sales tax in most states, and taxes are actually being paid on about 10 per cent of Internet sales. But ignorance is no excuse and you are obliged to be aware of your own state's tax laws, and follow them.

Related websites:

www.ecommercecommission.org is the website of the Advisory Commission on Electronic Commerce.

www.salestaxinstitute.com provides services and seminars dealing with sales tax issues.

www.e-fairness.org represents retailer organizations lobbying Congress for equal tax between offline and online.

www.in-fo.org is the website of the Independence Forum which is lobbying against Internet taxation.

www.ecommercetax.com for online paper *E-Commerce Tax News* featuring articles about taxation with e-mailed updates.

www.gppf.org/pubs/analyses/2000/Etax IA.htm is the Georgia Public Policy Foundation's very comprehensive issue analysis on the tax issue.

www.webcom.com/software/issues/1ec-sttx.html has links to papers about sales tax etc.

www.cbpp.org/12-13-99tax.htm provides a discussion forum on allowing tax-free Internet sales.

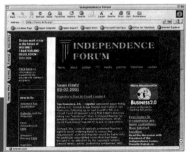

Internet taxation is a subject dear to many websites' hearts with the Independence Forum going so far as to lobby opinion on the subject with an on-site poll

**How to make sure
it's worth your while**

BUYING
FROM ABROAD

Buying goods online from an overseas
site may look easy but getting them into
the US could be a different matter

As soon as you buy a product from a foreign site, **you
become an importer** and are subject to the same rules
and regulations that govern importing. It is you who
must take responsibility for the goods complying with
both state and federal government **import regulations.**
For instance, if you import something which fails to meet
the **health code requirements** of that state, you could be
fined or penalised. And the chances are your online
purchase would be confiscated by customs.

Before you buy... and once you've decided

You'll reduce the potential for problems if you shop from
a well-known overseas vendor who's savvy with the
customs regulations in the US. The more interesting
purchases on the Internet may be from some of the smaller, more obscure sites but any joy associated with locating
that Moroccan smoking pipe at an entrepreneurial
Marrakech trader's website may be totally wiped out by
shipping costs and import duty, not to mention hassle.

If you're still determined to go ahead, phone the vendor

and suss out their credibility. Remember that you'll also be safer using a credit card for payment. Finally, if a **product is covered by a manufacturer's warranty**, make sure it is still valid in the US. You should also check the format and compatibility of items for the US. Next you have to find out if you're able to import the goods, how you do so and how much it's going to cost (you're exempted from duty on goods up to the value of $200, or $100 if it's a gift). Unfortunately, the procedures surrounding this can be complicated but the US Customs site has an excellent section on Internet transactions at ***www. customs.gov/impoexpo/inetrade.htm***. These are the main areas to be aware of as a starter...

Customs declaration

All goods sent through the mail must be accompanied by a Customs Declaration. **Goods not accompanied by a declaration will be subject to seizure**.

Shipping methods

Your options are the international postal service, a courier or a freight carrier. Be aware which method is to be used and how much it will cost you.

The import process

You, as the importer, are liable for paying the duty and determining it can be difficult but the US Customs site has an interactive database that will help you work it out.

Restricted/prohibited merchandise

Restricted items need a permit in order to gain access into the US. Prohibited items are those which cannot be brought into the country at all.

CHECKLIST

1 Know who you're buying from; a big company will be more familiar with shipping and customs procedures.

2 Pay by credit card to give yourself some protection.

3 Check whether manufacturers' warranties will still be valid and make sure goods are compatible with the US.

4 Ensure you know exactly how much you're being charged for shipping before you buy.

5 Use the US Customs interactive calculator to roughly work out the duty you'll be charged but remember – it will be customs officials who finally decide it.

6 Check your item isn't on the restricted or prohibited goods list.

7 If you have any doubt or queries, contact your local customs port.

How the Web helps you shop

USING THE INTERNET

Okay, you've been to your local PC World and put a snazzy beige box on your credit card. You've listened to your modem gurgling, clicked on the browser and you can see something which the manual describes as a homepage. And the rest, as they say, is a mystery. Don't click on the "Help!" button until you've read this

Searching the Web

A search engine is exactly that. A means of searching the Net for whatever it is that you want. Just type in key words and click on **"Search"** or **"Go"**. Hundreds of links of some relevance to your chosen topic should appear. But type in Madonna and you may find yourself reading reams of religious sermons instead of quirky facts about the Queen of Pop.

The granddaddy of all search engines has got to be **www.yahoo.com**. Its straightforward design gives you the choice of browsing through the categories listed, such as "travel", or just typing in your chosen topic. Yahoo can search sites in a specific country or the whole Web.

A wealth of young pretenders have emerged to challenge Yahoo with new technology and new ways of linking you to your request. For example, ***www.google.com*** delivers results based on those sites which have been linked to the most from other sites. So Google should lead you to the most useful, if you accept that the most useful are also the most

A wealth of young pretenders have emerged to challenge Yahoo

popular. If you want quantity rather than quality, ***www.altavista.com*** claim to hold the largest index available, with 350 million web pages.

From the best of the rest, ***www.alltheweb.com*** is a parallel search tool, exploring a range of other engines to find results, ***www.dogpile.com*** gets good word-of-mouth recommendations whereas ***www.askjeeves.com*** could be called the idiot's guide to the Net as you can type in the exact question you want answered. But Jeeves can focus on the "ifs" and "buts" rather than the real question.

Making sense of directories

If you lack the patience to browse the thousands of pages that most search engines list, directories provide a narrower field of enquiry. They group together URLs of like mind – so if you want to know about skiing, a directory will offer a list of sites all relating to the skiing fraternity. If you want a one-click process, try the online Yellow Pages at ***www.yellowpages.com***.

Shopping bots

With many couples' Saturday ritual being to hit the mall at 11am, have the men lose interest at around lunchtime and both head home at around 2pm with not a purchase in sight, shopping has ceased to be a pleasure. Shopping from your computer could ease the tension if you know how (and where) to look. But help is at hand.

Shopping directories are the online equivalent to shopping malls. Most, like **www.webushop.com** and **www.fingertipguide.com**, offer a list of popular shopping categories alongside reviews and ratings. Many are taking directories that one step further by creating shopping bots. Most sites advertise themselves as cutting street prices so you should get some kind of bargain, but a shopping bot searches cyberspace to find the best deals for you. This sounds too good to be true – and in some cases it is – but many good bots will do exactly what it says on the box.

All you do is tell them what you're looking for, they take a few seconds to scan the globe and return with a list of the best bargains. One of the best bots is **www.dealtime. com**. Categories include music, film, wines, electrical appliances and computing, and you can make your search as simple or complex as you like. For finding your item on an auction site **www.bidfind.com** will get you there. Or you can make yourself feel doubly good by combining shopping with charity: with **www.greatergood.com** up to 15 per cent of your spending will go to the charity of your choice.

If you're after a specific bargain, simply type "price comparison" and then key whatever you're looking for into your search engine. Most search engines come up with something, but try **http://wine-searcher.com** for the boozy bargains, **www.bookfinder.com** for literature and **www.ibuyer.net** for computers.

Some shopping bots only search the vendors with whom they have deals so

SHOPPING & MORALITY

If you feel you should be doing something more useful with your time and money than shopping, the Internet offers penance with sites that donate money to charity when you spend.

----

www.forafriend.com will link you to a number of reputable online shops including Amazon and Disney. If you buy from these sites using the link from For A Friend they'll donate 75 per cent of the profits to charity.

----

www.igive.com donates up to 15 per cent of sales from associated sites to a charity you choose. E-tailers involved include Walmart and Cold Water Creek. So now you can feel morally superior about shopping.

you won't always get the cheapest price. An easy way to check this is to do a simple search for a common item and see how many different stores are listed. If it's limited to only a couple you may be better off looking elsewhere to find better deals. Some companies such as ***www.prices-can.com*** and ***www.mysimon.com*** actually make a point of saying they don't accept money from vendors.

If you're still not convinced, both ***www.botspot.com*** and ***www.smartbots.com*** offer guides to the best around. In the future, bots will constantly e-mail you with new bargains. Some of them might even be relevant to you. Either way, you need never face a Macy's sale again.

What's a bot got? It's got the lot... or at least it's got both the time and the inclination to dig up lots of information and save you the hassle

Group buying power

If you've got enough friends, group buying is another way to save. Sites such as ***www.volumebuy.com*** work on the premise that the more people who buy an item, the cheaper it becomes. It's a bit more complicated than that, but not much – just make sure you look out for the Best Price marking. Even if you persuade your whole family to join in, you'll never knock the price so low you get a digital camera for $10. They usually state a cut-off price point which may be 40 per cent off the normal price. Volumebuy offers several ways of joining – a price based on the number of final purchasers within the time limit, or a guaranteed low price so you can decide in advance how much you'll be stung for. You can also tip off a friend about the latest great deals.

Getting the best reviews

The Internet is teeming with review sites for everything from film and music to computer and household goods. There are even sites reviewing other websites so you can find the best site at which to start your online search.

Of the more general review sites, ***www.epinions.com***, ***www.productreviewnet.com*** and ***www.consumer-guide.com*** are probably the best. Each covers popular online buys like CDs and computer equipment, as well as more unusual stuff like cigars, sleeping bags and shampoo. You can submit your own reviews or read those from independent buyers. Product Review also offers buying guides and shopping tips, and Consumer Guide offers a

You're never alone when you're online shopping: not with sites like Product Review around to advise

concise history of each item and a guide to what the technical nonsense in the handbooks means. Useful if you still can't set the clock on your video.

Don't be put off by the countless computer reviews that you'll find during your searches. There's a review site on the Net to cover every product and topic imaginable. Book reviews are posted on the sites of some e-tailers like Barnes & Noble and Borders. And all the major newspapers have online book review sites too.

Review sites give you what no retailer can: an objective opinion

For an alternative to the perhaps over-familiar movie reviews from Roger Ebert, you can always try ***www.unni.com*** which is chock full of reviews from the general surfing public plus critic reviews, a chat room and member's nominations for the next Oscars. ***www.odeon.com*** follows a similar premise with the added bonus that you can buy online.

If you want computer reviews and can't face looking at every Tom, Dick and Harry's entry, one of the best is ***www.zdnet.com***. Covering PCs, peripherals and digital technology, ZD collects reviews from different sources and offers simple overviews, full reviews and test scores for a good all-round picture of the product before you buy.

Internet review sites are infinite in number, especially if you're looking for something like a car or a computer. But even if you're after something more specialized, the Internet can help. If you're just getting into scuba diving but aren't sure what to use, ***www.scubadiving.com*** will help you decide if the Aqua Lung Impulse 2 or the Zeagle Flex is the best snorkel for you.

Review sites give you what you'll never get from the mumbling sales assistants who can barely recall the name of the products they're selling: an objective, informed opinion. A site like ***www.audioreview.com*** offers you the opinions of the public and experts. At ***www.usbuy.com*** they'll help you decide what deal best suits you, rather than what suits them. If you're after a mobile phone you just answer a set of questions, from which they'll then determine what kind of phone you should get, if any. They will then link you to reputable retailers who stock the product you need.

www.reviewfinder.com   Review Finder

And now for the bad news...

Christmas 1999 should have been a festive bonanza for online shoppers and e-tailers. Instead, seven online shops ended up agreeing to pay $1.5m in penalties for various failures to deliver the goods during the season and for generally behaving as the e-commerce equivalents of the Grinch who stole Christmas.

Since then online service has vastly improved but various studies have shown that the biggest problem wasn't anything to do with delivery or fraud, it was that the sites themselves didn't work. About 1 in 4 purchases, according to one of the growing tribe of Internet consultants, were halted by technical hitches. That figure has since fallen to 8 per cent.

Many customers, confused by sites which offered too much choice and too little guidance, left cyberspace's electronic aisles littered with abandoned shopping carts. But again, most shops have now simplified their sites. Indeed, Amazon's approach to online shopping, usually cited as among the Web's easiest to use, is now being used by Toys R Us.

And wonder of wonders, e-tailers are replying to shoppers' e-mails faster (in an average of 12 hours, not 48). So even the bad news is getting better.

AND THE WINNER IS...

Gone are the days of spending hours dreaming up the prizewinning combination of words to end classic sentences like "Shredded Wheat is the best breakfast cereal because..."

Online competitions are easy to enter and you don't need to hunt for a stamp. Some of the best offerings include *www. eSweepStakes.com*, *www.contestworld.com* and *www.contestguide. com* with prizes of hard cash, cars and Mini-Max workout videos!

Part two

How to buy everything online from
American quilts to zithers

THE DIRECTORY

Antiques

Fed up with the 21st century's disposable culture? Why not surround yourself with a few beautiful things that have stood the test of time? The sites below can help

Antique Fest

www.antiquefest.com

If you want to find out when and where all the antiques festival and fairs happen in New England, this is a must. Antique Fest also sells and auctions a good selection of interesting antiques and collectibles, ranging from 19th-century Italian pottery to a pair of original 1950s bowling shoes. They charge the actual shipping cost to get items delivered to you, and if you're not happy, they will refund your money (minus shipping costs) without question.

Antique Quilts

www.antiquequilts.com

An excellent site devoted to the sale of original American quilts, but which also stocks other collectibles such as Quimper and Bennington pottery. You'll find plenty to browse online, with all the quilts promised to be in good condition without serious stains or damage. Alternatively, you can buy the full catalogue for $10. There's a choice of shipping options and costs are calculated at the checkout.

Antiques.co.uk

www.antiques.co.uk

This speedy and beautifully laid out British site promises antiques that have been vetted and guaranteed by a team of experts for sale and delivery worldwide. You can build up your own portfolio wish list, arrange to view an item, or even just go ahead and buy it, all online. You can sort out paying for your purchase by credit card or arrange to wire the money. Delivery charges are calculated online so there won't be any nasty surprises in store. A very professional and impressive site.

Bath Antiquities Centre

www.bathantiquities.freeserve.co.uk

Another British site that has the facility to ship goods all over the world. If you like your antiques to walk on the ancient side, here's the place to get genuine antiquities with items available including flint arrowheads or Ammonite fossils at surprisingly affordable prices. For a more up-to-date treasure, an amulet of the Egyptian god Shu will cost you around $180 – and hopefully won't come complete with a Howard Carter-style curse. Purchases can be made via e-mail and the phone, and all items come with a guaranteed certificate of authenticity.

Dawn Hill Antiques

www.dawnhillantiques.com

Beautifully laid out site that mimics Dawn Hill's real-life store, with different items laid out on the Porch (where you'll find antique garden furniture and urns), the First Floor (which is full of 19th-century French furniture) and so on. The articles each have clear photos and descriptions, as well as prices listed so you know what you're getting into. If you live nowhere near New Preston, CT, you can e-mail or phone for further information or to purchase any of the items on the site.

Essex River Antiques

www.essexriverantiques.com

Browse through the wide selection of antiques on this site, many starting at very affordable prices for the novice collector. All sorts of treasures are available, from authentic shop signs to paintings to Sheraton chests. Prices are listed on the site, but you'll have to e-mail the company for further information and shipping arrangements.

Invaluable

www.thesaurus.co.uk

Not really an online shop, but a useful collection of news, articles, and info on forthcoming auctions and tips for antiques enthusiasts everywhere. They have a comprehensive search facility through auction catalogs and dealers' stock lists for folk who are looking for a particular item, as well as contact details for dealers all over the world. A great online starting point for amateur collectors.

Leigh Keno American Antiques

www.leighkeno.com

This very impressive and well-designed site is mainly for the serious collector, but a good place for less well-off shoppers to drool over Federal sideboards and Queen Anne clocks. You can e-mail the site for further details and costs for any of the pieces, although each is listed with a comprehensive description and clear photo to help you make your choice.

Mir Russki

www.russiansilver.co.uk

Should you find yourself with an overwhelming urge to collect Fabergé, this UK-based site can help you drop some serious cash on exquisite silver and enamelled pieces made in Imperial Russia. Not many people have £895 (around $1500) to spend on a matchbox cover, but if you do, you can contact the company through its website – though, for security's sake, they recommend the final money transaction takes place over the phone.

TIAS.com

www.tias.com

Huge resource for online antique hunters with more than 300,000 items now available to buy through their links with antiques dealers all over the country. There are also useful articles and information if you don't feel expert enough to go ahead with a purchase before doing a thorough check. It may take you a little while to find your way around the site, but it's worth persevering – you never know what's going to be on the next page.

Chock-full of your more serious items for your more serious collectors, the Leigh Keno site is still worth having a look at

Appliances

Whether your fridge is just barely managing to keep the milk below room temperature, you just blew up the oven, or are simply having a Griswald-style Christmas, there are plenty of websites out there which can rescue you from (almost) any domestic crisis

General **Because electrical shops are so dreary**

A-1 Maytag

www.a-1maytag.com

Maytag sells its own range of oven ranges and cooktops, as well as products manufactured by Hoover, Jen-Air and Magic Chef. Select a brand and browse, but make sure you stick to the online catalogue. Only cookers, vacuum cleaners and waste disposal units are available but there's an extensive choice, with prices to suit every budget going up to thousands for a cooking range. The ordering process is secure if rudimentary, and shipping is $1.20 times weight. More detail would be helpful.

American TV

www.americantv.com

American TV has obviously realized how dull shopping for essential items can be, creating a site to cut down on the boredom factor. Pick a category and they sort out the dishwashers from the cookers. You can add price and brand specifications, and all the usual images and feature lists are available. Delivery is the real bonus though. If you'd prefer no charges you can pick up from their nearest store – they'll even provide directions. Alternatively they do deliver, and whenever best suits you rather than the other way round.

The Sears site is everything you would expect from an old family favourite. Online shopping in the comfort zone

Compact Appliances

www.compactappliances.com

As the name implies, this is the perfect site for anyone living in a mobile home or studio apartment, with compact dishwashers to compact freezers. The usual browsing and ordering system applies, and the customer service section is worth a look, especially as upstairs delivery can add $75. Every item is discounted, luckily, as at $300 for a mini bar (empty), small doesn't equal cheap.

Cuisine Parts International

www.cuisineparts.com

Cuisine Parts covers your standard kitchen appliances, from microwaves and blenders all the way to yogurt makers and even a Programmable Urn. The degree of information on each item varies, and pictures are of poor quality but, again, you should be able to find something to suit your budget. And if you think that an urn is a promising gift, they will ship to an alternative address at no extra cost.

Repair Clinic

www.repairclinic.com

Hate it when you have to pay some guy 50 bucks just to tell you that a fuse has blown? Well, this site gives free advice on many appliance repairs and will sell you the parts you'll need. We don't recommend you start fiddling with your machinery unless you have some idea what you are doing – but if you do, you're sure to save a few dollars here.

Rex Stores

www.rexstores.com

Appliances available from this professional general store include microwaves, refrigerators, air conditioning units and vacuum cleaners. Sitewise they haven't quite got it yet – after a decent start the tiny picture of each item scattered across the following pages doesn't inspire a sale. The individual product pages are better, with enlarged images, useful spec sheets and shipping information. Most items shipped within 48 hours.

Sears

www.sears.com

A good option if you'd prefer to shop with a name you know and love. A safe and professional looking site, it's easy to search for all your appliance needs, from a fridge freezer deluxe walk-in model to replacement vacuum bags. And after selecting an item, they'll suggest similar alternatives. Shipping is free, generally within a week, and financing options are available. A good safe bet.

US Appliance

www.us-appliance.com

A member of Yahoo Shopping, US Appliance has created a professional looking site. Search for cooking, refrigeration or laundry, select the brand or the look you're after, and you'll get an extensive list, enlarged images, and stacks of information. Not a site for those on a budget, though.

Added extras To make your kitchen complete...

ABC Vacuum

www.abcvacuum.com

Security problems seemingly sorted with their rudimentary order form, this site features all the top brands, including Hoover, Bissell and Samsung, plus additional info and independent reviews.

Home Appliances

www.homeappliances.com

A site that allows you to ask the experts anything and everything about buying your next cooker, toaster or even ice cream maker. Just specify which appliance, the price range and when you're likely to be buying.

Miele

www.mieleusa.com

Funnily enough this online emporium focuses on Miele products, but worth a look if you're looking to buy a professional brand with a good reputation. Covers residential and professional models.

Ronco

www.ronco.com

Pasta makers, food dehydrators, bagel cutters and inside-the-shell egg scramblers. If you're searching for unusual gadgets, look no further.

Kitchen gadgets Modern day living made easy

Aabree Coffee Company

www.aabreecoffee.com

Whether you're thinking of setting up your own coffee shop, or just want to recreate that Central Perk atmosphere in your own home, Aabree sells everything from the grinders and coffee makers to the beans and frothing sticks. You can browse the entire store, but we suggest you stick to a particular brand – Solis Crema, Capresso and Gaggia are all included – and use their comparison charts to make an informed buy. Prices vary from $75 to $1,000 depending on whether you're looking at domestic or business models, but they do offer a lowest price guarantee and free shipping.

Americana From The Heart

http://shop.store.yahoo.com/americanafromtheheart

This site deserves an honorary mention even though it sells ironing boards not irons. These products are designed to leave a hole in the wallet and a lump in the throat of any right-thinking American. Their ironing board is described as "America with birdhouses" but you have to see it to gauge the full scale of the atrocity. The site says supply is limited. Right. As in "limited to the number we can sell".

Anomolee

www.espressoproducts.com

Anomolee doesn't hold anything like as extensive a range as Aabree but every item is tailored for home use rather than cafés. Prices range from $15 for a

StoveTop Espresso steamer up to $240 for a spruced-up Saeco machine. Images and brief descriptions are on hand, but there is only so much you can say about coffee. Ordering is easy and you don't have to register to do so.

Appliances.com

www.appliances.com

If you're the kind of person that regards household gadgets not so much as a trifling accessory but more a consuming passion, Appliances.com is the site for you. Not only do beverages and waffle irons each have their own section, but there's a selection of unusual, and possibly unnecessary, items including Henrietta Hen the Egg Cooker and the cookie and biscuit maker. If you're looking for major household appliances you should probably head elsewhere, with only dishwashers to choose from here. Top names include Rowenta, Cuisinart and Kenwood. Prices are standard and the customer services section is helpful.

Internet Kitchen

www.your-kitchen.com

Buried in among an array of kitchen clay pots, aprons and spices is a selection of kitchen gadgets and small appliances. Click on a product and browse the multiple offering within covering all budgets. The site itself and the ordering system is fairly rudimentary, but you can benefit from discounted prices – up to $40 off in some cases – so it's worth a look if you can't live without a ravioli maker one minute longer.

Kitchen Aid

www.kitchenaid.com

As long as it's state of the art, Kitchen Aid sells it, from blenders and cookers, to washing machines and dishwashers. For quick searches you can use the scroll down product menu, although the choice under each category is generally limited to between 3 and 5 items. Images are clear and the descriptions are based on a need-to-know basis.

APPLIANCE 411

www.appliance411.com

According to the experts at Appliance 411, after buying your own home and your car, appliances are the next most expensive purchase you're likely to make. Hence their site, which offers helpful advice on everything from making a purchase, to arranging those inevitable repairs. Check out who makes what before you buy, where to find a handy and reliable serviceman, and all those myths about appliances that cost you a fortune.

The Appliance411 site can help you decide if that extra $100 warranty is really useful. The site is easy to use and could even save you money.

The customer service section is full of particularly useful information and ordering couldn't really be much simpler.

Wal-Mart

www.wal-mart.com

Surprisingly, discount kings Wal-Mart can't fulfil your major appliance needs. There's not a washing machine, cooker or fridge freezer to be found. You can, however, buy kitchen gadgets galore online, and cheaper than those found at specialized outlets. Select your price range, type and brand in order to search using the product finder, or simply browse the store. Prices cover everything from cheap to relatively pricey; all the information you're likely to need is listed on one simple product page, including warranty details.

Vacuum cleaners Sweeping to conquer

Sanyo

store.sanyousa.com

If a regular cleaner just won't do justice to your Afghan rugs, the Sanyo store offers a limited range of super advanced vacuum cleaners at super cheap prices. They also sell more than vacuum cleaners, like a small selection of Dinosaur toasters for example, for when you just have to have that friendly dino print on your toast. Good for a bargain or something for the kids.

United Vacuum Brokers

www.unitedvac.com

United lets you choose the brand name you're familiar with – Hoover, Miele, Bissell – then browse the extensive ranges. You will be faced with a list of code names and very brief descriptions, so we advise you to stick to a price to suit your budget. Spec sheets are useful but don't overload you with information, and shipping is $8.99 anywhere in continental US. Easy.

Vac Shop USA

www.vacsrus.com

The site itself looks quite tacky and the annoying flashing symbols are hard on the eye, but they do sell online. Uprights, canisters, micro and cordless are all available, priced anywhere between $200 and $1,000. Top brands include Euroclean and Lindhaus. Accessories and spare parts are also sold.

Arts

The Internet is now the biggest art market in the world. You can buy just about anything, from a painting of Madonna and Child to furniture made out of old fruit crates

 For those with an artistic temperament

Art Crimes

www.graffiti.org

It's graffiti, Jim, but not as we know it. None of that "Kilroy woz 'ere" stuff, just an introduction to a network of artists who indulge in the world's biggest (and most debased) participation art, some of whom will do graffiti to order. All that and a catalog of magazines with great names like *Molotov Cocktail*. This site is definitely worth a bookmark.

ArtPlanet Gallery 2000

http://pages.prodigy.com/ArtPlanet2000/99gal.htm

Getting your work seen is the problem most artists face. ArtPlanet 2000 has links to a rotating stable of artists' homepages, where you can look at their work, get contact info and summit feedback. Quality and medium varies.

Art.com

www.art.com

The obvious address for all things arty offers limited editions, photographs, prints and posters, animation and even Mona Lisa mugs. The catalog is massive. If you key in Edvard Munch you will be bombarded with no fewer than 23 permutations of *The Scream* but you also get some of his less famous (but equally fine) work like *Vampire*. The site ships via UPS and orders of 7 or more framed items receive a 40 per cent discount on shipping.

One Lord and the Thin White Duke

Andy Warhol

www.warholstore.com

Andy's official online art mart has a massive range of stuff and much of it is at good discount prices. It seems no object is sacred – you can buy anything from Warhol decorated light switchplates, lip-shaped pasta and, er, camouflage condoms.

David Bowie

www.bowieart.com

The return of the Thin White Duke throwing darts into eyes of art lovers everywhere, but even hardcore fans might not be won over. UK-based, but the order form caters to US buyers. The site is uncluttered by any info such as a return policy, shipping details… when e-mailed, they responded that delivery is within 14 days of a credit card order and they will refund or exchange any item.

Jack Lord

http://sites.inka.de/sites/edruta/jlmaler.htm

In the 1950s Jack Lord, long before he found fame as Steve McGarrett of *Hawaii Five-O*, tried to make a living as a painter. On this Anglo-German site you can find a collection of his work in the style of masters such as Van Gogh and Gaugin, and it seems there was genuine talent before he turned into the world's most conspicuous consumer of hair lacquer. You can't buy his work online, but you can buy the work of another US TV cop Buddy Ebsen (who played Barnaby Jones) from www.buddyebsencreations.com/gallery/fine1.html – but please don't.

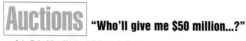 **"Who'll give me $50 million…?"**

Arte Primitivo Howard S Rose Gallery

www.arteprimitivo.com

Specializing in pre-Colombian Art, Classical, Egyptian and Asian Antiques and ethnographic art, this site allows you to download the current auction catalog and then place your bids online. An archive of previous auctions is well worth a look, though including final hammer prices would be one improvement. Beautifully designed.

Christie's

www.christies.com

The Christie's site takes you within touching distance of the finest fine art... as close as most of us will ever get

If you happen to have $82.5m burning a hole in your pocket or purse, this is the place to come to buy a Van Gogh. But not everything on this site run by the famous (and thoroughly wired) auction house costs that much: you can pick up a Warhol print for less than $9,000. Failing that, a subscription to the company's *Living With Art* magazine will cost you a measly $22. A word of warning though: once you've visited this site you will probably find that you keep on coming back, if for no other reason than to hang around in a very classy part of cyberspace.

Sotheby's

www.sothebys.com

It may be just the color scheme but this site feels more formal than Christie's. But you can register to bid online and, as with Christie's, there's no shortage of stuff to bid for. Famous people use both these auction houses as an upmarket equivalent to a tag-sale and you will find the catalogs intriguing, especially the one devoted to the estate of the Ambassador Pamela Harriman. After all, $85 is a small price to pay for such prurience.

Posters You owe it to your wall

1 Stop Poster Shop

www.1StopPosterShop.com

Want a cute puppy poster for your kid sister? A motivational golfing poster for Dad? Or one of those oh-so-atmospheric posters of travel as it used to be – you know the kind of thing, imperious Cunard liner setting sail for New York. Look no further. This site caters to all tastes, with everything from angels to the military to weather neatly in its own category. Navigation is simple and policies are clearly laid out.

Bare Walls
www.barewalls.com
Searchable by subject or style, this site has a huge range of posters to cover your bare walls. And once you've selected your own little reproduced masterpiece you can chose to have it framed, either in metal or wood. However, this will usually cost you quite a bit more than the poster itself. Other options include canvas transfer and matting.

Citiscapes
www.citiscapes-art.com
This unique idea involves taking a night-time panoramic skyline of the city of your choice, and replacing the major light points with fiber optics. Suddenly what was originally a static photo is now a hypnotic poster with waves of multi-colored light. You can choose the frame color to match your décor. A great idea for the office.

Contemporary Posters
www.contemporaryposters.com
This site's name is missing a key word, the word in question being "Polish". With that caveat, there are some very cool posters here including the classic Solidarity poster from 1980, and a great selection of Polish circus posters.

Paris 1903
www.paris1903.com
This quick and easy site specializes in reproductions of antique European advertising posters. The range includes huge (over 4ft), automotive and movie posters. Framing is an expensive option.

Rare Posters
www.rareposters.com
A vast collection of exhibition and museum posters, with more Roy Lichtensteins than even the Lichtenstein family would probably choose to have on their walls. Rare Posters is a nifty, unpretentious site which could lighten your wallet by $12 or a considerably more substantial $8,000 if you were tempted by a signed and numbered Lichtenstein limited edition print.

Virtual galleries Fine art, butterflies and flowers

Always Art

www.alwaysart.com

This virtual gallery has a wide selection, a handy glossary section helps the novice buyer, and there's a file of recent art and culture articles. No shipping or return information (though there is a stated no-quibble guarantee) but when you order, a standard $30 is added. The tax info lets you chose if you live in or out of the merchant's state, but no information as to what state that is.

Animation Art

www.animationartgallery.com

There aren't many works of art that Joe Public can afford but just $400 at this online gallery will buy you an original piece of animation art from *The Simpsons*. The site – which showcases cartoons and animation from *Dr Seuss* through to *Disney* and *Matt Groening* – is slightly chaotic, but there is secure online ordering (although you only find that out when you try to buy).

Art Flukx

www.flukx.com

The site design is so retro chic you'll want it as your screen saver. This UK-based site sells contemporary, yet useful art. Divided into bathroom, kitchen, furniture and accessories, you can view a wealth of items designed to bring art into your life, even that new fruit bowl you've been searching for. Profiles are on hand and prices are reasonable, most items below £40 ($60), but add £20 ($30) for US delivery.

Chesterfield Galleries

www.chesterfieldgalleries.com

This art glass gallery has a lovely selection of glass, from sculpture to bowls and vases and perfume bottles. A biography of each artist is a click away. A sensible layout makes this site a pleasure to use and buy from.

Guild Artists

www.guild.com

This site is reassuringly large and professional looking. The navigation bar has links to information about the company and security and privacy issues. When

The Guild: not only a massive range of art, but all the back-up stuff to boot – including an instant dispatch date

you click on "order" it calculates the shipping and estimated dispatch date straight away. Gift certificates are available.

Les Pabillons
www.galerie-dcor.com
This is a Swiss gallery that sells butterflies made out of banknotes. The almighty dollar has escaped such mutilation and you can't order online, plus the prices are in Swiss francs. But it just might be the next big thing. Or it could be the craziest thing to do with banknotes apart from set fire to them.

On View
www.onview.com
This is an online art gallery that brings together dealers worldwide. If you can't find what you want it will search the world for you. There is a good "Learn" section for those unfamiliar with the terms, movements and styles relating to art. The prices are negotiable and shipping depends on each particular item.

The E-Commerce of Art
www.ec-art.com
Many artists are not with galleries and here they have the opportunity to reach a much larger audience. With instructions on how to best present their work, the artist can then upload a selection of their pieces on to the site. If you have the right software you can zoom and rotate each object and also listen to an audio description.

Tramp Art
www.trampart.com
If art were a stock market, now would be a good time to get shares in "tramp art", the name given to making small bits of furniture out of everyday debris like fruit crates and pallets (it's how hobos allegedly used to amuse themselves). The Clifford A Wallach Gallery of Folk Art and Americana has a fine selection to buy online. No info on shipping costs or return policies.

Babycare & maternity

Call on the Internet to feed the baby's brain in the womb, ease the sting of childbirth (very slightly), reveal the sex of unborn babies and pamper those new moms

General For the before, during and after

Baby Center
www.babycenter.com
A great site with good solid information and terrific interactive tools. There is even a dads' zone which includes information on sexual positions and fertility tips! The shopping area is fantastic. Extremely helpful are the parent's favorite polls so you get firsthand info on merchandise. There is a related product section and reviews as well. Great gift ideas include the Special Deliverease Labor Kit at $39.99 – lip moisturizer, washcloth, foot massage cream, relaxation spray, breath mints and even a classical CD! Shipping time for all items depends on availability and the delivery method you choose (Standard, Premium, or Express).

Baby University
www.babyuniversity.com
A humorous parent-to-parent site with baby boards, hot topics and birth stories, practical budgeting sections and a forum for swapping those coupons you don't want for some you might. It also gives you a chance to have a go with a Chinese birth chart tool that is derived from a chart buried in a tomb in Beijing for nearly 700 years and is allegedly 93 per cent accurate in revealing the sex of your unborn child. You can order products from their affiliate www.geniusbaby.com. We liked the Wombsong pregnancy and massage video at $15.95 and the free gift wrapping selection and handwritten card is a nice touch. Your order goes out at the end of the next business day and costs a flat $6.95 to deliver.

Babycare & maternity

Parents Place

www.parentsplace.com

Part of the iVillage group of websites, this bright, informative portal has helpful articles and interactive tools for the family. The "Ask The Experts" section includes a birth guru, dentist and schoolteacher. There is interactive video on topics like infant pain and how to show boys affection. Shopping takes you to Shopping Central at iVillage featuring e-tailers like Disney and iMaternity. And their Personal Shopper service is a winner. Just fill in the request form and you'll get personalized links and suggestions within 48 hours. Shipping costs are reimbursed if you spend over $50.

Stork Net

www.storknet.com

A friendly pregnancy and parenting community online, this literary site features writers like author Elaine Moran and columnists Forrest Seymour, Jeff Stimpson and Linda Sharp. Writing about their parenting adventures, the site has its own customized electronic greeting cards and guest interviews with authors and experts. Particularly enjoyable is the huge shopping mall with a range of e-tailers from GapMaternity to classy Nordstrom. Be prepared to spend hours shopping here – and no aching feet at the end of it!

Baby Help for the bringing up of...

Babies R Us

www.babiesrus.com

This superstore is a fantastic experience. It claims to be the largest baby product specialty store in the world and you get a huge range of products and

services like special order department and state-of-the-art baby registry service. If you want to order a travel system you get all the info you need. Everything comes with its own experts' checklist and the search tools are really effective. Particularly useful is being able to shop by department, nursery theme, pattern, collection and brand.

Follow in the pregnant footsteps of the rich and famous and dress the little ones for success too

Baby Bloomers

www.babyblooms.com

A gentle, wholesome site peppered with biblical quotations. Everything available here has been painstakingly made by a group of handcrafters.

There are some very sweet gifts on offer like diaper bags and baby pillows, handmade pacifier clips and hand-smocked baby gowns. Almost all the products can be personalized. Orders take a maximum of 2 to 3 weeks to deliver due to the nature of the product. Shipping costs for all orders is $5.

Baby Style

www.babystyle.com

A must for celebrity-wannabe moms and babies, this chic site lets you dress your little darling in the latest trends. It has everything from maternity clothes to baby gear and nursery furnishings, but its big selling point is sections like Celebrity Closet which reveals the pregnancy style secrets of celebs like Cindy Crawford, Amber Valetta and Catherine Zeta Jones and then lets you buy similar outfits. You can also discover how to dress your son like Dylan Michael (Catherine's son) or Presley (Cindy's son). Labels include Ralph Lauren, DKNYBaby and Belly Basics, and each product comes with care instructions and sizing info. Style comes at a price though; Cindy's melange sweater is a cool $89. You can also write product reviews or tell a friend. All standard orders will be charged a flat rate of $4.95 for ground shipping.

Bare ware

www.bareware.net

A Canadian site that offers a great selection of guilt-free, eco-friendly cloth diapers. Also featured are breastfeeding accessories, slings and fashionable animal print maternity underwear. The prices are competitive and customer service is excellent. The site also offers "gently used" diapers and liners. Free shipping with all orders over $25, within 24 hours, and you can save up to 35 per cent with the Canadian exchange rate. (Prices are listed in US dollars too.)

Genius babies

www.geniusbabies.com

A bright fun-filled site catering to would-be geniuses, this one offers all types of products to help you bring up your own baby Einstein. From Embryonics products to encourage your baby in the womb through to nurturing your baby with Baby Massage Kits and My First Flash Cube, products are divided into appropriate sections. There's a flat rate $6.95 fee on your entire order when shipped to one address and free gift wrapping too.

Urban Baby

www.urbanbaby.com

The brainchild of a New York mom who was a former stylist and fashion editor, this fabulously trendy site offers wide resource guides, interactive communities and an online store for urban parents in the top metropolitan cities in the world. With hip illustrations by artist Ruben Toledo (he figures in the Metropolitan Museum of Art) the site has a cosmopolitan sensibility with distinctive products. It's not cheap but service includes free gift wrap in posh boxes and a personalized gift card. Regular delivery takes three days at $5.

The usual stuff: personalised sick cloths, etc...

Baby Bloomers

www.babyblooms.com

Everything on Baby Bloomers is handmade, specializing in ultra-twee memorabilia such as baby bracelets and personalized first curl boxes. Your baby can even have their very own personalized sick cloths, which may come in useful if you linger too long here. But if this is your (hand-embroidered) bag, shipping is a flat $5. You might have to wait two weeks for delivery because of the handmade nature of each item.

 **When there's a bun in the oven**

9 Months

www.9months.com

A website that grew out of frustration by a working mom-to-be who could not find stylish and affordable maternity clothes. It's purpose is to enable you to do as many chores as possible online (including banking). Registering only takes a matter of seconds and once you're off you can be smug in the knowledge that you're doing a good deed too: the site donates a percentage of its sales to The Children's Fund.

Anna Cris Maternity

www.annacris.com

A fashionable maternity clothing boutique featuring top designers, this fresh looking site retails maternity clothes for your career, casual weekends and for your holiday and special occasion needs. There are tips on how to shop for clothes during your pregnancy and a handy Q&A section where they will help you find whatever you are after, even if they don't have what you want in stock. The Passport wallet service stores credit card and address information so you don't have to retype it for every purchase and the site claims to have a no hassle return policy.

Baby Becoming

www.babybecoming.com

Baby Becoming provides maternity clothes for the plus-sized pregnant mom and the reviews from the members are glowing. The product range is not the biggest but it covers all the basics at very affordable prices: tops at $9.99, dresses for $19.99, nursing wear at $14.99. It also sells nightwear and swimsuits from sizes 1X to 6X. There is a helpful sizing chart and pantyhose guides for women up to 400lbs. Shipping charges start at $5.50, delivery takes three days and is free for orders over $200.

Belly Shop

www.bellyshop.com

Lots to fill your birthbag in this site, especially if you happen to lean towards doing things the natural way. Here you can buy Pregnant Goddess Pendants for $10 plus brightly colored birth balls and belly cream. A belly gallery lets you see your bump on screen and there are a few select articles about birthing communities and the likes. You only get e-mailed your shipping costs after the order has been dispatched to you, though.

Breastpumps For Less

www.pcez.com/~muralt/breastpump

This family-owned company promises fabulous savings on breastpumps (thanks to low overhead costs and bulk buying) as they aim to make breastfeeding affordable for all mothers. An Ameda Purely Yours deluxe model with tote kit, normal retail $240, is $144.99. There are also tips on how to choose a breast pump and how to store expressed milk. All products are shipped via UPS ground and your zip code decides the price.

From Here to Maternity

www.fromheretomaternity.com

A stylish, up-to-date, user friendly fashion site featuring versatile ensembles from bootcut pants to classic work suits. There is also a customized wardrobe service based on your budget, style and size, and the sizing tips and washing instructions are a great idea. Deliveries arrive promptly within 48 hours; any delay and you'll be contacted by e-mail or telephone.

imaternity.com

www.imaternity.com

Calling themselves The Maternity Everything Store, this straightforward shopping site has a large selection of bright, fun maternitywear for the mom on the go. Look out for seasonal sales where prices are slashed. Prices start at $9.99 and the sizing charts and bra guides are helpful. Check out the online outlet store that has great discounts. Free shipping within 2 days for all orders over $100, a $4.95 flat rate for orders below.

The Belly Shop is stocked to the rafters with stuff to ease your journey through pregnancy and childbirth

Maternity Shoppe

www.maternityshoppe.com

Perfect for the hedonist, the Maternity Shoppe promises to give women a pampered pregnancy.

Maternity gifts, skin care, yoga videos, pregnancy books, prenatal fitness and a whole lot more. Shopping is split into categories such as first time mother, birthing, labor aids and skincare. Ranked by ABC parenting as a 4-star site, standard UPS ground orders shipped within the US cost an average $5.50.

Maternity Zone
www.maternityzone.com
A nice site for great gifts. The "Honey, it's time" nursing and childbirth wardrobe is a complete kit comprising nursing nightie, an easy access cotton bra and full-cut panties. The best part is shipping is free. Easy to sign in and navigate, the site is not only about shopping – you get lots of info in the baby zone and not just frothy stuff but important issues like adoption and infertility.

Mother Nature
www.mothernature.com
Good for moms-to-be looking for a more holistic approach to having a baby. This mom-owned and operated website has information on topics like the role of herbs in nutrition and how to make your own baby food. Their shopping area is small but features a unique selection of breastfeeding accessories, baby slings, books on spiritual midwifery, cloth diapers, herbal remedies and more. Delivery takes 1-2 weeks but is free; 3-day delivery costs $3.99.

Pamper me Maternity
www.pampermematernity.com
Another site with products to naturally help provide comfort and pain/stress relief throughout and after pregnancy. The fragrant herbal aromatherapy relaxation products are a step above the usual basics. A handy tool lets you search for products according to your symptoms so everything from hemorrhoids to cracked nipples has an online solution. Shipping costs will be automatically calculated.

If it's a spot of pregnancy pampering you're after then why not click on to the Maternity Shoppe

Under Works
www.underworks.com
This site features an exceptional collection of maternity underwear, girdles, bras and much more, across a wide range of sizes and colors. There is also a plus-size bra collection featuring sizes from 34B to 52G. You can order online, via fax using the printable order form, or though snail mail. Delivery is efficient: within 24 hours. The shipping and handling charges really depend on how much you order.

Baseball

From Little League to the Majors, America's favourite sport has something for everyone so it's only fair that everyone should be able to buy something for it...

 **Bats, balls, baseball caps and much more**

All Coaches
www.allcoaches.com
Easy to navigate, this site sells everything that makes a coach's life easier like bags and ball holders. Its specialty is blank lineup cards and charts to keep track of the team's performance, plus extras like team stationery.

Baseball Express
www.baseballexp.com
Takes you down to the Ball Park which sells every item of baseball equipment you could ever possibly need, from bats, balls and gloves to those sandals you can wear in the shower or throw at those who have had a bad game.

Bats Unlimited(CHECK)
www.batsunlimited.com
Find the same bat cheaper elsewhere and they will try to beat the price. As authorized dealers for Worth and DeMarini they have an excellent selection, and you can buy from the range of promotional T-shirts and sweats.

Capsized
www.capsized.com
As Henry Ford might have said, you can have anything you want as long as it's a cap, from this site that bills itself as "the greatest cap store on the Net". Stock includes vintage caps worn by the likes of Hank Aaron and Babe Ruth.

Cooperstown Collection
www.cooperstown-collection.com/capsteam.html
This site is slightly bewildering but there's still a huge range of caps to quicken the pulse of the most hardened cap-aholic.

Kelley Baseball
www.kelleybaseball.com
Kelley's mission is "to provide you with the best gear on the planet!" and with gloves for every position and bats for every taste, the range is pretty wide.

Major League Baseball
www.mlb.com
The official shop on the official MLB is slick, well designed, and possibly just a bit over-branded but you can buy every item used by MLB teams.

The Jugs Company
www.thejugscompany.com
Keep getting hit on the head by pop flies? Erratic hitting a danger to the crowd? The Jugs Company thinks its trademark pitching machines, batting cages and accessories are the answer. Radar guns are also available.

The Lumber Company
www.thelumbercompany.com
This is one of baseball's big hitters but this site is a missed merchandising opportunity with only posters and sweatshirts with players' names on offer.

 **The things you can do with leather...**

Basehit
www.basehit.net
Al Young's vast baseball memorabilia site is vast but clear and easy to use.

Cooperstown Bat Company
www.cooperstownbat.com
Bats, bats and more bats. But not, as yet, any online ordering.

Hall of Fame
http://shop.baseballhalloffame.org
Everything that can be branded including a dress stitched like a baseball.

Mickey's Place
www.mickeysplace.com
Well-designed and folksy site including autographed items and prints.

Sports Accessories
http://sportsaccessories.com
They take baseball-mitt leather and produce other things from it...

The MLB team homepages have now been absorbed into www.mlb.com.

Bath & beauty

Mirror, mirror, on the wall, which is the loveliest site of all? While the newer, trendier brand names seem surprisingly shy of selling online, good grooming is there for those who know it's chic to click...

 Go on, treat yourself

Aboe
www.1Aboe.com
Not a huge range but the herbal and aromatic bath and body products are reasonably priced. There's also free shipping on orders over $25.

African Formula Cosmetics
www.africanformula.com
African Formula cosmetics stress their environmentally friendly nature with no animal fats or proteins. Prices for bath, hair and skin products are cheap at $6.50 per item but the $7 shipping charge quickly bumps the cost up.

Bath Factory
www.thebathfactory.com
Psychedelic colored bubbles spring from the homepage, and every scent imaginable can be found at this store, from honeysuckle olive oil soap to mustard bath soaks. Ordering is easy, but shipping charges remain a mystery.

Beauty Jungle
www.beautyjungle.com
Perseverance is needed here but once you get the hang of the system there are cosmetics, haircare, skincare and fragrances to be had from top names. The discounts are limited but the collection is extensive.

Garden Botanika
www.gardenbotanika.com
A standard site selling own-brand products from skincare to Aromatics,

cosmetics to something for the men in your life (but not, sadly, for the life in your men). UPS delivery costs $5.50. Dull but worth a look.

Lite Cosmetics
www.litecosmetics.com
Just $14.95 gets you Revive Refirming face cream, Wrinkle Lite cream and a host of other products designed to get your skin looking better.

Origins
www.origins.com
A comprehensive range of natural remedies for poor hair, skin and stress levels, featuring the majority of what you're likely to find in stores; prices starting at $11 for hair care, going up to a more extravagant $30.

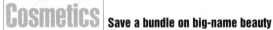 ## Cosmetics — Save a bundle on big-name beauty

Anna Sui
www.annasuibeauty.com
Anna Sui has a glitzy and sparkling range and the color swatches do the products justice but the site itself is a nightmare to navigate. Prices are average given that this isn't your everyday make-up.

Avon
www.avon.com
Bath, beauty, skin and haircare products online with more to come no doubt. The color swatches are small but they do offer helpful notes as to how to best apply. There are also weekly specials, free gifts and of course low prices.

Bobbi Brown began with just lips and now there's just no stopping the queen of neutral cosmetics

Bobbi Brown
www.bobbibrown
cosmetics.com
If you've just realized your ice pink eyeshadow is a little too Barbie girl, Bobbi Brown has the answer with the Looks & Tips section – shades for every skin tone from African-American to Asian. Prices are steep, but you are paying for expertise.

Cosmetics Mall
www.cosmeticsmall.com
A chaotic opening page but worth sticking with for the

bargains. Names include Sally Hansen, Revlon and Clarins, at a fraction of their regular price. However, this is a site that's best for those who stick to what they know.

Mac Cosmetics
www.maccosmetics.com
How not to sell cosmetics. The Mac site looks flashy but doesn't work. Every product has a silly name, an unnecessary introduction and blurred color swatches.

New York Cosmetics
www.nycos.com
An attractive site with simple scroll down menus offering own-brand cosmetics and face products at average prices. More thought needed but a good start.

Strawberry Net
www.strawberrynet.com
Top names include Anna Sui, Clarins and Chanel, discounts are generally between 35 per cent and 50 per cent and shipping is free if you can wait 4-6 days.

Urban Decay
www.urbandecay.com
A funky, well put together site, but definitely not for the shy and retiring. Shades include Cash, a lovely green hue, and Frostbite blue.

Zhen
zhen.fastcart.com
Amateur-looking but well thought out with products tailored for those with Asian skin tones at half the price of their competitors.

EYEBROWZ

Definitely one of the more unusual sites, Eyebrowz is the DIY site to perfect eyebrows. Advertised as "painting by numbers", Eyebrowz offers 60 eyebrow shapes to choose from, helpful advice and Hollywood celebrity visual aids including Madonna and Jennifer Aniston, to help you choose the best shape stencil to suit you. Choose from the whole package for $22.95 or just the powder refills at $5. Men can also get in on the act with their own kits. They ship within 2-5 days for a mere $2.

www.eyebrowz.com

Fragrance The sweet smell of the Web

Atomizers King
www.atomizersking.com
So you've got your bottle of the latest Gaultier fragrance, half the price it should be. Why not now get yourself the ultimate 1940s glam accessory – the atomizer. Choose from discreet models to collectible works of art for display.

Fragrance Net
www.fragrance.com
Virtually every difficult-to-find fragrance lurks on these pages, and each one

comes with recommended "when to wear" information, just in case you aren't sure when Rumba is appropriate. Shipping is always free.

O-Shipping Fragrances
www.0-shippingfragrances.com
Free shipping on all products with designer names ranging from Abercrombie & Fitch to the lesser known Bill Blass, plus old favorites Mr Klein and Chanel.

Perfumania
www.perfumania.com
Top brands, discount prices, and even perfume for the kids, what more could you ask for? Search for a brand or simply browse alphabetically. All the top brands are there and discounts offer up to $25 off the RRP.

Perfume Warehouse
www.perfumewarehouse.com
At $10 an ounce it must be fake, and it is! Worth taking a risk? Up to you...

 Get in touch with your softer side

Menaji
www.menaji.com
The homepage flaunting buff men isn't exactly subtle but this is one of the few online cosmetics stores exclusively for men who need a concealer to hide nasty blemishes, bruises or nicks. Most items are priced between $20 and $30, but shipping is cheap at less than $1.

Norelco
www.norelco.com
Norelco accommodates all your shaving needs with Double, Micro, Reflex and even Quadra action razors on offer. On the downside you're expected to buy without knowing the cost – that isn't revealed until you begin the ordering process. The 2-year warranty makes (slight) amends for this.

 Reddy, steady, go

Redhead's Fancy
www.redheadsfancy.com
Should really be called "Redhead's – and those of a fairer complexion's – Fancy". Top-to-toe cosmetics for those who fall into both those categories which are, says the site, not available "anywhere but here". Standard $2 shipping charge per order.

Bikes

Whether you have aspirations to follow in Lance Armstrong's footsteps and make the Tour de France your own, or you just fancy pedalling to the office every now and then, there's a bike site to suit

Bicycle Buys

www.bicyclebuys.com

OK, so the neon yellow design can be a little offputting, but at least Bicycle Buys is easy to use and there's a good chance you'll come away with a not too expensive model. Products are categorized by type and then brand; names include Fuji, Ciocc and Free Agent BMX. Information is limited to a few descriptive lines and images that can be enlarged. Prices vary, but with a catalog heading into the hundreds you should be able to find something to suit your budget. Do, though, read the small print: prices listed can only apply to the frame, add an extra $500 in some cases for the whole ensemble.

Bike Smart

www.bikesmart.com

If you're an in and out kind of shopper Bike Smart is just the site for you. From each page you can link back to every other category, customer services and the checkout, and your shopping basket is displayed at all times. Descriptions are brief, and advice on how and what to buy is limited, but images of every product from jerseys to skewers and tires are available. You are encouraged to join the Bike Smart club, but unlike a lot of other sites there are benefits, like 10 per cent off every purchase, free shipping and updates on any interesting developments in the world of cycling. An excellent online venture.

Bikes Direct

www.bikesdirect.com

Not all of us are aiming to be the next Tour de France winner but if you're interested in trading in your now grown-up daughter's rusting Bluebell, with or without grocery carrier, Bikes Direct is designed for the simple sell. Categories consist of mountain, road, cruisers, kids and best of all, comfort cycles. Images are clear, with no obscure shots of state-of-the-art pedals, alongside easy-to-read features tables. Oh, and there's also the small matter of discounts up to the $500-off mark, free shipping and no added sales tax.

Bulltek Sports
www.bullteksports.com
If this truly is the biggest bike store, it hasn't done itself any favors creating a text-laden and difficult to navigate site. Our advice is to stick to the scroll down catalog index at the top. With everything from the gear to wear to frames and handlebars, it's only a pity they don't sell complete bikes. But they do offer helpful guidance on selecting the correct frame size and so on. Worth the trouble if you can take advantage of the sale prices and you can always individualize your new steed. E-mail orders only for the time being.

Excel Sports Boulder
www.excelsports.com
Standard site offering road and mountain bikes, accessories and tools. Search by product or brand, including Gios, Cervello and Merlin. Descriptions are adequate, but you can always link to their partner site, www.bike.com for more in-depth information and news surrounding the world of pedal transport. Prices vary but shipping in most cases doesn't break the $20 mark.

North Shore Cycles
www.nscycles.com
A Trek 2001 cycle or nothing this year? That's lucky as North Shore deals principally with these very items. If you're just in the market for any old ride it may be best to avoid this tedious online offering. With no obvious link that works to view the catalog, you're left solely with whatever feature items they're selling this week and special deals generally consisting of cut-price helmets. Die-hard Trekkers only.

SuperGo
www.supergo.com
A useful buying and general information site. Parts and complete bikes are available to buy from manufacturers Mongoose, Fuji, Gary Fisher and many more. Otherwise if your old faithful bike isn't being as faithful as it used to be, Mr SuperGo is on hand to answer any queries and hopefully save you the time, trouble and money of contacting a specialist for repairs. Prices obviously depend on the brand, but they generally lie between $1,000 and $2,000 – so probably one for enthusiasts only.

Boats

Build your own, buy your own and earn the right to say "Hello sailor!" and be saluted by your shipmates (if you must)

Buying a boat
Fancy a sloop? Look no further

Bluewater Sales

www.bluewtr.com

The classified ads cover a wide selection of crafts, from a basic dinghy for $850 to a long-range cruiser for a cool million and a half. Not all the ads have pictures, but you can e-mail for further details. The site also sells instructional videos on sailing, cruising, boating and salt and freshwater fishing.

Boat Hunter

www.boathunter.com

Online yacht brokers with a listing of boats to buy all over the world. You can e-mail them with the details of the exact boat you are looking for, or just browse through current listings and imagine yourself sailing away on the deck of an $80,000 cruising sloop. The site will act as your broker, checking title deeds and registration documents for each sale, as well as acting as stake holders to ensure that money changes hands smoothly.

Cape Yacht Sales

www.capeyachtsales.com

East Coast sailors should head for this well-designed site featuring new and used sail and powerboats. There are good pictures and specifications of most of the boats on offer, plus a monthly payment estimator for you to work out how much it will cost you to get finance, and you can make an immediate online enquiry about anything that catches your eye. The site also features a useful guide to the process of boat acquisition for first time buyers.

Sea Eagle

www.seaeagle.com

Not the most slickly designed site you'll ever see but nevertheless a terrific boating resource from this sport and fishing boat retailer. You can view some of their inflatable boats from all angles and even download RealVideo clips to see them in action. They also sell kayaks, separate motors and other accessories, and there are often hefty discounts and special offers for online buyers. All boats are available on a 30-day trial basis and come with a 3-year warranty. Shipping charges range between $6 and $75 and goods should arrive within 7 to 10 days of ordering.

Equipment — Roll up for your sat nav...

Maritech Marine Electronics
www.maritech.com
Based in Stamford, CT, this nautical electronics store can sell you everything you need in the way of on-board navigation, security, communications and entertainment systems and, if you want, install it for you.

Performance Yacht Systems
www.pyacht.com
Online yacht supplies from rigging to Gore-Tex jackets to two-way radios. Prices are comparable with discount catalogs, but there's lots of advice here. There are also a bunch of message boards for swapping stories. A rate calculator will give you an idea of shipping costs before you buy.

Starpath School of Navigation
www.starpath.com
How about learning to navigate the old way, using the heavens? Starpath can

sell you a classroom or home study course on sextant use for offshore navigation or all the plotting tools you need for safe passage within sight of land. Shipping costs between $8 and $28.

Waypoint
www.waypoints.com
Marine navigation and communications equipment and software for serious sailors. The company claims to have tested all the kit under real-life cruising conditions. They have a downloadable library and catalog of boating items, plus an informative newsletter.

Maritech Marine Electronics has everything to make sure you never get lost again. Unless you want to

Books

They're the most popular item to be bought over the Net, so it's odd how many sites have badly designed homepages or don't allow you to order online. Here are some of the best – and some of the weirdest

 The big names and biggest stocks

Amazon

www.amazon.com

The most famous name on the planet when it comes to online shopping and while it has long branched out beyond its original niche, it is still synonymous with books on the Web. It remains one of the easiest-to-use online shopping sites and a one-click system lets you buy in seconds. The search mechanism is quick and simple although you sometimes get different results depending on which page you access it from. User reviews are normally well worth reading.

Barnes and Noble

www.barnesandnoble.com

If you're based in Manhattan, B&N can whizz your order round the same day. The rest of us lesser mortals have to wait a little longer but there's still plenty of reason to shop at this site, such as the Readers' Advantage scheme, which will save you 5 per cent on online purchases (10 per cent in their stores). It also gives access to invitation-only events such as signings while other perks include a free canvas B&N bag. And if you're at or leaving college, B&N will kindly buy or sell your used textbooks.

Bookstreet

www.1bookstreet.com

Free shipping and a free book with orders over $20 have made this a real contender in the book price wars. It also offers 30 per cent off *New York Times* best-sellers and there are some bargain 2, 3 and 4-book multi-buy bundles which offered up to 72 per cent off when we visited. If you know the category of book you're after, head straight for the appropriate "street" –

Wander off the beaten literary track with Borders – which comes complete with its own TV channel

MysteryStreet, RomanceStreet, or CookbookStreet. If it's Christian books you need, try 1 JesusWay.com. Seriously.

Bookzone
www.bookzone.com

Bookzone is not just an online bookstore, it's an online book community where you can rub shoulders with the literati. This site also acts as a gateway to publishers who will sell direct to you. There are 3,500 publishers listed; the SuperCatalog lets you search for what you want and a Literary Leaps link section will let you search outside of the site. If you fancy publishing your own work online, you'll find plenty of advice here.

Borders
www.borders.com

Well worth keeping as a bookmark because it reaches parts of the book world that some of its bigger rivals don't, featuring more obscure, often-overlooked American authors. Drop into the Netcafé where it's easy to while away the time with interviews, features and a true multimedia literary experience: read excerpts from various selections in the Reading Room, hear some poetry in the Listening Room and find out what's playing on Borders Vision, the site's own TV channel, which was showing a video of Anthony Hopkins talking about *Hannibal* when we visited.

Contentville
www.contentville.com

A site for people who just love "content", whether that be books, screenplays, study guides, dissertations or speeches (there's even a Charles Dickens speech you can download for $1.85). Certainly one for the more erudite book buyer. You can go behind the scenes with Contentville's book scout to find out what you're going to be reading next year. There is also a good stack of free first chapters to read online.

Iron Kettle Books
www.ironkettle.com
No Barnes and Noble or Amazon, as it's the first to admit, Iron Kettle started off selling remaindered books to American schools. It now delivers to individuals and often sells its small, but interesting, stock for a third of the listed price. It's always worth checking out its latest catalog for bargains and there was a fiction clearance sale when we visited with hardbacks going for just $2. No secure server when we dropped by but you can e-mail your order and put a check in the post (remember that you should never send credit card details via e-mail).

Powell's Books
www.powells.com
A Powell's shopper can choose to pay "$24.95 for a new hardback or $15 for the same volume used", says the *Philadelphia Inquirer* on the site. So unless you're completely anal about books and must have them in mint condition, the used option has to be worth a try, especially since Powell's guarantees every book for quality. The biggest new and used bookshop in the world cuts a similarly imposing figure on the Internet and should certainly be in any booklover's top 5. You can also sign up to a regular newsletter which, says Powell's, smells like a day among wet Douglas Firs and sounds like feisty salmon orating at town meetings about hydroelectric power. Mmm...

Waterstones
www.waterstones.co.uk
The book chain that changed the face of main street bookshops in the UK is also in the business of selling to overseas customers, including US residents, and while you might not be bagging a bargain by the time you've added shipping and

handling charges, the packed site is worth a bookmark. Lots of editor's recommendations (across a variety of different categories) books of the month, and "buy two get a third free" offers. You also get the opportunity to order pre-publication bestsellers at
a discount. Watch delivery charges, though.

Wordsworth.com
www.wordsworth.com
The online incarnation of this well-known independent bookseller may not be bursting with special offers and features like some of the big Internet superstores but it'll appeal to the independently minded book-buyer. It also features one of the longest running weekly contests on the Web, in which it gives the first line or the last line of a book. Your mission, if you choose to accept it, is to figure out what the book is. Be warned, it's strangely addictive.

Also worth a mention if you're into that sort of thing:
www.comedybooks.com for a range of rib-tickling books about professional rib-ticklers.
www.digitalguru.com for those who like reading computer manuals.
www.dogbooks.com for dingo, coyote, purebreds and generic dog owners.
www.eastwest.com is reading for those on a spiritual inner quest, whatever their desired path.
www.hopefarm.com for native New Yorkers, who can't get enough of reading about their state.
www.hungrygulch.com for lovers of the American West; e-mail orders only.
www.killerbooks.com for whodunnits of every genre.
www.io.com/~aylott for space-crime continuum travellers.
www.napoleons.com.au/ for fans of the French general, everything ever written about him.
www.sherlock-holmes.com for fans of deductive reasoning, elementary sleuthing and the curious incident of the dog who barked in the night.

The vast selection of Powell's used books is a real winner, providing a bargain route to beefing up your library

E-books
Reading at the click of a button

Books you can usually download from the Internet for a small fee and either read on screen (fine for shorter work) or print out. The queen of e-authors is Lee Nolan Childers, who writes romances and detective stories starring a cat.

E-Book Ad
www.eBookAd.com
With more than 10,000 titles, across all genres, in any format, even the most resolute e-book sceptic can't deny there's something to this. Search by price, category, author, publisher or the format you need. Esquire's *How To Be A Better Man* is not the literary pinnacle of the free section and only titles like the *Cisco Router Handbook* are featured in the $50 plus section.

E-Book Mall
www.ebookmall.com
The title won't blow you away, but the E-Book Mall is all about efficiency. Well-organized with the usual search modes and prices generally around $6 plus free e-books with every order. Concentrates on literary classics rather than new titles but it'll help you swot up on some of the masters.

E-pulp
www.e-pulp.com
Great title and suitably hard-boiled design raise expectations for this store of new mystery and sci-fi writing. Sadly the authors don't quite live up to them.

FictionWise
www.fictionwise.com
Dedicated to those looking for escapism. The literary offerings, mostly short stories, are divided into suitable categories but you really have to have a pretty clear idea what you're looking for.

Stephen King
www.stephenking.com
The horror maestro's online serial offering, *The Plant*, had, in the words of the site, "furled its leaves" when we visited but a return was promised.

Universal Download
www.udownload.com
Most e-book sites are partial and populated by authors you've never heard of. Not this one. It allows the user to peruse TS Eliot's *The Wasteland*, inspect the *Treaty of Versailles* or download *War and Peace*. A thoroughly impressive selection of electronic texts with a friendly, ersatz Yahoo-style homepage.

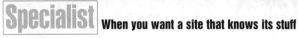

Specialist When you want a site that knows its stuff

Business
McGraw-Hill Bookstore
www.bookstore.mcgraw-hill.com

This is a "real professional bookstore", aimed at outstanding professionals who simply can't wait to delve into its archive of 35,000 business titles. Although it is owned by a leading business and academic publisher, this store sells titles by all publishers. You can even find a title that tells you how Genghis Khan and Bill Gates made their fortunes, although you suspect competition was a bit less intense when Genghis was pioneering his own particular brand of monopoly capitalism.

Culture
Essential Media
www.essentialmedia.com

Counter culture rather than culture in actual fact. We were given an ID cart number even before we started shopping (or expressed an interest to do

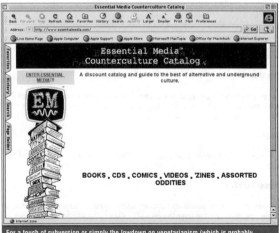

For a touch of subversion or simply the lowdown on vegetarianism (which is probably regarded as subversive by those of a carnivorous nature), head for Essential Media

anything but browse) which seemed a bit too much like Big Brother. However we'll forgive them since this is the place where you can buy the esteemed Rev Macklin's booklets of joyous guerilla letter-writing to corporate giants such as Coca-Cola, Kellogg's and Proctor and Gamble. A fantastic emporium of books, videos and ephemera on all things alternative and underground (categories span African American studies to Vegetarianism and Ecology), with enough books on conspiracy theories to keep Mulder in holiday reading for the rest of his life. Good clean, ordering instructions too.

Films
Read the Movie
www.readthemovie.com

You would think this Amazon-associate site would help you find the book of the movie. Well, almost right, except that films like *Chopper Chicks in Zombietown* (starring Billy Bob Thornton) obviously didn't require any literary inspiration, although they're still listed here. In fact, this site also sells audiobooks, soundtracks, videos, DVDs and laser discs of popular movies (plus a few TV series) all at discount prices. There is also a small archive section of certain actors and actresses. If you're desperate to know how *A Bug's Life* inspired enough titles to outnumber an ant colony, this is the place for you. Compelling in a very odd sort of way.

Medicine
Priory Bookshop
www.priory.com/prbkshp.htm

UK-based Amazon-affiliate site that has a quick and easy to use front-end index, neatly categorized. It lists every medical title you could ever want, including a *Companion to Hypertension* and a handy *Pocket Guide to Electrocardiography*. There's a family section if you want more consumer-oriented books but wherever you select your purchase, you'll be taken to the familiar Amazon interface to order and pay for it.

Political
Midnight Special Bookstore
read.msbooks.com/MSBooks/homepage.html
Online version of the Santa Monica-based bookshop,

A WORD IN YOUR EAR

When buying used books online, remember to check:

1 Shipping costs and policies. They're not always easy to find but it's worth the effort.

2 The condition the books are in. Good sites offer ratings or tell you if the title's worn or damaged.

3 The book you're buying. When you're scrolling down your umpteenth text page, it's easy to misread the short description of the book you think you're looking for and get an unpleasant shock when it actually arrives.

4 The policy on returns. Understandably, sellers of used books don't offer the kind of "no quibble guarantee" you'll get from bigger stores. If you can't see a policy, ring or e-mail them before you hand over any money.

5 If the site's secure. A disturbing number of smaller US stores seemed to expect you to key in your credit card details on unencrypted sites. If in any doubt whatsoever, ask.

which specializes in social and political titles. More than 100,000 titles to browse, with both obscure and mainstream tastes catered for. If you want to see what the bricks and mortar shop is like, take a QuickTime VR tour. And just in case you happen to be in town, the site features a full itinerary of in-store author signings and other events.

Sports
ShopSports
www.shopsports.com
A one-stop superstore whatever your sport and it has the advantage of letting you hop across to the video section, or maybe treat yourself to some new kit, all in just a couple of clicks. Plenty of how-to books (performance kayaking, anyone?) as well as celebratory ones. Our only criticism is because they include a thumbnail picture of each book, pages can take a while to download, especially in the big sections like baseball and golf. Free shipping on all orders.

Travel
Book Passage
www.bookpassage.com/travel
All the big names in travel are covered – *Baedekers*, *Compass*, *Eye Witness*, *Lonely Planet*, *Michelin*, *Rough Guide* – as well as lesser-known ones. Quick and easy to use site: click the destination you want on the homepage and it takes you to a list of titles dedicated to that place (factual and fictional). Shipping is free in the US on orders over $20. BookPassage is part of the BookSite network of independent resellers.

 **Used books** Out of print but not out of mind

Advanced Book Exchange
www.abebooks.com
The Advanced Book Exchange describes itself as the world's largest network of independent booksellers, and its homepage has been designed as a homage to Amazon's. You can search its list of 20 million titles and find some pretty obscure stuff, such as the out-of-print autobiography of 1970s glam-rock icon Bryan Ferry or the European diary of a wealthy young American called John F Kennedy. Probably the best place to start if you want old, out-of-print books, even if they're paperbacks.

Antiquarian Book Dealers and Associations on the World Wide Web
www.connectotel.com/books/wwwbs.html
Gateway to the wonderful world of dusty old antiquarian and rare booksellers. The backbone of the site is its huge A-Z database of online dealers around the world who specialize in everything from the Ottoman Empire to the Beat

Generation. There are also links to the world's major rare book search engines, plus fellow bookish associations.

Bibliofind

www.bibliofind.com

A site which spans an impressive network of booksellers – it claims to have 10 million titles in its archive. This site is associated with Amazon, so you know you can order with confidence.

Maps And Prints

www.mapsandprints.com/manuscripts.cfm

If you're interested in some rather older used books, why not take a trip to the Maps and Prints site and splash out $200 on a medieval manuscript of a *Book of Hours*? Art Source International's rather limited stock of old manuscripts sits alongside a more impressive array of maps, globes and such. This site positively encourages you to order online, uses a secure server and is upfront about its shipping costs.

The Antiquarian

www.theantiquarian.com

Plenty of holy grails for booklovers to search out here. For real classics (and we mean classics), head for Bibles, religion and philosophy where you can bag a Bagster bible from 1827 (first edition), complete with fully gilt dentelles and red moiré silk end papers for just $3,000. Or $900 buys you Longman's 1845 copy of *Sermon on the Mount*. The Civil War, children's literature and the 20th century are

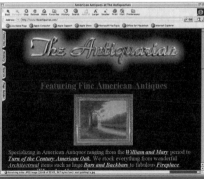

The Antiquarian's idea of fun might not exactly tally with yours but you'll probably still find plenty of seriously old items to marvel at

also covered and there's even a section entitled "A few fun items", with signed letters from both Conan-Doyle and TS Eliot; they may not be everyone's idea of side-splitting humor but they will obviously bring a smile to a book collector's face.

The following are also worth a look although not all offer online ordering or have a secure server so check payment and shipping information first:

www.austinsbooks.com Lists old books on General Custer and fly-fishing among its specialties. Good for general US history.

www.edicionesgrial.com This Anglo-Spanish site contains a limited edition facsimile of the *Quest For the Holy Grail,* complete with a reproduction of the original binding for $2,510 plus shipping. Ordering is via fax, e-mail or snail mail.

www.eskimo.com/~recall/ Of more modern relevance, leaning towards radical and social political books. It features a checklist of more than 5,000 Vietnam books.

www.hrkahnbooks.com This is a Canadian shop which specializes in old books on travel. Stock varies and prices can go well into 5 figures, but most are between $400 to $2,500. A search feature would help. Ordering is via e-mail.

www.needleworkbooks.com There is obviously a demand for out-of-print sewing books or else the Hard-to-Find Needlework Book company wouldn't have been in business for over 20 years. Your best shot for that elusive first edition of *Quilt World.*

Poetry Get off your horse and write a poem

You don't have to be Walt Whitman to publish your poetry on the Web (though it would help, of course), which is why cyberspace is full of badly penned verse. Thank heavens then, for literary guardians like the Cowboy Poets Society at www.cowboyrudy.com/cbyptsoc.htm. It's not enough to don a ten-gallon hat and a pair of spurs to get in: "The honesty of their presentations cannot be imitated unless the performer has lived the life," says the site, which has links to greats such as Jeremiah Johnson from Texas, Bo Boggess from Tennessee and Tena Coker Bastian, the cow gal from Ohio. And if you're looking for a cowboy poet to entertain at your party, the wordsmith behind the site, Rudy Gonzales, is only too happy to oblige. Fear not about his credentials: he was the first cowboy to perform at the Kennedy Centre in Washington for Idaho State Day, having been nominated by Idaho senator Michael D Crapo.

Cameras

Whether you want to take better snaps or become the new Cartier-B it's worth logging on. There's even a site featuring a type of camera that predates the venerable French photographer

4 U Digital
www.4udigital.com
Whether you're looking for digital, 35mm, APS or SLR models, or just a new bag or lens for your existing model, 4 U Digital offers a comprehensive catalog of cameras and accessories. All the top brands are available, Nikon, Canon, Kodak, Olympus and more, with detailed descriptions and spec sheets, and clear images. They also offer every model at a discount price.

Abbey Camera
www.abbeycamera.com
Bit hit and miss this one. On the one hand it has a fair selection of equipment and film and paper laid out in a clear format, but on the other there is little information and no specs, and no digital cameras. Shipping is calculated each time you add to your basket.

Cambridgeworld
www.cambridgeworld.com
What an incredible resource. The description and specs for the cameras are exhaustive to the point where you'll feel you know the camera inside and out before you take a picture. There is also a used section but it claims that the selection is so vast and constantly changing that you're better off calling with your specific requirements and you're bound to find a match.

Camera Zone
www.camerazone.com
With a clean layout and easy navigation, the Camera Zone offers a large selection of digital and point and shoot cameras, along with all the necessary and unnecessary accessories. On the downside the site's speed of response

isn't quite as super as you might expect from a company which bills itself as "your online photo superstore".

Craig Camera

www.craigcamera.com

Found an old camera in the attic and wondering if you can get it to work? This is a great resource for instruction manuals and those pamphlets that came with the camera but which you've long since mislaid. A variety of collectible cameras and equipment are also for sale. Sadly ordering is the annoying fill-in-the-form type. As for the "Basic Computer Lesson" well if you haven't already seen this example of toilet humour we won't spoil the "gag".

Focus Camera

www.focuscamera.com

A bit fiddly but this site has most things you may need. The shipping details are rather long-winded as the site calculates it for you but you can see it adds a fair bit to your total. Prices are all discounted. You might find yourself overwhelmed by the volume of "incredible deals you won't want to miss".

Kodak

www.kodak.com

If you're a one camera kind of person, and that camera has to be a Kodak, you can put your mind at rest with the knowledge that they boast one of the slickest and most comprehensive digital camera stores online. Simply browse the selection of models and accessories, or use the advice section for a little background knowledge. There are few discounts but the reconditioned section offers the latest models, revamped at discount prices.

Order a camera from Cambridge World and you get given so much detail that when it actually arrives it will feel like an old friend

LH Systems

www.lh-systems.com

This is a specialist site, so specialist in fact that you have to be an account customer before you can buy from it, but as it sells aerial and photogrammetry equipment (if you have to ask, you don't need it), it isn't exactly targeting those hoping to take better holiday snaps. If you use this stuff at all you're probably a commercial or military customer. Still, it's reassuring to know it's out there.

Pacific Rim Camera

www.pacificrimcamera.com

This is a good source of used and collectible cameras and other photographic equipment but it could be made a bit easier to use. The company claims it doesn't want its site to suffer from an online equivalent of urban sprawl and to speed up downloading the pages are low on images. All of which would be fine if it was easier to buy stuff. There is an e-mail option and a phone number but no ordering form to help you. The site says it does most of its business by e-mail but you might wish to phone or fax your order.

CAMERA OBSCURA

Finer Times at www.finertimes.com offers a different kind of camera, the collectible kind.

Prices vary from far less than you'd pay for a new model to $1,349 for a mint-condition Leica M4-2. The descriptions are faultless and you can always e-mail the seller for the personal touch.

Photo World at www.photoworldweb.com offers a mainstream approach to collectible, used and camera accessories. No online ordering however and you will need to e-mail for more info.

Ritz Camera

www.ritzcamera.com

This site does more than sell camera equipment at discount prices – it will even advise you on how to take better pics, from basic techniques to how to photograph a swimsuit model. If you are happy with the results, the site sponsors a photographic competition with some decent prize money. Sections include one-use and children's cameras. The clearance section has some incredible deals.

Smile

www.smilephotovideo.com

One for the experts. Smile offers a huge range of both your average APS and 35mm models, and professional lighting equipment, filters, flashes and tripods which is great if you're looking to buy the whole shebang but not so good if you're a novice. Beginners may also be flummoxed by the absence of any extra info. That aside, you can make your search as detailed as you prefer and with such a large selection, every price range is catered for.

The Hungary Eye

www.leicasource.com

This Leica specialist site expects you to do all the work – none of the cameras, lenses or other

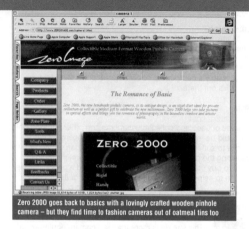

Zero 2000 goes back to basics with a lovingly crafted wooden pinhole camera – but they find time to fashion cameras out of oatmeal tins too

equipment has any sort of description or spec details, just a name and a price. You even have to fill in the order form yourself. The test reports section, which might reassure buyers, wasn't available when we visited.

Wolf Camera

www.wolfcamera.com
An easy to navigate site, with a large selection of cameras and equipment and there is a "recommended section" but when you press for "more info" you can get as little as 15 extra words on a product. Shipping by ground is free.

Woodmere Camera

www.woodcam.com
You have to know exactly what you want here, as this no-frills site is not going to help. It sells used equipment, graded cosmetically, with optics and mechanics in perfect order unless otherwise stated. It also auctions equipment through eBay. Could do with a more legible typeface and layout.

Zero Image

www.zeroimage.com
This site was created in Hong Kong, but is in English, and the type of camera featured, a wooden pinhole in various formats, is beautiful and unique. The translation is endearing, yet comprehensible. The cameras themselves look like works of art and the gallery displays a few examples of the kind of photographs that can be achieved using them.

Cars

Keen to get a
new set of wheels
but more worried about
saving money than getting a feel for your
new automobile? Then skip the showroom
salesmanship and check these sites out

 Back when chrome was king

Caddy Daddy

www.caddydaddy.com

A site that sings to you while you're browsing and a downloadable catalog of spares for every Caddy made from 1936-1978. You can save yourself time and find other fans who have whole Cadillacs for sale, although not all are shown. Added bonus: the world's first comprehensive list of Cadillac songs.

Classic Auto World

www.classicautoworld.com

A huge range of classic autos, including imports like an English 1969 MG GT Coupé, and plenty of pictures. The vast number of cars from the 1920s to the present day can make it all a bit bewildering, but it's worth looking for the bargains – and the utterly disturbing "time out dolls" for your fender.

Classic Car Mall

www.classiccarmall.com

The definition of "classic" may be pushing it and the design won't win any awards but the site puts buyers in touch with sellers and leaves them to it.

Findamustang

www.findamustang.com

Search for the Mustang of your dreams by state and the site will tell you which types are for sale, and where they are. It will also give contact details of the vendor, but after that it's down to you. Should you need to make room in your garage for your latest purchase, you can also place ads yourself.

Lost n The 50s
www.lostnthe50s.com

Back to the days when songs had lyrics (like "awopbopaloobop"). Lost n The 50s stresses it's a work in progress so you can't buy online yet, but you can e-mail the owners in Missouri if you've seen a car you want on the site or want them to search for one. On sale, everything from a mint condition 1955 T-bird ($28,000) to a Route 66 clock ($24.95). Pity about the online furry dice.

 Brand names which sell online

Chrysler
www.chrysler.com

Chrysler wants you to buy anything from a PT Cruiser to an owners' manual but while this is a sleek, well-designed site, it's also slightly misleading. Rather than being the "fast lane to acquiring Chrysler vehicles", it's more of a nice shop window to look through. Once you've chosen your car, they e-mail your request to one of the 5-star dealers in your area.

Ford
www.ford.com

This looks promising – you can buy cars, but they're die-cast metal and about 3ins long. With "Build and Price" you can custom-build your dream car or truck – no crazy wings or jets, sadly – and request a price quote. Ford is confident enough to offer a link to impartial reviews at Yahoo! Autos, but doesn't feel the need to explain things like front- and rear-wheel drive to first-timers.

General Motors
www.generalmotors.com

GM tells you what nice responsible people they are but won't sell you a car online. Use the muscular GMBuyPower search engine to find the car of your dreams and then decide on the (detailed) spec. Keying in your zip code gives you the address of the dealer where you can find your new car and a number for the member of staff who's waiting to sell it to you.

Lexus
www.lexus.com

This drab site will find you a Lexus CPO (certified pre-owned), or,

Want to pick your new Chrysler? Off you go then. On a budget? Forget the car, just buy the manual

surprise surprise, build your own from scratch. You just have to stay awake.

Nissan

www.nissanbuydirect.com
It's probably easier to spend a quick $300 here than in Vegas, but that $300 deposit does mean you can pick up your new Nissan 24 hours later. Albeit probably from San Diego.

Volkswagen

www.volkswagen.com
An absolute joy to use. VW will find your local dealer, find the dealer selling your dream car and shock, horror, it does all this with a sense of humor.

 ## Just smell that upholstery

1Click Auto Brokers

www.1clickautobrokers.com
Decked out in attractive white and beige combo, this site might not look that good, but it's disarmingly simple. 1Click acts as a buyer's agent. Use the site to tell your 1Click broker what you want, pay them a refundable $100 deposit and leave the rest to them. If they find a car you want they keep the deposit; if they don't it won't cost you a cent.

Autobytel

www.autobytel.com
Another site that acts as a middleman, Autobytel has a search engine that will find what you're after and find someone near you who's selling it. It's a one-stop shop with financing, insurance quotes and warranties all under one roof on this clean and clearly laid out site.

Autoweb

www.autoweb.com
The bright and friendly pastel shades make you feel like buying a new car is the least you can do for this lot. It's all smiley faces and a customer care team who'd just love it if you e-mailed them. Once you've found the car you want, "an Authorized Autoweb.com Dealer or online car selling partner" will e-mail you back with a quote. And they'll e-mail you again 3 days later just to make sure you're happy. Bless them.

THE FIFTH BEETLE

www.geocities.com/
herbielove53/

At the HerbieLove site you'll find everything you need to turn the Beetle languishing on your driveway into the world's most famous car with a heart. Admittedly all you get are several blue and white stripes and the number 53 in a big white disc (called a gumball in the trade) to stick on your vehicle, but it does the job. Why stop there? You can also buy Herbie's famous license plate OFP 857 and a pin. The point of all this? "To spread the joy of Herbie and Herbie's products throughout the world." Can't argue with that.

Bored of gridlock? Bored of big men kicking sand in your face when you go to the beach to get away from it all? The answer is at Auto Haus Buggies – www.autohausbuggies. com/ – where you can get your very own dune buggy for a meagre $6995.

Where to go when they're not all in working order

CarParts
www.carparts.com
There are a lot of parts here, and a lot of menus. Once you've found your way round you can use the shortcut and enter the keyword and number of the part you're after, or just browse. The site sells recycled parts, as well as Chilton's manuals to tell you what to do with them.

e-Parts Source
www.e-partssource.com
You can find everything you want here from whole cars to stereo equipment and memorabilia. Essentially a site of searchable classified ads, you can tell it to auto notify you when someone places an ad for that clutch you can't find. Or you can download a "babe" browser skin if that's more your kind of thing.

Wrenchead
www.wrenchead.com
Not a David Lynch film but somewhere to buy parts online, Wrenchead divides its parts into 3: replacement, accessories and performance. Search results come up with a range of alternatives from different suppliers. Or you can just meet other Wrencheads in the "Hangout", which sounds like the name of a groovy nightclub from a truly bad Elvis movie circa 1968.

 Just one previous owner. His name? Jackie Stewart

iMotors
www.imotors.com
"The best way to buy a used car on the Internet" is a big claim but it's one that iMotors can back up. Tell them what kind of "pre-loved" car you're after, place a $250 deposit, and they find it and give it a 269-point inspection.

AutoTrader
www.autotrader.com
With 1.5 million cars on this site, you'll find the car you want or just have to accept the fact it doesn't exist. It's fast, easy to use and wholly excellent.

ZoomCar
www.ZoomCar.com
ZoomCar is every couch potato's friend. They'll not only find that Mercury you want, they'll drive it to your door. They also arrange finance over the phone.

Celebrities

Whether you're after a Liberace poster, an Elvis doll, or a T-shirt from a bygone TV show, the Internet is your friend

A Remembrance of Marilyn

www.remembermarilyn.com

Marilyn occupies a (un)healthy portion of cyberspace all by herself. This site has an impressive selection of authentic and reproduction memorabilia, including vintage magazines and promotional movie posters. There's no shopping cart, nor does the site state that its online order form is secure, so you may prefer to phone your card details through. Domestic shipping is a standard $6 including insurance and you should allow 4-6 weeks for delivery.

Baby Jane of Hollywood

www.babyjaneofhollywood.com

Betty Grable, Esther Williams, Montgomery Clift – this site conjures up memories of a raft of old stars through their posters, photos and autographs. Some of the items are not cheap. An original costume design sketch of Ursula Andress by Edith Head will set you back a cool $200, a rare Liberace poster is on sale for a "mere" $95. But for serious celebrity collectors looking for something unusual, this is a great site.

Celebrity Merchandise

www.celebritymerch.com

Lots of official merchandise on sale here from a host of current stars and celebs. Choose from stuff like membership to Paula Abdul's fan club, a free photo of Michael Douglas, or an entire Elvira costume. Information on shipping charges is somewhat vague, but it seems that there is a single flat rate charge, regardless of the size of your order. The exception to this is if you happen to live in either Alaska or Hawaii, in which case they will e-mail you with the bad financial news.

Celebrity Signings

www.celebritysignings.com

Online catalog for you to snag the John Hancock of your favorite star without having to follow them around like a crazed stalker. Great offers include a signed color photo of Muhammad Ali, and there are autographs from other screen and sporting stars like Jeff Bagwell and Sean Connery.

Classic TV Shop
www.classictvshop.com
If you loved Lucy, always left it to Beaver, or longed to join the gang on *Gilligan's Island*, this is the site to stir all your memories and give you the chance to buy a few trinkets along the way. You could be after a Lassie lunchbox ($14) or a Daisy Duke T-shirt ($16); whatever old show you loved, there'll be something here for you. Shipping charges depend on your location and are calculated at the checkout (a shirt would cost around $6 to send).

Elvis Shop
www.elvis.com/shopelvis/default.asp
The official online Elvis mall has enough product to satiate even the most ardent fan's appetite. Swinging hips telephones, Taking Care of Business jewelry (complete with lightning bolt insignia), a life-size stand-up of Elvis in his *Jailhouse Rock* outfit, Action Man-style Elvis dolls, it's all here. The biggest surprise is that the shop's nav bar links to his onetime rival, Ricky Nelson.

Music Memorabilia
www.visionaryrock.com
Tour programmes, concert tickets, T-shirts, posters and even guitar picks from some of rock and pop's greatest names. There's a speedy search engine to pull up what you are looking for from the extensive database, so if you're after an original ticket to an Andy Williams concert ($5), or a 1982 Judas Priest *Screaming For Vengeance* poster ($55), this is the place to surf. Small items cost up to $16.50 to send FedEx, or you can contact the site for costs of shipping framed and larger orders.

Got one last space on your bedroom wall that's just perfect for a *Screaming For Vengeance* poster...?

Chocolates & candy

Bars, fudge & humbug! Is this the Internet or is Congress back in session?

 From the classic to the simply very classy

Godiva Chocolates
www.godiva.com
The most sophisticated chocolatier has also managed to produce a sophisticated website. You won't find balloons and multi-colored sweet wrappers here, just premium chocolates in gold ballotins. Browse the entire collection or search by occasion, prices are standard, ranging from $20 to $100. More unusual items include the dessert chocolates, including Crème Brûlée and Mochacinno mouse. If the shiny boxes aren't tempting enough you can click on individual truffles for close-up shots and descriptions.

Hershey's Gift Shop
www.hersheygifts.com
Everyone loves Hershey and now you can buy Hershey bars and Kisses online. This site is aiming at the special occasion market, search by event or holiday (or just invent one) and then choose from a huge catalog of boxes. Prices range from $15 for a 1lb tin, to $80 for a mountain of Hershey Nuggets, Almond bars, Reeses Pieces and Kisses. Ordering is simple, but take care to note additional costs for taxes and shipping.

 Still not sweet enough?

Candy & Stuff
www.candyandstuff.com
All your childhood favorites are here, candy apples, jawbreakers, cotton candy, popcorn, all at bargain prices, although probably more than you

remember – $3 an apple, $6 a box of jawbreakers. The site assumes you
know what cotton candy looks like – you're only offered a limited range of
images – but the items really sell themselves. Who could resist a white
chocolate and peanut candy apple? Ordering is standard but check the
information page for taxes and shipping.

Candy Depot
www.store.yahoo.com/candydepot
Very similar to Candy & Stuff, the Candy Depot focuses more on your hard
candy needs – Nerds, Skittles, Pez – and anything and everything sour: sour
bears, sour worms, sour cherries. If you think you can manage a pound of
sour apples they'll only cost you $4, but to order from here you'll need to do
more serious damage to your waistline as they have a minimum order value
of $15. Useful for celebrations and gifts but maybe a little much just to keep
your cravings satisfied.

Creole Creations
www.creolecreations.com
Originally based in Louisiana, Creole Creations is basically devoted to
(almost) everything you can do with praline including praline candies, candy
apples, and a variety of gift items. Prices are cheap at $9 for 6 praline bars
and shipping is respectable at $3.95 no matter what the amount. Worth
a note, the order form may put you off by making it look like you need to fill
everything in manually, but click the GB box next to your choice of items and
they take it from there.

Good Lollipops
www.goodlollipops.bigstep.com
Although you can only order via e-mail, Good Lollipops is definitely worth
a mention for sheer originality of the site. Despite the kid's style rainbow
homepage, the array of lolly flavors featured within are definitely not for
children. Amaretto, jalapeno and kahlua are just a few of the stronger

Happily there's no sign of Shirley Temple
on the Good Ship Lollipop, a site full of
goodies with definite adult appeal

varieties, with dill pickle and wintergreen taking top honours in the bizarre stakes. Don't expect to find your standard selection of round shapes either; there's everything here from cowboy boots to a cloverleaf. On the downside you do have to buy in bulk; at $84 for a selection of 240 lollipops you could well begin a new craze.

Grace Gourmet
www.gracegourmet.com

"Delight the soul!" proclaims Grace Gourmet, but even if you don't find spiritual fulfilment here it's certainly a useful site if you have a gift to buy and no idea where to start. Search through the adequate array of products or alternatively use the budget guide or sampler section to pin down the perfect gift. Tasty choices include cherry, choc-apricot and blueberry poppers, pecan caramel turtles and cheesecakes in every variety. Shipping charges vary from free to $24 so be aware. Otherwise this is a particularly tempting site.

 **Chocolate** The world's favorite stress-relieving drug

Chocodelphia
www.chocodelphia.com

If you're after a box of chocolates but want something that little bit special, at Chocodelphia you can choose the chocolate selection to suit your loved one. Pick and choose favorites from a wide selection of milk, dark and white chocolates, truffles and pralines, sugar-free for the health conscious and everything nutty for those nut-lovers. Prices start at around $13 a box. And if you can't make your mind up, you can always go for a "little-bit-of-everything and little-bit-of-heaven" in the shape of the Chocodelphia Sampler. As ever, don't forget shipping which starts at $6.

Chocolate Potpourri
www.chocolatetruffles.com

Don't be put off by the fragrant name. Calvin Klein hasn't (yet) produced a range of perfumed chocolates. What you will find is a deliciously chocolate brown homepage leading onto a limited, but gourmet, selection of truffles and toffees. Each tasty morsel is described in terms of the

Chocolate Potpourri could use Internet scratch 'n' sniff but there's still plenty to get the juices going

number and the different flavors. If you're not content with the image of the box, click on a truffle to find an enlarged picture of each chocolate, from Irish Cream to swirling pralines. Prices range from $12 for a box of 15, to $100 for the largest gift basket any stomach could handle. Remember to view the shipping however, as there is a minimum charge of $5.

River Street Sweets
www.riverstreetsweets.com
The site itself is basic: choose a category, browse through Christmas gift baskets, chocolates, nuts and their famous pralines and make your selection. The products are what make the site worth searching with southern delicacies such as glazed pecans, chocolate pecan pie and boxes of pecans to choose from. Prices are reasonable but don't be fooled by the blank space next to shipping charges. Once you make your selection the shipping charges are added – $5.95 is the standard charge, increase the price for the "in desperate need of a fix" rush service.

Fudge & toffee   Be tempted

Enstrom's Almond Toffee
www.enstrom.com
As the name suggests, you can only buy Enstrom's brand of almond toffee, but such an unusual sweet deserves a mention. A lot of effort has been put into the site, despite the curious lack of items to choose from. Click on toffee to see a close-up shot and description of the sweet cream butter and almond, chocolate-covered delight. A pound box will set you back $12, and if you become totally addicted, the 5lb box at $55 should tide you over for a week.

Fort Fudge
www.fortfudge.com
If you suffer from an insatiable sweet tooth, stay away or you may end up buying the shop and making history as the first person to overdose on fudge. Black walnut, chocolate black raspberry and rocky road fudge, salt water taffy and mint wafer bark are just a few of the toothache-inducing items on offer. Just to make matters worse, shipping charges encourage bulk buying, $3.50 for one item, just a dollar more for two. Very, very, tempting.

Clothes & fashion

Desperate for a new bag?
A suit to knock 'em dead at
that next power lunch? Or even
a matching mom, baby and doll
ensemble? Size up the Web...
it's tailor made for the task

 Essential collections for all the family

Bugle Boy
www.bugleboy.com
You can't go wrong with $14 for a pair of Easy jeans. If you're after basic clothing essentials, Bugle Boy can fulfil the whole family's needs. The site has been well thought out with close-up shots of every item. There's the option of separate billing and delivery addresses, and a 10 per cent discount on your first order. On the downside, delivery is slow at 10 days.

Gap
www.gap.com
Luckily for us, Gap has realized that it's the perfect store from which to buy online. After all, if you've seen one Gap fleece you've seen them all, so there's no need to worry that the online offerings won't live up to expectations. The site has everything from men's clothing to newborn baby outfits and toiletries; the images are clear, and the descriptions include sizing and style comparison charts. It's worth noting that searching via image pages is quicker and easier than by lists of items. Prices are standard, but they do sell sale items online (particularly useful at manic times) and Gap maternity wear is exclusively available online.

Old Navy
www.oldnavy.com
Despite the bargain nature of the store, Old Navy has produced a stylish and

vibrant site selling cheap essentials and catwalk copies. The collection varies from cerise turtlenecks to logo print "Disco Fever" and "Rock Star" tank tops. Prices can be summed up as cheap; so too is shipping at only $5 for $50 worth of clothes. An essential stop unless money is no option.

Accessories — Those all-important finishing touches

Chic Bags
www.chicbags.com

Bit of a mish-mash of bags here, divided into evening, everyday, leather and vintage. The evening and vintage selections are generally stylish and timeless, with good prices – beaded chic for $10, 1920s glamour at $60. The everyday and leather selections are admittedly dated, but with the 80s enjoying a

Special requirements — Fitting the bill

Not all of us are blessed with perfectly proportioned bodies. In fact it's a struggle to think of many who are, beyond the odd supermodel, and even they probably have to have their pants extended. You're unlikely to find a mall of stores dedicated to proportionally challenged men and women, but the virtual mall is a different story. Long Elegant Legs specializes in, you guessed it, clothing for women over 5ft 9in. The clothes are mainstream yet fashionable, and e-certificates are available. The site itself works well and the quality is better than average. At the opposite end of the scale Short Sizes Inc stocks clothes for the vertically challenged – or men under 5ft 8in. Maybe you'll have the honor of sporting the same slacks as Dustin Hoffman. At Marks Warehouse you submit your measurements and they'll hunt through their warehouse for items to suit. Best of all, however, is the Hanover Clothing Company, where you can use boxer shorts-clad "Dress Tim" to showcase garments before you buy. This is probably only useful in reality if you actually resemble the muscle-bound Tim.

Catering for those non-mainstream sizes:
Abundant Big & Tall www.abundantbigandtall.com
Big At Heart www.bigatheart.com
Hanover Clothing Company www.bigandtall.com
Long Elegant Legs www.longelegantlegs.com
Long Tall Sally www.longtallsally.com
Mark's Work Warehouse www.marks.com
Short Sizes Inc www.shortsizesinc.com

revival, you may pick up something kitsch enough to pass as fashionable. Enlarged pictures available, with easy ordering and free shipping over $50.

Ciara Nichole
www.ciaranichole.com
Ciara Nichole is actually a flutist, doubling up as a jewelry and accessory designer. Every one of her bags, shawls and necklaces resembles something from a 20s movie, with silk, satin, beading and taffeta featuring strongly. Unfortunately the amateur images don't do the items justice. Prices are competitive and shipping costs start at $3.90 but delivery takes 2-3 weeks.

J Tiras
www.jtiras.com
The bags and jewelry at J Tiras are ideal for ladies who lunch. Few designer names but plenty of replicas, from the classic tote to snake bejewelled evening bags. They also sell an extensive collection of jewelry; Egyptian designs meet American Indian. Most items were half-price on our last visit.

Louis Vuitton
www.vuitton.com
The classic tote bag is only available online in the US via a direct link to the eLuxury site (also in the designer section). No discounts here, just an easy way to complete your wardrobe with those Vuitton matching handbags, luggage, writing sets and even dog collars. If you're feeling really flush, there's a Vuitton monogram wardrobe for a few dollars shy of $20,000.

Price Control
www.pricecontrol.com
With up to 90 per cent off the RRP, this lot can be forgiven for forgoing design awards in favor of bargain prices. The designer accessories include last season's Prada and Gucci bags, but at these prices you can't help but leave the diva temper tantrum for another day. A useful one-stop shop.

Stella Pace
www.stellapace.com
This independent operation is better organized and more stylish than those posted by some multi-million dollar companies. The catalog of beads, bracelets and bags is limited, but the attention to detail on both the products

Not one of the bigger sites, Stella Pace proves not only that smaller is beautiful, but that it works too

and the site itself (the close-up images are close enough to practically smell the leather and you don't have to make do with poor color swatches) makes this a fab find. The ordering process is simple, too.

Sunglasses 2000
www.sunglasses2000.com
This is the ultimate shades warehouse. Designer ranges include Gucci, Ray Ban, Fendi and Nike at affordable prices, generally from $50-$100. There are 40-50 different designs for each brand, all with clear images, a choice of colors and precise measurements so you can find the perfect fit. Only shipping prices let the site down – remember to add an extra $20 to your order – but it's still far cheaper than buying on Rodeo Drive.

Ties & More
www.tiesandmore.com
Just like the name says, this site offers ties, plus briefcases, caps and even golf grips. Prices for ties start at $50, although the lack of sophistication of the sport and novelty offerings will save you a good $20. Ordering is simple but shipping charges remain a mystery till you reach the checkout.

 The original mail-order concept, updated

Boston Proper
www.boston-proper.com
This very proper site exudes elegance and style. The tone-on-tone type is a bit hard to read but the photos are great and you can choose an alternative view of each item (even the back if it has special detailing), a different color, or just a different view. Annoyingly you have to choose the size and color of the products before you can see the price. Shipping and returns as normal.

Eddie Bauer
www.eddiebauer.com
Another great source of casual and outdoor wear, Eddie Bauer also makes shopping online a breeze. The site is clearly laid out with sensible sections. There were several incentives when we visited, including free shipping on orders over $100 and 10 per cent discount on purchases if you apply for an Eddie Bauer credit card. The outlet page has plenty of bargains. Returns are easy and you may also bring online purchases back to an offline shop.

Just My Size
www.justmysize.com
Featuring underwear and fashions from the Playtex, Bali and Hanes brands for sizes 16 and above, although the models sometimes look smaller than a size 16, thus not giving a great idea what these items will actually look like.

Returns are always accepted, even on underwear, a pleasant contrast in service to other sites who refuse returns on intimate apparel, citing health regulations.

Lands' End
www.landsend.com
You're unlikely to see Madonna wearing Lands' End as it sticks firmly to the middle of the road in terms of design, but it's good for long-lasting cotton T-shirts and wrinkle-resistant chinos. The stock is all good value for money, with regular sales and special offers. One feature with a difference is the Virtual Model, where you create an online model of yourself on which you can try some of the clothes, though this can take some time. Color swatches are available to order, and delivery is speedy and efficient.

LL Bean
www.llbean.com
Get this trademark New England look without braving the snows of Maine, by ordering from your desk. These styles are never going to get your heart racing, but neither are they going to break the bank. Quality from such a well-known brand is assured, and returns are no problem. A nifty gimmick allows you to specify who the item is for when ordering.

Long Elegant Legs
www.longelegantlegs.com
This site, for women, has clothes not just bigger, but taller. Sleeve lengths and leg lengths are proportionately longer and swimsuits have a longer torso. The initial photos could be a lot bigger, and some photos do not illustrate the items very clearly. But this site manages to combine style with a good fit.

Newport News
www.newportnews.com
The online version of this budget catalog has the same trendy clothes designed to offer you the latest fashion without breaking the bank. You can only choose sizes and colors that are in stock. Items are clearly illustrated and matching items are displayed to complete your outfit. Returns are always accepted too.

Boston Proper staff appear to be pictures rather than words people – but then when you've got pictures like these...

Spiegel
www.spiegel.com
You'll know this name from the telephone book-sized catalog on sale at newsstands, and ordering online will save you carting it home. The pictures tend to be on the small side, however, and the layout of items could be improved. The same policies apply as to the mail order process, and these people have been in that business for a long time. Good for home items, electronics and lifestyle products too.

Sundance Catalog Company
www.sundancecatalog.com
Robert Redford's Sundance community extends to this online version of his printed catalog which sells clothing, jewelry and home items – generally western in style – made by artists and crafts people of the region. Returns have no time limit. The site is also full of info about the Sundance Institute.

The Territory Ahead
www.territoryahead.com
Great for outdoorsy type clothes, this beautifully designed site has enough items to find what you want, without swamping you with choice. The "availability" check lets you know what's in stock and what has sold out.

WinterSilks
www.wintersilks.com
This online version of the well-known mail order catalog offers the same quality clothing made, naturally, of silk. Shipping charges are just a click away and returns are happily accepted. You can get live customer service between 8am-8pm EST. The only complaint is the design: tiny type and a dull layout.

 How to keep them hip and happy from 0-16

Alhambras School Uniforms
www.alhambras.com
Standard school uniform items for boys and girls, from pants and skirts to polo shirts and accessories including backpacks and hair scrunchies. Prices are mostly cheaper than their offline options: blouses from $6 and pants from $12, with a standard $5 shipping charge.

Baby Gap
www.babygap.com
Ever-reliable Gap have covered all the bases here. Search by age, outfit or trend of the moment, with classic Gap wear featured throughout. Prices are standard and returns can be made by mail or in-store.

Ebrats
www.mymama.com
Bright and cheery site selling the perfect play clothes for babies and kids up to the age of four. Prices are good, and shipping charges are $5.

Estyle
www.estyle.com
Hectic but well organized site, through which you can link to baby and kids' wear up to 10 years old. Brands sold include DKNY, Ralph Lauren, Baby Go Go and Urban Fleece. Standard shipping starts at $4.95.

InStyle Kids
www.instylekids.com
Classic kids' clothing with sweet floral dresses for the girls and smart polo shirts and chinos for the boys. Prices are good – most outfits are under $35 – and the site is a cinch to search. They also stock boys' school uniform items.

Jordan Marie
www.jordanmarie.com
A beautiful site matched by a selection of beautiful clothes for special occasions (birthdays, christenings etc) rather than playing in the mud.

Kid Stitches
www.kidstitches.com
Personalize your kids' clothing with embroidery designs from the catalog of thousands, or suggest your own designs. Search their product range of clothing and gifts, or e-mail them for customized items.

Koala Konnection
www.koalakonnection.com
Each pair of shorts, T-shirt and swimsuit offers protection from both UVA and UVB rays up to 100+ SPF and prices are cheap – there are items on sale at under $5, but most are priced around $15. Orders by phone.

Plowshares
www.plowsharesltd.com
Matching outfits for mother, daughter and doll. Scary but true.

Polar Babies
www.diapercovers.com
Ideal for those living in the north: baby clothes, booties, hats and even diaper covers made from the snuggliest but lightest PolarTec fleece material.

The Little Artist
www.thelittleartist.com
Artist smocks, shirts and T-shirts for the creative genius in your midst.

Designer | More labels than your local wine store

AnyKnockOff

anyknockoffs.com/cgi-bin/SoftCart.exe/anyknos/index.html?E+scstore

Despite what the name might suggest, Any Knockoffs don't deal in anything shady, only accessories that resemble designer goods. Chanel, Fendi, Gucci and Prada are just a few of the brands providing inspiration. You shouldn't worry about this, however, just focus on the prices: mock-croc Fendi bags at $39 rather than $800. Prada boots for $42, a saving of $400. The ordering process is simple and if you spend more than $100, delivery is free.

Armani Exchange

www.armaniexchange.com

One of the few catwalk designers to embrace the Internet with enthusiasm, Mr Armani has produced a suitably stylish site selling his more casual wares. Select the male or female side of the site to view scrolling pictures highlighting the numerous sub-categories including denim, novelty knitwear and accessories. From here, select whichever scrolling image takes your fancy in order to view descriptions and more detailed images. Prices are cheaper than expected – $80 for jeans, $200 for leather outwear. Ordering is simple, with the registration process kept blissfully short, and shipping is only $5. Added extras include a style guide, useful if you're after that scene-stealing look but have no idea how to get it.

Betsey Johnson

www.betseyjohnson.com

Judging by the site, Betsey has recently transformed herself into a Jessica

The Guess homepage is a tribute to the power of orange. The rest of the site is damn good too

Rabbit character: the wild pink, yellow and rose-laden site features a lounging lady handing out the orders. Sadly it looks far better than it works, as each page takes forever to load – unless you're using Explorer in which case nothing loads and if you make the mistake of clicking "back" you'll head for the homepage rather than the previous page and the loading will begin again. The clothes are pure Betsey – lots of frills, vibrant colors and scary mannequins as models. For diehard Ms Johnson fans only.

Designer Exposure

www.designerexposure.com

It may seem extreme to import your clothes from New Zealand, but if it's a hard-to-come-by Alberta Ferretti skirt, it could be worth it. Browse through the entire catalog of hundreds of designer wares, or narrow your search down to simply finding that 70s Fendi bag. Prices vary, but you can certainly pick up some good bargains – a CK cool white mac for $150 for example. Just remember to factor in those shipping costs.

Gianfranco Ferre

www.gianfrancoferre.com

View the latest Ferre collections through his own site, or link to Lux Look to view and buy a limited selection of bags and accessories. Images can be enlarged and ordering is easy but the prices, over $1,000 for some items, make this one for Ferre addicts only, although there are some discounts. Lux Look also features Vivienne Westwood, Versace and Paul Smith accessories.

Guess

www.guess.com

Guess excels online. The vibrant orange homepage practically forces you to browse the extensive collection of clothes and accessories. New ranges are added frequently, helping to make this one of the most comprehensive sites going, with every catwalk craze from Rodeo fashion to the Snow Bunny look and 80s chic. Despite the label, prices are reasonable – around $50 for jeans and pants and $100 for coats. In fashion and in budget, descriptions are adequate and enlarged pictures of clothing details are available.

Kenneth Cole

www.kennethcole.com

Best known for his elegant, not to say sexy shoes, Cole has branched out into men's and women's clothing and accessories, all featured here. The site is as stylish as the products. You can either simply browse the catalog, or view catwalk images and then see what Kenneth can offer you of the same ilk. Ordering is simple, with no designer flash plug-ins needed, and even prices aren't too over the top – $150 for shoes for example.

RECYCLED CHIC

Owning a Prada tote bag or a D&G catsuit is old hat these days. Everyone can get hold of one, or at least a decent copy. Even celebs like Ms Lopez and Donatella Versace end up wearing the same dresses. But Piece Unique has the answer, with new and pre-owned designer garments and accessories. The site itself is rudimentary – simple lists of what's in stock linked to extended information and clear pictures. They only stock one of each garment, so scrolling through for your size is the easiest option. Designer names include Chanel, Armani, Versace and Valentino, all at discounted prices even if brand new. You could save yourself thousands.

----

www.pieceunique.com

Ralph Lauren Polo
www.polo.com

Polo is said to represent the casual side of Mr Lauren, but don't mistake casual for cheap. The site is stylish, with clear images, concise descriptions and handy additions such as sizing charts and the chance to "Ask Ralph" about your latest fashion mistake. Other sections of the site include vintage, travel and *Runway* – an online women's fashion magazine. Although there is a speed shop option, taking in the lifestyle of the whole range is easier and more enjoyable. An online slice of Ralph cool.

 ## Serious streetwear for your inner hipster

Abercrombie & Fitch
www.abercrombie.com

Having been eulogized in many a rap song, Abercrombie & Fitch clothes have become a must-have with those in the know. Skate and urban wear dominate but don't worry, you shouldn't be mistaken for a homeboy. Relatively inexpensive, jeans and fleeces are priced at around $50 with T-shirts for $19. Shipping takes 5-10 days, costing from $5. A little more original than a pair of Levi's and a Gap fleece.

Andrew Marc
www.andrewmarc.com

Andrew Marc specializes in leather goods for men, women and children, with prices ranging from $300 to $800 for jackets and coats. The range is limited but the styles are contemporary. We're not totally sure about the "jacket with underwear" look however…

Banana Republic
www.bananarepublic.com

Banana Republic has proved beyond any doubt that it is far more than just a useful place to shop for separate essentials. Easy to use but chic to boot, the company hasn't forgotten that for the average shopper practicality is high on their list of priorities, therefore washing instructions – or, as is more often the case, instructions not to wash – are provided. There are enlarged images of the products, ordering has been made easy and prices are good – $200 for leather jacket – with many items at sale prices. On the downside, delivery can take up to a week.

Free Country
www.freecountry.com

Free Country have yet to embrace online shopping, but their site deserves a mention for 2 reasons. Firstly, they don't assume you're a technical whiz kid who shops online everyday. The upshot of this is they spell everything out for you. You can select men's or women's clothing to view small images of their latest collection of everything fleecy, padded and leathery, then move your mouse over the small images for enlarged views. Secondly, once you've selected an item they can tell you whether it's available in a store near you, saving you half the hassle at least.

Porn Star Clothing

www.pornstarclothing.com

Porn Star clothes are fast becoming the name to be worn both here in the States and in the UK. The extensive online catalog offers everything from men's jackets and women's baby T-shirts to condom cases and wallets. The majority of items are standard shirts and pants with variations of the Porn logo emblazoned across the front, although a few motifs are slightly more explicit. The site is easy to use with clear images and secure shopping, and prices have yet to be inflated in line with popularity ($18 for T-shirts). Shipping is cheap at $4 throughout the US. Only an invitation to click on a non-existent "catalog" button spoiled it. Get in there quick before everyone else does.

Zoza

www.zoza.com

Never heard of Zoza? Well, they sell "urban performance clothing" for men and women. Don't be put off however; this doesn't simply translate into skate and boardwear, but into funky and stylish pieces with an emphasis on the cut and fabric – there are no synthetics here. Each description comes complete with enlarged images, detail and fabric views, and the elaborate descriptions go down to whether the fabric will pill. Prices are currently reduced, but still remain fairly expensive – in the region of $70-$90 for a pair of men's khakis. Could be a name to note for for the future.

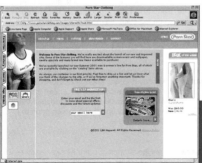

Seems Porn Star is where everyone wants to be right now, and with a mix of good prices and a good site, that trend looks set to continue

Clothes & fashion

 **From formal to low-slung crotches**

Brooks Brothers
www.brooksbrothers.com
You can't get much safer than a Brooks Brothers shirt. There's no chance of controversy in the boardroom if you turn up in their latest strip. The Brooks site is, not surprisingly, just about as interesting as their products. Prices for the play-safe men's suits begin at around $400, with dress shirts around the $40 mark. The site itself is easy enough to search if somewhat slow, but we were disappointed to find that you can neither see nor read about what materials each item is made from, and even the enlarged images are poor quality. One for devotees only.

Discount Designers Menswear Inc
www.menswear-discounts.com
Based around stylish black and white shots of smart young men and equally suave older gentlemen, the extensive range of menswear featured here is for the smart rather than casual dresser. It's easy to search – simply select from everything from suits and shirts to tuxedos, and scroll through the collection of names, Ralph Lauren and DKNY included. Descriptions are adequate, and the images could be improved, but the emphasis here is on discounts, and most items live up to expectations with prices reduced by hundreds of dollars. There's an added bonus of free shipping too.

Purple Pants
www.purplepants.com
The male equivalent to the Purple Skirt site sells a range of menswear that, contrary to what the site name might suggest, is designed to suit all tastes. Top names include Samsonite, Burro and Theory; prices vary depending on the designer. It's simple to search, so even the most fickle man should manage to last long enough to buy something.

Urbanix
www.urbanix.com
Street and designer wear from urban designers including Phat Farm, Rocawear and Ecko. If your office policy is liberal enough to allow carpenter jeans and logo tees into the dress code, the prices here are cheap enough to revamp your entire work wardrobe in one swoop. Hooded tops are the most expensive items at $60. Ordering is easy and they've even gone to the trouble of providing enlarged and 3D images.

Y2G Shop
www2.y2gshop.com/?style_letter=A
If you like having the crotch of your pants down around your knees, and

jackets three sizes too big, Y2G can meet your needs as the only official re-seller of FUBU clothes. Everything from jean jackets to sweatpants and T-shirts is on offer here, and the site is funky and colorful, only letting itself down on the images – the initial pictures are too small and the 3D view is temperamental. Prices are reasonable, $85 for jackets and $65 for jeans, and shipping starts at $4.95. If FUBU is too tame, Y2G also sells Willie Esco clothes for those with a taste for puff and shine rather than denim and leather.

 Making that difficult age a whole lot easier

Delias
www.delias.com
Don't be put off by the link to study guides – Delias is strictly aimed at the fashion conscious teen. The site is well laid out with scroll down menus, enlarged images and detailed descriptions. Prices are standard, although the sale section often produces real bargains. Shipping begins at $4.99 and can take anywhere from a few to 10 days. Worth the wait for exclusives.

Girlfriends LA
www.gfla.com
Fun and funky teen clothes that should head off any "you're not going out dressed like that" arguments. The site is easy to use and the prices are good ($18 for trendy logo T-shirts), but best of all they don't assume every teenager is a size 4. Most items are available up to XXL or size 25, and are designed to suit every shape and size.

Tee Zone
www.tee-zone.com
We won't go as far as agree with *InStyle* that this deserves a place in the top 50 online stores (many items featured can be found at Gap at more appealing prices), but teenagers can be picky so pay attention. Teen brands include Juicy Couture, Buffalo Jeans and Three Dots, but remember to check with the hormonally erratic one in question before you buy. A bit pricey considering what you're paying for, but searching is easy and ordering is via Yahoo.

A decent selection of sizes from Girlfriends LA, taking on board the real size and shape of your average teen

 **All you might imagine... and more**

Beautiful Queen
www.beautifulqueen.com
Big and beautiful is in, and these lacy numbers will showcase your assets to
the best advantage. The size chart leaves nothing to chance – a good idea as
health regulations mean that opened packages cannot be returned. Shipping
is free, but you have to allow 2-4 weeks.

Becoming
www.becoming.com
With 1 in 10 American woman being diagnosed with breast cancer, it is
no surprise that there is a site dedicated specifically to women who've
undergone surgery. Treating the customer with delicacy and respect, the
site aims to allow women to wear good-looking underwear that supports
prosthesis, thereby boosting their confidence. Medicare claims are explained,
and 2 per cent of each sale goes to breast cancer awareness.

Bodyaware
www.bodyaware.com
The men on this site are very, er, impressive, which distracts you from the
fact that the pale lavender type on white background is very hard to read.
Decidedly on the fetishist side, the site puts enough on view to get even the
most liberal surfer to blush. But if kinky undies in mesh, rubber or lace are
what you want, then you'll probably find it here. Beware: the returns policy on
intimate apparel is strict and you may get socked with a restocking fee.

Deffego
www.deffego.com/Merchant/index.htm
Pantyhose galore. Whether you need total control or just some good support
for everyday wear, Deffego could be the low cost answer. You can buy singly
or by the dozen (12 pairs for $30). Better still, you no longer have to put up
with bra straps showing or put up with uncomfortable strapless numbers, not
with the Adhesive bra, or "Free Bra". The funny little cups come in various
shades and represent a bargain in new technology at $3.95 for three pairs.

Edible Undies
www.edibleundies.com
So, always fancied giving it a try but too embarrassed to walk into your local
sex shop? You'll have to take a leap of faith with this site as you can't actually
view any of the items on sale. But chose your item from the suggestive yet
discreet photos, and then the flavor, and in a few days a brown paper packet
will get you salivating. Despite the declared shipping costs, it always comes
out a lot more on the secure order form. Not for dieters.

Frederick's of Hollywood

www.fredericks.com

This online version of the famous lingerie store offers the same sexy items it always has offline, and at very reasonable prices. These products need no introduction – you have to do a bit of clicking to get what you want, but shipping is free and the photos are always enjoyable.

Hippie Skivvies

imerchants.cc/hippieskivvies/home.html

Hey, all you 60s throwbacks! These tie-dyed undies are just the thing to get your groove back, man. The site is a bit limited on style but all the basics are covered and each one comes in a psychedelic array of colors. And if you take pride in wearing your skivvies, then you can take a snap, send it in with the printable release form and share yourself with the world. Shipping is free in the continental US.

Lingerie Mall

www.lingeriemall.com

Whoa! Anything lacy, satiny or rubbery can be found on this site. Their exceptional selection of sexy costumes will fulfil any fantasy from Wonder Babe to Sexy Bunny to FireFighter, although bondage and other sex toys make this strictly an adults-only site. Ordering is simple and arrives in that inevitable plain wrapping (as if the mailman doesn't know…).

Underneath

www.underneath.com

It's busy, and you'll ponder where to start for a few minutes, but with such a

Frederick's may have "Hollywood" in their name but you don't have to be on a Julia Roberts-level income to be able to indulge

vast selection of underwear for men and women it remains an essential stop-off point. Search by style, specialist category, or brand; top names include Wonderbra, Guy Laroche and Maiden Form. Prices vary depending on the brand, but shipping is a $4 flat rate.

Victoria's Secret

www.victoriassecret.com

Okay, so more men than women may read the offline catalog but contrary to popular perception this site is much more than a gallery of skimpily glad beauties. It's actually a great place to buy underwear. The products are shown on catalog-type pages, and there's a customer services page that takes the word "comprehensive" to new heights. Shipping costs start at $4.95 and your order should arrive within 7-10 days. Nightwear, swimwear and other stuff as well as the trademark lingerie.

 Women's Paint-splatted trousers? They're right here

Bisou-Bisou

www.bisou-bisou.com

Bisou Bisou is all about keeping up with the latest trends, so if mesh and lace are all the rage this season, that's what they'll be offering. Select a category to see clear images of each collection, see something you like and click on it. From here you can view enlarged and detailed images of each item, the detailed view being useful when you're dealing with fabrics like corduroy, lace or angora. Prices vary, but trousers are generally around $100, with dresses closer to $200. But shipping is cheap and delivery is usually next-day.

Escada

www.escada.com

As yet nothing to buy online, but you can view the latest Escada collection in its entirety before you head out to the boutiques.

Esprit

www.esprit.com

Your first port of call for quick and easy shopping. Nothing revolutionary in terms of design and layout but there are simple search categories, enlarged pictures, and sizing and ordering guides always on hand. The clothes and accessories themselves are all fashionable copies of catwalk styles but at standard commercial prices – $48 for sweaters, $60 for dresses.

Left Gear

www.leftgear.com

The *Sex and the City* line is that the gulf between angry New Yorkers and sunny Angels is too wide to bridge, but Left Gear gives it a go with hip designs from LA's hottest new designers. Floaty skirts from Ruby Mae, funky Mick and Mad's T-shirts from Smashing Grandpa… there's something to suit every taste and fashion conscious vixen, plus info about the designers so you can really sell your exclusive merchandise to envious friends. Prices are good, $30 for stylish tees up to $150 for that ubiquitous little black dress.

Little Black Dress To Go
www.lbdtodo.com
As the name says, the classic little black number in all its forms for $90.

Purple Skirt
www.purpleskirt.com
Owned by, among others, comedian Tracey Ullman, Purple Skirt showcases items from designers and stores worldwide. Searching can be time consuming (there are 37 pages of tops alone and each page displays only two items) but if you're looking for something special it is worth it – top names include Whistles, Jet and Trina Turk. Enlarged pictures are available, ordering is simple, many items are shipped the following day and gift-wrapping is free of charge.

Shop 45
www.shop45.com
Based in Chicago, Shop 45 showcases the work of a number of emerging designers, including Miah y, Lotto and Veronica M. Each designer has submitted an outfit for you to buy, so the collection is sparse, but you're guaranteed something more original than what you find in your average mall. Prices range from expensive ($160 for a T-shirt) to reasonable (only $75 for a little black dress). Details about the garments are limited but they do include enough information about the designers for you to launch into a convincing conversation over dinner about the chic outfit you're wearing.

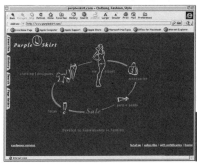

With 37 pages of tops, it could take you a while to have a browse round Purple Skirt, but it's probably worth the effort

Clothes & fashion

Tag Rag
www.tagrag.com
Currently worn by various "where are they now actresses" (Kelly McGillis, Natasha Kinski, Sara Gilbert) the Tag Rag range is fashion rather than essentials. Pants are "shiny", "stretchy", "ostrich". Then there are those best described as paint splatted. Prices match the likely shelf-life of the designs: pants at $40, tops for as little as $25. Excellent for a striking yet bargain outfit.

Vintage clothing Looks proven to last

Fashion is great, and having fashion icons is even better; that way you can explain clearly to your friends the sort of look you're going for. The only drawback is everyone has the same idea and we all end up as Brad and Jennifer clones. The best option therefore has to be vintage clothing. Every season fashion designers head back to bygone eras for their couture inspiration. Go for the chic of vintage clothing and you'll still be the fashion diva of your hometown but with some originality too. Some of the best online offerings are featured below; obviously we accept that star spangled hot pants aren't everyone's idea of fashion, but stick with it…

5 and Dime Vintage
www.510vintage.com
True fashion divas change the shade of denim they're wearing every season so pick yourself out a few classics for that retro cowgirl look.

Cats Pajamas
www.catspajamas.com
Back to the late 19th century to make that Merchant Ivory fashion statement.

Enoki World
www.enokiworld.com
Pages and pages of vintage women's clothing and accessories, including a to-die-for Chanel quilted coat and a 70s Pierre Cardin blonde clutch bag.

Hemlock Vintage
www.hemlockvintage.com
Men's and women's clothing from 1800 to the 1980s. Try the cocktail dress section for pure sophistication and glamour.

Just Say When
www.justsaywhen.com
Groundbreaking news of Clark Gable's secret love child perhaps takes the nostalgia idea a little too far but this is one of the cheaper stores around.

Collectibles

...as in Marilyn light switch plates, *Howdy Doody* lunchboxes, *Star Trek* medals. Oh, and a few old coins and stamps

 Eastern Airlines coffee pot, anyone?

1886 Company
store.yahoo.com/1886
These aren't originals, and prices are highish, but this pretty little site has a small selection of reproduction tea, linen, sewing and desk accessories. Ordering is easy, but you won't find out shipping charges till the end.

4 Collectors
www.4-collectors.com
You may think this is a site just for collectors of the terminally cute Puffkins and teddy bears. But delve deeper and you'll find the auction section full of interesting stuff, though no pics. The free classifieds are worth a browse too.

A and A Antiques
www.tias.com/stores/aanda
Remember California Raisins? Here you can get your mitts on Captain Toonz or CB Stuntz for $10 or less. This site also sells other collectible figurines and even furniture, but it really shines when it comes to glass. Whether you are into Depression, Carnival or Ruby Red, you can add to your collection here.

Affordable Antiques and Collectibles
www.tias.com/stores/afford
This New Zealand-based site (prices in US dollars) specializes in English and continental ceramics and porcelain – your basic Lladro, Royal Doulton and Hummel figurines plus many more. The descriptions are clear and ordering is easy. After sending your details, they will e-mail you final costs including shipping and insurance for your approval, with delivery in just 8 days.

American Favorites
www.americanfavorites.com
All things Coca-Cola here, from model trucks, airplanes and clocks to

furniture like tables and chairs. You could almost furnish your house with the stuff. Betty Boop makes a few appearances too.

American Logos
www.americanlogos.com

Fancy a Marilyn Monroe light switch or a telephone magnet? There's a variety of inexpensive collectibles here. A vast range of replica tin signs focuses on car-makers, oil companies, sports and celebrities – basically anything with a recognizable image or logo. A number of John Deere items are for sale too.

Antiques by Rasberrys
www.tias.com/stores/rasberry

A collection of vintage handkerchiefs is the highlight here, at very reasonable prices considering the craftsmanship. Also ephemera, sewing accessories, musical instruments and the usual ceramic figurines and kitchen collectibles.

Betsey's Collectibles
www.newcookiejars.com

Betsey's has cookie jars of every conceivable shape, color and character, some of which are of questionable aesthetic value, but could be the pride of someone's collection. Many items are retired and there are discounts on larger orders. Ordering is through the fill-in type of form.

Brettun's Village
www.brettunsvillage.com

Fabulous selection of old trunks and suitcases with each one lovingly described. Tools and accessories for restoration are also sold. Payment through PayPal.

Cyber Imports
www.cyberimport.com

Japanese snuff boxes take pride of place on this site, along with carvings, bottles and jewelry. Ordering is a bit fiddly – you have to e-mail your selection and then, after confirmation of item availability and final costs including shipping, pay through PayPal.

The Franklin Mint
www.franklinmint.com

Every Sunday paper magazine advertises Franklin Mint collectible plates, coins and dolls and you can order products from the ads, and the printed or online catalog, through this site. Focusing on "icons from our culture", expect to see legends such as Princess Diana, Jackie Onassis and Princess Grace.

GT's Hallmark Shop

www.gohallmark.com

Come here to fill in the gaps in
your Hallmark collection with
Dr Seuss and *Peanuts* in many
guises. A great line of lunch
boxes include *The Jetsons*,
The Beatles' *Yellow Submarine*
and *Howdy Doody* reissues.
Payment is through PayPal.

Marion Antiques and Collectibles

www.tias.com/stores/ma

A neat line of *Star Trek*
collectibles here, including
a Lieutenant Uhura mini-plate

Two great American icons collide as Coca-Cola meets
Betty Boop – and all in the name of making a cup of tea

and action figures. Unusual items include a carved cherry wood Chinese
warrior figure from the late 1800s and an 8-day clock from a WWII bomber.

Ole Coyote

www.olecoyote.com

Can't imagine life without your collection of beer cans and other beeriana?
You can add to that aluminum mountain through this site, which also has beer
trays and collector steins. Crack open a six-pack and start browsing.

Soda Pop Shop

www.sodashop.com

Remember Moxie? Like root beer with a weird after-taste. You can relive
those days of hot summers and a cool drink of soda pop by checking out this
site. Can phones, key chains, signs, pins etc… marketing your favorite thirst
quenchers means that logos are plastered onto everything from T-shirts to
playing cards. Go ahead, give those drinks giants some free advertising.

The Relic Shack

www.relicshack.com

You can't order this stuff through the Net but it is unique so it has to be
included. Native American collectibles abound here – arrowheads by the
score, baskets, jewelry and pottery too. All are guaranteed authentic. The
site itself is well designed and the photos clear. Phone to order.

Valino Antiques and Collectibles

www.tias.com/stores/valino/

This site is a treasure trove of fun collectibles – battery-operated tin toys,
robots, superheroes and even dress sets for the original *Charlie's Angels*.
Shipping varies from item to item, and is sometimes included in the price.
This is the place to check out if a Mr T ring would complete your life.

Collectibles

Coins & stamps — Buy them while they're hot

American Coin and Stamp Brokerage
www.acsb.com

This is an auction site that could yield great coins and stamps. There is a massive amount of advice and a whole stack of bidding guidelines provided here, and you really should follow them to get the best deals and to save time-wasting. Payment is through the mail or PayPal after you have been notified of winning bids.

Island Stamp and Coin
www.usstamps.com

Ducks are the specialty here with lots of stamps featuring our feathered friend, but there are no pics, so either you have to do some research or just trust you'll like the stamp when it arrives. Shipping and ordering is clearly explained. We're not sure how you can get your hands on the coins though, as there is no sign of them except in the site's name.

The Stamp and Coin Shop
www.stamp-coin.com

This site has a decent selection of stamps but you have to know what you are looking for as it starts with a search rather than a catalog list. No sign of coins here either, just a vague promise for the future. It's also really annoying to have to go through the whole purchase process to get any shipping information. An overall disappointment – but then there are surprisingly few stamp and coin shops that let you buy over the Web.

Treasuretime
www.gibraltarcoins.com

A bit of a confusing site, this one, but then coin collectors seem to have their own language, so if this is your hobby, you'll probably have no problem. The design is a bit heavy but the coins are there and, hurrah, ordering is pretty straightforward, although it says it will only ship to the credit card address, then gives the option of sending to another on the order form to make for maximum confusion. Credit cards are not accepted for bullion orders.

Like any auction there's no guarantee of a bargain but follow the guidelines and you never know...

Honest Abe Souvenirs of the premier Prez

Bricks
www.abelincoln.com
If walls could talk they'd have some stories to tell, but until this happens, be satisfied with a genuine brick from Lincoln's Illinois home. Yours for only $15.

"Floaty" Pen
www.thelincolnmuseum.org/main.html
Impress your *Time* magazine-reading friends with your Lincoln pen, complete with floating stovepipe hat. $2.50 with a 10 per cent discount on orders of 20.

Lincoln "The Musical" CD
www.sparxecho.com
According to *Rock Beat International*, In Spite of Reason "succeeds admirably in offering a musical portrayal of Abraham Lincoln and the Civil War". Judge for yourself by buying this double CD.

Medal
www.polikicks.com
It may just look like a bronze picture of a former president but Polikicks insists there's a lot of history in this tiny medal, which not only shows Lincoln as the first photogenic president, complete with his trademark beard, but also that "OK" was a familiar word by the 1860s. All that history for only $119.

Mouse pad
www.yahoo.com
We can't guarantee this mouse pad with a tasteful mug shot of Mr Lincoln, dates back to the 19th century, but it's up for grabs at Yahoo's auction area.

This is a new mouse pad of President Abraham Lincoln. The image is from an

Just think how much more fun Abe would have had running the country using a mouse pad of himself

Paper doll
www.ebay.com
Winners in the kitsch stakes are Abraham Lincoln & Family paper dolls, complete with a "large assortment of outfits to choose from". These delights are up for grabs on e-Bay, only $5.50.

Collectibles

Memorabilia — First Lady buttons by the bucketload

American Resources
www.tias.com/stores/amres
This site sells the usual collectibles, but where it really excels is in political memorabilia. When you come to a site with 37 pages of political bumper stickers and 27 pages on First Ladies, you know you are on to a business that knows its stuff. Because the inventory of around 25,000 items is so high, it is impossible to illustrate each item (there are even four pages of butter pats, for crying out loud). The site is regularly updated with news on fast sellers and suggestions. Well worth a look.

Collector's Post
www.collectorspost.com
Theater playbills and programs are the primary featured items in this site, though it also has other theater-related pieces. Don't be put off by the fact that it's an English site – all prices quoted are in US dollars, and the productions are all from US theaters. The site also has a good amount of American and English political memorabilia and autographed documents. Flat shipping fee.

The Den at Peddlar's Village
www.thedenpv.com
This site has a good line in Civil War collectibles – mostly reproductions of cannons and books – plus Hudson pewter Civil War soldiers and village characters. Harley-Davidson and other collectibles are available. The one big drawback is you have to fill in all the catalog numbers to order.

From Hudson pewter to Harley-Davidson, it's not so much a Den, more an Aladdin's Cave of collectibles

Do Wah Diddy
www.dowahdiddy.com
Ever had a hankering to live in the *I Love Lucy* apartment or feel like the *Happy Days* house would suit you down to a T? Here's your chance to buy vintage 40s, 50s and 60s items for the whole house and its occupants. A pink Vesta stove from the 50s to go next to a turquoise vinyl dinette set? No problem. Some new but retro accessories will fill in the gaps. Ordering form requires you to fill in the details.

Comics

They may be very
collectible but
fans may be
disappointed by what they can
actually buy over the Web. But among all
the sites which have a "look but don't buy"
policy, you can find a few bizarre curios

The Comic Box

www.thecomicbox.com

This stylish site offers a wealth of added attractions including an online comic art gallery, a handy subscription service and issue reviews, and a massive online store selling everything from original comic art and figurines, to trading cards and, of course, actual comics. Browsers and those looking for hard to find editions are both catered for with prices starting at a dollar, although signed editions will obviously make more of a dent in your wallet.

Comics One

www.comicsone.com

Admittedly if you're a collector you're not going to be interested in mere electronic versions of your favorite comic heroes, but if not Comics One offers an impressive enough catalog of US and Japanese comics to help you while away a few hours. If you don't already have Adobe eBook reader installed, the quick and easy link here can sort that out before you start downloading the latest Kazan, Weed and Sarai adventures, all for just $2.95.

Comic Store

www.comic-store.com

Okay, so the Comic Store won't blow you away when it comes to web design, but the 8,000 DC Comics up for sale should captivate any *Superman*, *Batman* or *Green Lantern* fan. Pick a character to view reams of adventures, old and not-so-old. Prices are generally around the $3 mark with $5 shipping your cheapest option, with PayPal on hand for secure online ordering.

Comics Unlimited

www.comicsunlimited.com

A site which almost lives up to its title, with an impressive array of products from Marvel, DC and Chaos, a resumé of the latest comic news and even an issue of a psycho circus magazine based on the rock band Kiss. Prices are just as impressive, starting at only a dollar.

Compal Comics

www.compalcomics.com

Auction site that's a must for serious collectors. It allows you to bid online on a secure server and sells such fascinating items as the original model for the Dan Dare rocket ship, made in 1951 and used by illustrators. Only flaw: the auctions aren't held often enough, but if there's nothing going on when you visit they'll happily e-mail you a notice when the next one comes around.

Demolition Comics

http://demolitioncomics.com

No online ordering, back to mail and phone we're afraid, but Demolition is worth bookmarking for the huge catalog of comics from DC, Marvel, Image and more. Simply select a publisher to view the list of titles available. Free delivery on orders of $150 or more in the USA.

English magazines

www.englishmagazines.com

This site offers British classics such as the *Beano*. Not for the collector because it sells current issues, not classic titles of yore, but with worldwide delivery you can get your hands on some quintessential British humor.

Marvel

www.marvel.com

The official site for what is still the best known name in comics has a decent

comics and collectibles section and a search engine to help you find your nearest comic shop, assuming you don't know already.

Online subscriptions to titles like *X Men* are offered at pretty reasonable discounts.

And there's a link to www.davescomics.com to help you fill in the gaps in your collection. The comparable site for DC isn't quite as useful but check it out on www.dccomics.com if you're a fan. Images fans are best keying the name of their favorite title into their fave search engine and following the trail from there.

Comics Unlimited is the place to go for news and comics from Marvel and DC. Prices are low too

Computer games

There's no better (or cheaper) place than the Internet to get gamed up, whether you're into Barbie, bingo, or "blast into oblivion" type games

General You may have heard of these guys...

Barnes and Noble

www.bn.com

Not a huge selection, but there is something reassuring about shopping with a huge brand name like Barnes and Noble. The site is easy to navigate, the ordering simple, and you can be sure that this site will be around for some time. You can also return your goods to any Barnes and Noble offline store.

Games without guns "Peace, man!"

Argos Gameware

www.gameware.com

This site should get an award for original presentation, with its fun cartoons giving you an instant idea of the games on offer. There isn't a particularly large selection, but the descriptions include reviews and screen shots and specs. A fun site, but we had problems getting the cashier to recognize the purchase.

Deck Wizard

www.dw4pokemon.com

Get the inside info for all Pokémon trainers including new cards, powers and strengths. This is a must-have child-friendly addition to any fan's collection.

Something of a victory for style over content, Argos is nonetheless a good place to hop off for a peek into the wackier side of things

Lance Haffner Games
www.lhgames.com
Text-based strategy sports games that span football, car racing, wrestling, basketball and baseball – a must for any dedicated sports fan. There are free sample downloads but no online ordering as yet – you need to e-mail them or phone for policies or to order. The message board is a great feature.

MacTreasures
www.mactreasures.com
A large library of mostly educational and non-violent Apple Mac games.

MG Software
www.mgsoft.com
This site has non-violent, kidsafe games. You can download samples of mazes, puzzles and strategy games for both children and adults, then download the game and get the code e-mailed to you, or order a CD.

Soleau Software
www.soleau.com
Billed as non-violent strategy logic games for the entire family, this site has the advantage of offering downloadable games that you then need a registration code to activate. Ordering is secure and the more games you buy, the bigger the discount you get.

Starship Titanic
www.starshiptitanic.com
Hilarious, but still taxing game from the endearingly knotted mind of the late Douglas Adams. Rescue the stricken starship using only your wit, a few hopeless robots and some roast chicken.

Tutor House
www.tutorhouse.com
A panel of moms and kids has approved all the titles here. A well thought-out design lets you see system requirements, and there's a money-back guarantee.

Online retailers Out there in cyberspace

Ace Toys
www.acetoys.com
It claims the best selection of games on the Net: Barbie to Rugrats, Sega to Playstation and everything in between. All the legal stuff is up front. You get a five per cent discount on your first order or if you introduce another customer.

Activision
store.activision.com
A decent selection of games but descriptions are a bit thin, and there are no system requirements or customer reviews. Ten per cent off your first order.

Chips & Bits
www.cdmag.com
Another online game superstore. The main complaint with this site is the tiny type, but the good thing is that you can chose your system or media to avoid setting your heart on a game only to find it doesn't come in DVD. An extensive collection, but little by way of descriptions and few illustrations.

Gamers
www.gamers.com
You can't buy games through this site but it deserves a mention as the

Gamers.com's vast database of games makes it an ideal start point for a trip into gaming cyberspace

Computer games

definitive resource on computer, video and unplugged games, gaming news and features. It has more than 25,000 games in its database, and each one comes with a synopsis and review. You can also post your own review. This site is a must for any gaming fan.

Electronics Boutique
www.ebworld.com
You don't have to do much clicking to get going on this site. Each game is illustrated with a description and customer reviews. Screen shots and features of the games are revealed in detail, letting you chose from the huge product list with confidence. The shipping info is just a single click away and they have anticipated pretty much any question you could have concerning ordering, returns and delivery dates.

Gamescan
www.gamescan.com
This site, beautiful as it is to look at, needs a bit of attention. Half of the featured games on the homepage were not available when we last visited, and the information page uses white type on a pale gray background, making it virtually impossible to read. There are no reviews or screen shots, but it

Game over? Have consoles had their day?

Once upon a time Nintendo and Sega were the big hitters in the battle of the gaming consoles, but now the entire future of those swish boxes which once seemed to offer endless entertainment seems to be in jeopardy. Sega's Dreamcast will soon be hitting the bargain bins of every mall in the country, and game production too will come to a halt. Sony's Playstation 2 extravaganza might be doing better if the company had built enough machines to cover demand, and Nintendo appears to have vanished save for the GameBoy and its grip on the Pokémon franchise. Not satisfied with its stranglehold on the computer industry, Microsoft is now looking for a piece of the gaming action with the X Box – if it ever finalizes a date for the product's debut. Could this be the end of gaming as we know it? Will we soon have to head back down the arcades again to play Space Invaders and Pac Man? Serious gamers panicked by such bleak prospects should check out the links below for news and views...

Nintendo	gamespot.com/gamespot/filters/0,10850,6013220,00.html
Playstation 2	www.sonyweb.com
Sega Dreamcast	www.planetdreamcast.com
X-Box	www.x-boxed.com

130

ore categories would save a lot of search time. The ordering process seems straightforward though, and with help this could be a great site.

PC Software Store

www.pcsoftwaregames.com

Now here's a site that has some good and bad features. Let's start with the good. The homepage makes shopping through this site sound like a bargain: "five per cent accumulative discounts", "Buy 10 games within one year, get one free" and so on. It doesn't explain, however, how this works. There is a Game For Life program which allows you to get a game a month, regardless of cost, for one up-front payment and the site estimates you will save more than 50 per cent buying this way. Now for the bad – which is essentially the catalog of games. It's not the content that's the problem – it's the lack of any description or illustrations, let alone screen shots or reviews. The most you can expect is a one-line description. Prices are discounted, but not by much.

Software Zone

www.softwarezone.com

The spartan design of this site is great for no-nonsense shoppers who like to download their software direct from the Internet, including game demos and shareware options. You can see straight away that any purchase you make is secure and the process is easy and fast, as long as you chose the correct download for your operating system. The range of titles available here is absolutely mind-boggling, and even extends to some out-of-date (but still dearly beloved) machines such as the Sinclair Spectrum. At first the site seems difficult to browse, but stick with it. Of particular note is the nifty

SoftwareZone really does look out for everyone – even those still tinkering with those quaint little Sinclair Spectrums

"staff picks" button which, if you click on it, gives you such details as how long a game takes to download and what operating system is needed to run it.

The Networxs
www.thenetworxs.com

This busy site has the usual catalog of games with good descriptions and screen shots, but no customer reviews. There's a very expensive return policy – you will be charged 35 per cent restocking fee of your total order (including shipping, handling and tax), and if you reorder the same item, they charge you an extra five per cent credit card transaction fee, which seems harsh, as you're paying additional shipping and handling charges already. Plenty of other online games stores are much more customer-friendly.

Tronix Web
www.tronixweb.com

This is a site for serious gamers – ones who know what's coming out and when: there are no user reviews and only minimal descriptions. Specializing in Japanese imports, this site has a pre-order form which allows you to "reserve" a copy of a new release, even if the actual launch date or price is unknown. Policies are fair and clear; the only problem encountered was an inability to actually place anything in the shopping cart!

 **Specialists** For the serious gamer

Dexterity Software
www.dexterity.com

Makers of the popular Dweep games. You can save on shipping by ordering it to be e-mailed direct to your desktop, and you can have your money back if you're not totally satisfied with these games. T-shirts, mugs and mousepads featuring Dweep are also available. Good FAQ page too.

Diana Gruber's 3D Casino Las Vegas
www.3d-casino.com

Only one game available here – the 3D Casino Las Vegas game, which claims to bring you the sights, sounds, and thrills of the Nevada gambling mecca. There are free download samples, and if the "improved slot machine action" takes your fancy you can either buy the downloadable version or get it shipped to you (that costs 50 per cent more). Ordering is easy, but the policy statement is through Digital River which unhelpfully says you have to contact the vendor.

Double
www.pcv-soft.com/double

Loosely in the vein of Pokémon – or at least that's how you can sell the game

to your children when they complain – Double is actually based on the old Chinese game of mah jong, the purpose being to educate and intellectually stimulate the whole family. The Pokémon link comes in as you yourself can easily create new themes within the game and exchange these with friends. A tenuous connection we admit. Downloads are available online.

Flight Sim Central
www.fscentral.com
Always dreamed of being a jet pilot? These simulator games may well be the closest you ever get. You can choose from final approach, combat, scenery, or even taking the controls of a particular type of airplane. Some of these games have even been tested by pilots for that authentic feel.

GamePro
www.gamepro.com
This is the online version of *GamePro* magazine, and the aim behind the whole thing is to sell you subscriptions rather than the games themselves. But it is still well worth browsing this site as it's jammed with facts, figures, user reviews, news and features all about computer and video games. There are free downloads too.

MacTreasures
www.mactreasures.com
A dealer in unique or unusual Apple Mac products, this site has a large library of mostly educational and non-violent games. Though it claims to provide illustrations, reviews and screen shots, none were available with the dozen or so games we selected at random. But a decent description of each game and required systems is provided.

Computer games

PCAviator
www.pcaviator.com
This site has a fantastic range of flight simulator games, with in-depth descriptions and specs. As well as games, it sells books, multimedia, and add-ons. The site is well designed with good screen shots and easy-to-read type, and shipping is calculated each time you add to your cart. Information on their returns policy was hard to track down, however.

Sega
www.sega.com
Sega games, Sega consoles, Sega peripherals… if it's Sega you want, this is the place. This online store is easy to use, with policies and shipping info easy to access plus a reasonable return policy. There's also no doubting the quality and that the manufacturer will back up the warranty. Pre-orders are available for those who want to be the first on their block with the latest release.

Strategic Studies Group
www.ssgus.com
This independent gamemaker prides itself on its select number of quality strategic games, which continue to have a dedicated following. They make it plain that they don't like complicated websites, and their site duly keeps things simple. They offer a no-quibble returns policy, next-morning shipping, and each game is an award winner. A 25 per cent discount was available when we visited. The real only annoyance was the order form where you have to fill in all the fields yourself.

Tolkien Games Page
www.lysator.liu.se/tolkien-games
Tolkien fans should check out this site. It's more a resource for all things concerning Tolkien computer games, but it also has a truckful of downloadable games, plus a good technical Q&A page for players with difficulties. Any game that even vaguely relates to Tolkien-type characters is listed here, as well as facts on things such as availability, system requirements, screen shots, reviews and distributor information.

Your Move Chess and Games
www.icdchess.com
Chess fans will drool over the selection of games here. There are a few mass-market games too, but most are aimed at the professional player and the specifications and descriptions are exhaustive. Ordering is easy and a five per cent restocking fee is waived on exchanges. You can even buy real chess sets too.

ROUTE 66

For those of you who find computer games baffling, Yahoo Games has kindly provided an environment where you can play such classics as mah jong, Chinese checkers and, er, bingo. Yes, there is even a Net equivalent of an electronic voice yelling, "Clickety click! 66."

Chess and backgammon are proving something of an online mecca. As long as you've got a browser which can handle Java software you can join in the fun by registering at games.yahoo.com

Computers

Can you get good deals
on a PC online? Is software
soft? The Net positively
hums with computers
and computer stuff,
and we're here to
help you carve a path through
the maze of conflicting data

 It is so a proper computer

Apple Store
www.apple.com
With products this glossy and seductive, it's no wonder Apple offers its own
loan or lease scheme; the temptation factor, heightened by great site design
and photography, is enormous. If you need the latest iMac, spec sheets and
lots of helpful advice are available, as with all the products on offer here.
Caveats: Apple is a bit mean with the RAM at the lower end of the range,
and the RAGE graphics cards need updating. No, we didn't care, either.
Delivery can take up to 14 days, but is usually much quicker.

AuctionMac
www.auctionmac.com
This Mac-only auction site goes to a lot of trouble to reassure users of security.
Not many items are on sale at any given time, but it has an "alert" service that
will inform you via e-mail when your requested item comes up for sale. Bidding
is by proxy – you bid your maximum and the site will bid for you up to that
amount – so you don't have to keep checking in. You can also see the final
bid on closed sales. Like all auctions, a bid is a contract – you are obliged
to buy the item if you post the winning bid. It's not much use if you need a
particular model immediately but bargains can be had if you have time.

MacResQ
www.macresq.com
This is an independent reseller but the user-friendly site inspires confidence.

Computers

Prepare to be seduced. Apple's sleek, stylish site could very well persuade to you splash out

Again there is not a huge inventory, but it is always changing and you can e-mail them if you don't see what you need. Technical support is available for most products they sell, and you can download diagnostic freeware and some free driver software too. Usefully, they also offer a repairs service.

PowerMax

www.powermax.com
This authorized Apple reseller sells new and used, and offers a trade-in too. The Bargain Basement has good deals. Shipping details are missing, though there is a whole page on returns, but the truly annoying feature is you can't just register to buy – you have to call and talk to one of the consultants too.

Internet appliances Fools rush in...

Compaq

athome.compaq.com
The trouble with the Net is that you need a computer to access it – at least you did until now. Internet appliances are now starting to appear as an alternative, based on the premise that if you don't need all those bells and whistles on a computer, why pay for having them? Compaq have produced the iPAQ to fill this particular niche. You can't buy it online, and it's not all that portable. But its main difference from a computer is that it works with the ease of a TV and the screen on the IA-2 model is a nice user-friendly 15ins.

The best bit is, like a mobile phone, the hardware is reduced or even free when you sign up for the Internet access package (limited time offer).

eDevice

www.edevice.com

Although there seems to be as much life in the Internet appliance market as there was in General Custer's cavalry after the battle of the Little Big Horn, eDevice is persevering with its efforts in this area. Buoyed partly by the fact that it sells to companies rather than consumers, it has developed the world's first Internet-connected espresso coffee maker with Lavazzo. And everybody was betting on fridges as being the appliance most likely to get wired.

MSN

devices.msn.com/msncompanion

This site couldn't be less helpful if it tried. From the homepage the link to the MSN Companion isn't immediately apparent. When you do get where you want to go there are only minimal features, no specifications, no warranty or service information, no links, and you can't even buy the product online. All you know is that a product called the Companion exists.

Netpliance

www.netpliance.com

The I-opener from Netpliance comes with a 10in screen, and the keyboard is helpfully labelled with text, like "news" and "weather". There's no mouse, just a keyboard pad. The monitor displays a few sports and news links, a web browser links to a few dozen more, and there's also an address bar to insert any URL. The downside of this machine is that a lot of sites are geared to Internet Explorer or Netscape for either Windows or a Mac, so you won't get much joy with those, or with sites that require certain plug-ins to display. You pay $299 for the hardware and then a monthly Internet fee. A good example of an Internet appliance – but one that you may, ultimately, find limiting.

The IPAQ, which looks like a PC but works like your TV, is one of the few appliances to have survived the spring

Computers

Sony eVilla
www.evilla.com
As with the iPAQ, Sony's eVilla looks remarkably like a computer, the only real differences being the miniature keyboard and the vertical rectangular monitor (to reduce scrolling). The eVilla is so new that this launch site wasn't finished on our last visit, with only a few facts about the product and no prices on display. However, what you can add to your technological knowledge is that this is a complete e-mail, Internet and ISP rolled into one, with state-of-the-art flash technology and the potential to accommodate four separate users.

 **Computer trinkets & Harley mouse mats**

Compu-Crafts
www.Compu-Crafts.com
Specializing in sets of matching mouse pad, coaster, monitor pocket and wrist rest, this site has styles and patterns to customize any desktop. There is one flat shipping fee, but the order form is an annoying "fill in the fields" type. The returns policy is not explained and the site does not appear to be secure.

Computer Gear
www.computergear.com
Everything from chocolate CD-ROMs and computer pasta to denim computer covers and Harley-Davidson mouse pads. There is also a line of Christmas ornaments featuring a laptop and desktop ornament. The gifts are neatly separated into sections such Gifts for Her (sterling desktop earrings, no less), Cat Corner, Executive Office gifts, and even a food section, making it easy find the perfect gift for your computer-addicted buddy.

Classic Apple design is not restricted to Macs.
There's "Think Different" posters for a start...

Cybertrash

www.cybertrash.org

At last! Bits of old computer recycled into jewelry, wind chimes and fridge magnets! Surprisingly attractive, too, especially the earrings made from pre-loved inductor coils, resistors, diodes, head amps and switches. Ordering is secure and all major cards are accepted but their shipping policy seems non-existent. At an average of only $5 per item, it must be worth a try though.

Red Light Runner

www.redlightrunner.com

Apple collectibles, from towels and sandals with the Apple logo to mugs, pens and even a "Steve Jobs for President" sticker. Red Light Runner also sells those classy "Think different" posters, featuring Miles Davis, Alfred Hitchcock, Maria Callas, Lucy & Desi and Martha Graham, among others, all at classy prices.

USG Works

www.usgworks.com

Unique little gifts made from a combination of motherboards and wire and stained glass. You can have your corporate logo made out of a board too. You can't buy this stuff online which may be why there is absolutely no information on shipping or returns. You have to print off the form and send or fax it, along with a money order. There is a space to add shipping costs but just what could those be...? The site says it will add a secure shopping facility soon.

 Sites where the consumer is king

Circuit City

www.circuitcity.com

This electronics company has a great site that either lets you specify your requirements and it will show you matching options, or browse the complete product list. A customer ratings chart is useful and there are several shipping options, including a store pick-up as Circuit City operates in most states. Price guarantee means if any store has the same product advertised for less within a 30-day period, Circuit City will refund 110 per cent of the difference.

Radio Shack

www.radioshack.com

This online version of your local Radio Shack is designed like the store – in other words, busy and a bit confusing. It sells components rather than complete systems, and unfortunately two of the three monitors clicked on were no longer available to buy online or in stores, begging the question, why were they still featured? Otherwise you can shop here with confidence.

Computers

Accessories For the tastefully garnished PC

Now you've sorted yourself out with your new computer toy, you might think you're set to get your mortgage repayments back on track – but somehow it doesn't work like that. Okay, so you've got your entry-level PC complete with all the essentials – monitor, keyboard etc – but you're just not satisfied. It looks like everyone else's. A relatively simple way to put your stamp on it is to customize your keyboard. Access Keyboards and the Keyboard Company sell customized keyboards to your specs, or you can simply choose one from their range of large, small, waterproof and industrial models. If the South Park mouse pad you got free with your PC just isn't giving out the right messages, you can pick up a fine-art mouse pad for just $9.99 (including shipping) from The Mouse Pad Shop. Or if you're worried about RSI why not pick up a preventative ergonomic harness (from 4arms) for just $49.95. Face it – once you're hooked, you can say goodbye to all your spare cash.

4arms
4arms.com
Support for your arms, shoulders and back to keep RSI at bay.

Computer Fun
www.computerfun.com
From mouse pads – an animal theme prevails – to stress relievers.

Kuebler and Company
www.kueblerandcompany.com/
Be nice to your computer with a kangaroo dust cover.

Note Float
www.notefloat.com
Spinning your Notebook 360° has never been easier.

PC Coordinates
www.pccoordinates.com
Ever wanted to "beautify your work area"? Now's your chance.

Sunrise Multimedia
www.sunrisemm.com
Meet stress head on with the PC Hammer or Mac Hammer.

Mouse Pad Shop
www.mousepadshop.com
Fine art, calming scenery, or ergonomic gel-filled mouse pads.

From the big names to the little guys

Barebone

www.499pc.com

Most prices are under $500 here but this site is really geared to people who like to build their own component system, so it's a bit techie for your average user. If you know what you're after, however, the customer testimonials declare this to be a winning site.

Computer Discount Center

123cdc.com

This site claims to be able to offer computers as close to manufacturer price as possible but as it lists no RRP it is hard to compare. Each product has a long list of features, but doesn't say what those features actually do. Ordering is easy and shipping is calculated before you complete the order.

Computers4sure

www.computers4sure.com

Not only does this site feature a massive inventory covering every computer need, but it also has some interesting features – for example, click on an item and not only are the price and shipping costs right there, but it also gives you a "price drop alert" option, where you can state the price you want to pay and the site will e-mail you if it subsequently drops to that point through a sale or rebate offer. User ratings, extended warranty and recommended alternatives are also displayed with each item. Busy site with lots of great features.

PC Namd: their customers love them, it seems, and not just because they ship for free. It's because they're just nice people

Computers

BIG BLUE & THE REST

The manufacturers' sites are worth a visit for those with a high boredom threshold. The key URLs are:

www.compaq.com
www.dell.com
www.gateway.com
www.ibm.com
www.hp.com/country/
  us/eng/hp_store.
  htm
www.honeywell.com/
  eventures/index.jsp
www.csd.toshiba.com/
  cgi-bin/tais/pd/pd_
  home.jsp

Honeywell's eVentures is a, pardon the pun, gateway to its "e-merging" (their gag, not ours) sites where you can buy online.

Insight
www.insight.com
A little gold mine, though this pure-PC site is stronger on individual components and peripherals than it is on complete desktop PC systems – its partners here being Toshiba, Hewlett Packard, and Compaq. Those whose eyesight is not what it once was may struggle – the type is so small that it's hard to get at all the relevant shipping and warranty information without incurring major eyestrain. Battle through, however, and you'll discover that shipping is via UPS or FedEx with the usual options. The site also offers same day delivery for the really desperate.

PCDC
www.pc-techs.com
The people behind this site have gone to great lengths to explain their various policies on everything from order limitations to "typographical, photographic, or technical errors" to the point where it actually says that products on the site are not intended as an offer to sell. Huh? This seems to indicate that they have had problems in the past with accuracy. However, the rest of the information is taken to such a highly detailed level that it is probably more a case of them making sure they're covering all the bases. It claims to have comprehensive descriptions of all items, but these must only be available once you have clicked the "buy" button. At this point most systems protected by a firewall will be prevented from investigating further.

PC Nomad
www.pcnomad.com
Some small sites just seem to have a good personality and you feel like you are dealing with a trusted friend. This one sells new and refurbished portable computers (Apple included), personal organizers and related items – not a huge selection but from testimonials they appear to offer a customer-oriented service. Click on each product for technical specs, and you can search by price. Better yet, the products will be shipped ground completely free.

PCWebShopper
www.pcwebshopper.com
This hardware site has a clear layout with a navigation bar that guides you through all the terms and policies with a minimum of fuss. Products have an editorial description, good features and specification lists, plus a useful "content of package" list.

Sale On All

www.saleonall.com

No pictures or technical guidance with this site, so you have to know exactly what product you want and who makes it (search by manufacturer or category), but prices are well below retail so it works if your mind is already made up.

Superwarehouse

www.superwarehouse.com

As billed, this is a huge online catalog of all things computer-related, including refurbished and bargain sections. Product descriptions are thorough but unless you go for the special deals you will only be getting a small discount off retail. There's no shipping info up front, and you must register to check out.

 The world in the palm of your hand

Club PDA

www.clubpda.com

Easy to navigate, with plenty of products, all of which have good descriptions and compatibility warnings. There's a useful list of recommended add-ons accompanying each product selection, and a good support system too.

Mobile Mania

www.mobile-mania.com

This is what shopping online is all about – great product selection, excellent descriptions and specifications, good illustrations, fair and clear return policy, good support system, order tracking and same day shipping. No complaints.

PDA Mart

www.pdamart.com

This site has a news section that keeps you up to date with the latest technological advances and news gleaned from different sources. In the product section you can read user reviews and add your own. A good site with more than just an online catalog.

 **Before you splash the cash, read this...**

CNET Computers

computers.cnet.com

Editors as well as users review the products featured, and the categories are broken down to lists such as "Editor's Top 5 Cheap PCs". Chock full of specs

Computers

and even company profiles, this site is about as comprehensive as it gets.

Computer Previews
http://compreviews.about.com/compute/compreview
User reviews as well as Editor's Picks, plus links to magazine sites.

Computing Review
www.computingreview.com
Find your product and you get a snapshot rating; then one click lets you access all user reviews. These are real users, too, not journalists or "experts".

Product Review
www.productreviewnet.com
A summary of product reviews from a variety of other product review sources, and given the thumbs up by Yahoo Internet Life.

Review Finder
www.reviewfinder.com
Easy-to-navigate site searchable by categories, plus a small discussion section.

Ziff Davis
www.zdnet.com
Not the easiest site to find your way around with the links getting a bit lost among the adverts, but there's no shortage of information here.

Big on reviews and, better still, they're user reviews so you can find out which torments people just like you have suffered – and then avoid them

Crafts & hobbies

Okay, crafts have never been what you might call groovy but thanks to the Internet, they're starting to shake off that image of stuff that grandma might do. Slowly.

Arnie's Arts 'n Crafts

www.arnies.com

Not Mr Schwarzenegger's latest commercial venture to try and restore his bank balance after Planet Hollywood (although we'd dearly love to see the Terminator indulging in a spot of rock painting). Instead, it's a useful site to visit if you're looking for a variety of craft projects, including glass painting supplies and ready-to-decorate wooden boxes. The site is a little dull visually, but it's easy to use with a speedy shopping basket system. UPS delivery charges are calculated for you online before you confirm your order.

Art Store

www.artstoreplus.com

An online store that offers art papers, brushes, pens and other specialist supplies, including bookbinding tools and glass paint. There are excellent photos of all products including the wide range of specialist papers, so you can see exactly what you're getting. There's no online ordering as yet but it's promised soon. In the meantime, you can print out the site's order form and fax it over to them with your card details.

Baskets of Joy

www.basketsofjoy.com

Refreshingly modern and well-designed site selling tools and kits for making a wide range of designs of basket, from Shaker-style log baskets to tiny trinket holders. They also sell a range of wrought iron and porcelain handles for those finishing touches. Prices are good with wholesale deals for businesses and craft teachers. For shipping, the site will add the actual UPS charges to your order, so check what these will be before you buy.

Bent Needle

www.bentneedle.com

Great Arizona-based site for machine quilting enthusiasts, with kits and tips for a wide range of quilts, wall hangings and other patchwork projects. They also offer a very reasonably priced finishing service for people who have done the patching but can't face making up, hand quilting and binding the final article. Delivery costs depend on what you order; goods are sent by US mail.

Collectible Doll Company

www.jeannordquistdolls.com

Doll-lovers will adore the range of porcelain doll-making equipment and molds on offer here (non-doll-lovers will be terrified by them). There are kits to make reproductions of antique dolls as well as plenty of paints, brushes, books of tips and other accessories, including eyes. Shipping costs vary depending on the size of your order and delivery is via UPS.

Cotton Pickin' Quilt Shop

www.cottonpickinquilts.com

Fabric, patterns, and kits for quilters of all abilities on an easy-to-use site that features great illustrations of the kits, plus tips and a supremely useful fabric calculator for people wanting to make up their own designs. US mail delivery charges depend on the weight of your order, and goods should be with you in 7-10 days.

Craftopia

www.craftopia.com

Vast site with projects and craft supplies for every room in the house, as well as personal and gift items. There's a great section for kids' crafts and all projects are rated for the level of skill required to complete them – "dabbler", "enthusiast" or "expert". There's also clear and helpful information at all stages of the buying process. Shipping costs range between $4.95 and $18.95 depending on which UPS service you select.

Shipping from Crafty Chick comes at pretty much bargain rates – good going given that the site is based in the UK

Crafty Chick

www.craftychick.com

This site is based in the UK but all prices can be shown in US dollars, and it's a great resource for finding craft supplies and kits that you might not come across at your local mall. Sections include mosaics, stencilling, rubber stamps and decoupage. Shipping costs vary depending on the cost of your order – not forgetting the exchange rate – but are pretty cheap considering they're coming from the UK.

Global Outlet Hobby Store

www.hobby-store-online.com

Huge selection of model kits to browse here, with everything from vintage cars to state-of-the-art tanks to railroad engines, all lovingly reproduced in miniature. There is also a wide selection of paints, brushes and other supplies to help you complete your masterpiece. The site can ship overseas if you want to sent a kit as a gift, and prices are even available in a range of worldwide currencies.

Hobby Shop Mall

www.hobbystores.com

Nothing actually for sale at this searchable mall site, but it does provide a useful list of online retailers specialising in supplies for a variety of hobbies, including model-making, miniature railroads, and radio-control toys. Whether it's BC Hobby in Battle Creek, MI, or Tom's Trackside Racing in Plaineville, CT, each site is helpfully coded according to the kind of hobby equipment it stocks.

Miniatures Discount Dollhouses and More

www.miniatures.com

If small things are your big thing, then check out this wonderful site, which is pretty much guaranteed to provide you with loads of inspiration – not to mention practical supplies – for your next miniature project. Desperately searching for a dollhouse kit in Colonial style for under $100? Use the excellent search facility to go straight to what you're looking for, or just browse the whole site for ideas and tips from other dollhouse and miniaturist enthusiasts. Regular delivery costs $6.95 on orders under $150 (over that and it's free) or they can arrange a FedEx service for an extra charge. Their returns policy guarantees complete satisfaction too.

UNUSUAL CRAFTS AND HOBBIES

Forget woodwork or sewing – there are folk out there making stuff out of things you'd never expect. Check out the sites below for some, er, interesting craft projects.

Antler Creek Wildlife Creations

www.antlercreek.com
Tables, chandeliers and other home décor made from deer, moose and elk antlers.

California Gourd Society

www.calgourd.com
Get instructions and supplies for turning the humble gourd into a work of art.

Shell-A-Rama

www.shellarama.com
Been wondering what you can do with a barnacle cluster? This site loses points, though, as it also sells coral pieces, robbing some poor fish somewhere of its home.

Key West Soda and Beer Can Creations

gay-guide.com/clients/kwc.htm
If you drink a lot of soda, check this out for how to use those empty cans.

Mormon Handicraft

www.mormonhandicraft.com

Traditional craft patterns based on sewing and quilting are available from this Salt Lake City online store. Even if you're not religiously inclined, you can get craft tips from Crafty Cathy or just browse the patterns and books on Christmas decorations, clothing and soft toys. Shipping costs between $5 and $25 depending on the cost of the order and the service you choose.

Orbital Dynamics

www.orbitaldynamics.com

If making rockets is your thing, this site can help you to find the newest designs in complete rocket kits, or motors and other peripherals to help you build your own. There's some serious hardware here, some of which is restricted, so there's a fairly hefty Agreement and Release form to sign, and many items require you to provide a copy of your driver's license before your order will be accepted. Shipping is via UPS Priority Mail Insured and charges start at $6.95 for small orders; otherwise it's 15 per cent of the cost of your goods on orders over $100.

WhipperSnapper

www.whippersnapperdesigns.com

Bright and fun site selling a host of unique rubber stamps that are refreshingly different to the usual run-of-the-mill designs. There are theme stamps for the holidays, or for making cards and decorating gift wrap for new babies, weddings and birthdays. They also sell clip-art CDs of some of their designs. Prices may be a little higher than for regular rubber stamps, but the quality and detail of these designs more than make up for that. Please note that there is a $25 minimum order, but shipping charges are calculated for you online before you enter your card details.

A good few steps removed from quilts and basketweaving, Orbital Dynamics brings together cyberspace and outer space

Department stores

Traditional stores have taken to the
Net with all the reckless abandon with
which the film industry embraced TV

Bloomingdales

www.bloomingdales.com

As you would expect, Bloomingdales has managed to produce a stylish but
functional website catering for men, women, children and the home. Simply
select a category and browse through the comprehensive list of offerings.
Not only can you view enlarged images of items, you can also select which
aspect to zoom in on. It also offers True Internet Color, so you don't find that
the ruby red shoes you just paid a fortune for are actually pastel pink.

Macys

www.macys.com

Understandably, Macys has set things up so that if you want to browse the
decent selection of its online range you must visit a number of departments.
But why Nine West women's trousers only feature in the Nine West section
and not the women's department is a mystery. This aside, the reputable
department store has produced a comprehensive site, complete with zoom
facilities and essay-length descriptions as to whether the black polo sweater
is in or out this season. Orders are shipped within 7 days, and if they aren't,
Macys will contact you. Shipping varies from $8 for 7-10 days to $18 for
overnight delivery, but after processing rather than receipt of your order.

Neiman Marcus

www.neimanmarcus.com

Neiman Marcus has produced a particularly stylish site full of designer wares
from Anne Klein and Manola Blahnik to name just two, but the site is blighted
by its need to use fur as a supposedly attractive selling point. Still, if you truly
feel that what's missing in your life is a pink mink bathrobe, a snip at $1,995,
then this is the site for you. If you're shopping here, prices probably aren't an
issue, though why the company feels the need to stress the nationality of the
recently butchered animals remains a mystery.

Nordstrom

http://store.nordstrom.com

Bright and shiny – and that's just the models. Nordstrom, established as America's supreme shoe store, also holds its own with gifts, accessories, men's and women's wear. They make it possible to search by every means – category, brand, specialist item or trend. The images and descriptions of the products are clear, even down to the washing instructions, and although standard prices apply, the sales section offers a respectable selection of bargains.

Already in a healthy position offline, Saks has gone all out to blitz the online opposition too

Saks

www.saksfifthavenue.com

The mother of all department stores has put a massive amount of effort into their site. Their entrance is stylish, with a simple black-and-white homepage linking to searches via brand or product type. All the top names are here, at all the top prices, but the most impressive aspects are the images. Fendi shoes and Bulgari perfume bottles never looked so good. You can click to enlarge and then zoom in on the aspect you choose, creating a better and altogether less hassled experience than you'll ever get in-store. Add to this price, brand and category sorting for each section, and detailed information right down to dry-cleaning instructions or wear it once and throw it away, and you have a dream site for online shopping.

Sears

www.sears.com

Considering their reputation we expected a rather more distinctive site, but Sears have opted for the information overload approach. They don't sell clothing online (school uniforms excepted) and the range of electronics, computers and hardware on offer isn't as comprehensive as you might expect. What they do display, however, is easy to find and comes with clear images, sometimes enlarged, full descriptions and discounts. It's advisable to read the multiple pages of delivery information as charges vary according to type of product, size, weight and address. You will need your wits about you here.

HARRODS

Despite its "seven floors of service" claim, the range of goods you can buy online from the UK's most prestigious (that's British for "expensive") store is extremely limited. There are no clothes, for example, and choosing bedlinen brings up only a London number to call.

Being very wealthy helps. Select wine and a bottle of 1947 Cheval Blanc can be yours for just $6,500 (plus shipping: you have to call to arrange this). Clearly, shopping (online or not) is still something that the servants do.

---

www.harrods.com

Eco living

You don't have to chain yourself to a giant redwood to live an environmentally sound life (but don't let us stop you). Online you can buy stuff that spans the green spectrum, and will help you to help the planet

Abundant Earth
www.abundantearth.com
Great site offering everything for a natural and eco-friendly lifestyle, from state-of-the-art water and air filters to fun clocks made out of recycled bicycle parts. There are lights and appliances that will save energy and save you money, and it's all laid out on clear and simply designed pages. They have a no-quibble 30-day returns policy and most orders are sent out within 48 hours. If there is going to be a substantial delay, they will notify you. Standard shipping costs $4.95 with a surcharge for Alaska, Hawaii and US Territories.

Amazing Recycled Products
www.amazingrecycled.com
Recycled glass, plastic, wood and fabric come together on this site to provide a host of useful products, such as reclaimed plastic "lumber" for decking and landscape gardening, office products, golf shirts and lunch bags. There are some lovely glass paperweights on offer, too. If you too are starting to get concerned about how much stuff you throw away each year, this is the perfect place to come to even up the balance.

Composters.com
www.composters.com
You will be astounded at just how many ways there are to turn household waste into earth-friendly plant food thanks to the gadgets that proliferate across this clear and easy-to-use site. Compost bins and wormeries of all shapes and sizes (there's even one cunningly built into a garden seat) are available to help even the smallest backyard become a recycler's paradise. We were particularly impressed with the Doggie Dooley, a digester that will safely dispose of pet waste. Delivery and shipping varies depending on your order, but most items will be sent via UPS.

Eco living

Earthbath
www.earthbath.com
This site also belongs in our Petcare section since it sells a range of gentle, biodegradable dog and cat care products made from ingredients like tea tree and orange peel oils. Some of the products have a natural flea repellent quality. Online ordering is not yet up and running, but there's a guide to retailers who stock the products and a promise of additions to the site soon.

Forests of the World
www.worldforests.com
Ethically traded and environmentally sound products from the rainforests of the Amazon, Costa Rica and Madagascar. The range includes stationery, raffia bags and jewelry. The site also acts as an educational resource and there are rainforest kits and learning products for schools. There's no shopping basket facility at present, and the online order form is lacking in instructions, but it's a good site for gifts and unusual bits and pieces for your home.

Gaiam
www.gaiam.com
Chic but environmentally sound lifestyle company selling natural, sustainable products for the ethical consumer. Clothing, organic foods, and health supplements rub shoulders with yoga books and air filters. The site is beautifully designed (you feel more calm and centered just by spending a few minutes looking at it), and the online shopping cart is efficient and speedy. Orders arrive within 7-10 days, and shipping is calculated at 10 per cent of orders up to $100 and five per cent of orders over that amount.

A Happy Planet
www.ahappyplanet.com
Plenty to choose from on this organic cotton/hemp clothing and recycled

Style meets substance on the Gaiam site, which offers seriously stress-free, eco-friendly shopping

products site. There's an excellent section for eco-babies which includes reusable diapers with none of the chemicals that infest the disposable kind, plus some very cute soft toys and towels. The adult section, for once, has organic cotton clothes and underwear with some real style, rejecting the plain Jane veggie-burger style of some eco-sites. They even do organic cotton bedwares – mattresses, comforters and pillows. Shipping varies with the price of your order, but will not be more than $12. You should allow 2-4 weeks for delivery.

Kids Nature

www.kids-nature.com

Start them off young and kit your kids out in organic European clothing (we're not sure of the European significance either). Items range from baby romper suits to accessories and bedding, with a few things for moms as well. Given that their selling point is natural clothing, with the emphasis on natural, little is made of fabric details, with only adequate descriptions and enlarged images. Prices are generous, particularly the sale items, and shipping starts at $6.50.

Mad River Clothing Company

www.madriverclothing.com

This Canadian site sells "clothing with a conscience" for kids from six months to 14-years-old, made mostly from locally produced organic cotton, hemp and eco-spun fleece. The clothes are stylish and look hardwearing, and have the added advantage that you can be pretty sure no one else will be wearing anything similar. Mad River will ship anywhere (charges start at CA$9.50) and they donate part of their profits to Unicef and The Children's Wish Foundation.

Paperhaus

www.paperhaus.com

Demolishing the myth that recycled products can't be stylish, this stunning site features beautifully designed products made from recycled paper, by-products of the leather industry and other post-consumer waste. Main ranges include stationery, photo albums and frames – those from Pina Zangaro are particularly striking – and presentation materials. They also sell reusable and refillable pens and technical instruments. There's no shopping basket, but the online order form is simple to fill in and shipping appears to be free via UPS ground.

Planet Hemp

www.planethemp.com

Billed as the fibre of the future, hemp is an eco-crop par excellence and fast becoming a totally separate issue from its controversial cousin marijuana. Its uses range from making natural shampoos to sofa throws and Planet Hemp stocks the lot. You'll be amazed just how many products are on offer – we especially like the hemp canvas hanging CD rack. Shipping costs $9.50 and is via Certified Mail, taking around 2-4 weeks to reach you. If you're in a real hurry, phone your order in and they will arrange a FedEx overnight delivery.

Sustainability Source TM, Inc.

www.greenpagesstore.com

This eco-shopping portal brings together merchants from all over the earth-aware spectrum. From recycled coffee-bag neckties to handmade keepsake boxes, there's plenty of variety here, and all the sites are subject to serious scrutiny to establish that they're as environmentally responsible as they claim. You can even check each merchant's rating on a number of criteria, such as whether or not their products are certified by a recognised eco-organisation.

Educational

The Internet began as an educational tool for academics. These days, the definition of learning seems to have broadened somewhat, as it now includes detective stories starring Barbie and epidemic simulation kits...

General The e-tree of knowledge

The Education Station
www.theeducationstation.com
Making learning fun is the philosophy behind this site, and the limited but well chosen products on offer do just that. The multimedia and electronics items will delight your computer addict, and there are several old-fashioned games and toys that let your child learn while playing. Phonetics features heavily.

Discovery School
http://school.discovery.com
The Discovery Channel sells a huge range of educational videos, books and software aimed at adults as well as children. Browse through hundreds of products, including craft activity kits and the rather more exciting Epidemic Simulation Kit, on this plush, well-designed site.

Family Communications
www.fci.org
From the producers of *Mister Rogers' Neighborhood*, this site offers a wealth of information. The contents range from using Mr Rogers to help in the education of your child all the way to how to deal with issues surrounding adoption, divorce and even migrant children. You can be sure that the books and other materials will be of high quality and the advice sound.

Let Them Learn
www.letthemlearn.com
The mission here is to help 6 to 12-year-olds acquire good study skills. Making learning enjoyable helps to focus a child, and the kits for sale here aim to do that. Subjects are limited, but there are promises to expand soon.

Superkids

www.superkids.com

Nothing actually for sale at this well organized if plain review of learning titles, but there's a useful searchable directory plus articles, free educational tools, fun (*Detective Barbie's Mystery of the Carnival Caper*) and reviews with links to suppliers. The price survey is great if you don't have time to shop around.

Wieser Educational

www.wieser-ed.com

This site sells "high interest instructional material" (aimed particularly at remedial and special needs students) to both institutions and individuals. Topics range from independent living skills to health and drug education.

Home schooling If school's out...

Aztec Home Schooling

www.aztec-hs.com

Home schooling has become increasingly popular, but it's not for everyone. This informative site will help you decide if your child would benefit from it. While Aztec is not a school, it has products and testing materials that will help you, most of which can be downloaded after payment. A great resource.

Homeschool Associates

www.homeschoolassociates.com

This site has a slightly more professional ambience – there are certainly more things going on than just curriculum packages. You can get a high school diploma through North Atlantic Regional Schools, which will allow you to transfer your home-school credits. Links include Bookmobile Online where you can order educational books and other educational materials.

Home Parents Students Prep School

www.homeschool-hps.net

A resource for homeschooling all grades, with a more controlled curriculum for older students "in harmony with Christian principles". Offering guidance, this school (run from Washington state) is service-based. It's more formal than some programs with regular reports and feedback. The site was changing web hosts when last visited but promises to return to its former glory.

Mommyschool

www.mommyschool.com

A decent collection of books and tools to help you school your child at home, but there are no formal curriculum packages since they believe that getting out of one restricted system means that you don't want to get into another.

My Education At Home
www.myeducationathome.com
Christian and secular home-school curriculum packages and books, with a good section for special-needs students. Check that your state's requirements are met before purchasing, however, as no additional information is given.

Distant learning — Stimulating your grey matter

Educational Correspondence Training School
www.ectschool.com
Distant learning over the Internet makes a lot of sense. This site provides courses in many fields, although only to certificate and diploma level at the moment. Each course has a real teacher with whom you can communicate by phone, fax or e-mail. There is a lot of information on this site, so check it out if you want to change careers or advance in your current one. Registration is through a downloadable form, and financing is available.

Guided Correspondence Study at the University of Iowa
www.uiowa.edu
This university offers accredited courses that you can do online. Lessons are e-mailed to you, and a proctor near you supervises exams. Research can be done through the online library, and supplemented by your own books etc. There are other distant courses too that are administered offline, including a Bachelor of Liberal Studies (BLS) external degree program. Courses start the month after you enroll and you have 9 months to complete them (there's a chance of a 3-month extension).

The Internet is ideal for distant learning. The options aren't always cheap but you can get financial help

University of North Carolina at Chapel Hill
www.fridaycenter.unc.edu
A whole variety of online programs and courses are available. These either follow the school calendar with weekly assignments and online discussion groups, or are self-paced (you can start a 9-month course at any time and submit your work by e-mail). You have to provide yourself with the right technology, and an approved proctor must supervise final exams. Strangely, you must print out the registration form and send it in to enroll.

Food

Martha, Julia, Les et al
have taught us to expect more
imaginative cuisine these days and
the Internet is a great way of tracking
down that elusive ingredient to turn
a simple recipe into something special.
Or you can just use it to get a stack
of baked beans delivered to your door

 For what we are about to receive...

Fabulous Foods

www.fabulousfoods.com

Site devoted to good food in all its forms. If you're trying to steer your family away from hotdogs and fries, these healthy-eating and vegetarian delights are tasty enough to tempt even the most determined meat-eater. You can sign up for a newsletter tailored to your eating requirements – diabetic, low fat, low carbohydrate etc – and there are selected features and sections with kitchen, fitness and camping tips. Or you can just surf with your mouth watering.

Simply Food

www.simplyfood.com

Huge UK-based portal site set up by the Carlton Food Network and packed with recipes, foodie competitions, cookery advice and links to food shopping or cooking sites. A great place to start if you're seeking culinary inspiration.

Supermarkets Online

www.supermarkets.com/Entry.pst

Why not ease the burden on your wallet by getting your hands on a stack of money-off coupons? At Supermarkets Online all you have to do is enter your zip code and they'll locate offers in your area (covering a variety of stores, Pavilions, Food 4 Less, Albertsons and so on) and then you print out the money-off coupons you want. Simple as that.

What We Eat
www.whatweeat.com
Well-organized food portal with links to grocery and gourmet food stores, recipe sites, health and nutritional information, and restaurant guides. Direct links are provided, as are reviews and star ratings for each site. Includes international, recommended reading and children's sections.

Yahoo Shopping
http://shopping.yahoo.com/Food_and_Beverages
The comprehensive offering you would expect from the ever-popular Yahoo. Shop for groceries, gourmet items, gift baskets, recipes, appliances and restaurant guides, and collect Yahoo Points while you're at it.

Coffee & tea From Starbucks to St Helena

Any Coffee
www.anycoffee.com
Its design may be a bit clichéd, but Any Coffee is simple to search and offers almost any flavor and type of bean. Choose from whole beans, Espresso, flat-bottomed and filter, with flavors ranging from the hills of Mexico to good old artificial Snickerdoodle. Prices are generally under $10. You can also find out how to get the most from your beans with instructions for storage and brewing.

Barnie Coffee
www.barniescoffee.com
This great-looking, mercifully simple site doesn't bother with fancy graphics. Navigation is clear and easy: the products are listed on a sidebar with each one described in enough detail to get your tastebuds going. Prices vary from $10 to $50 depending on the roast, and shipping starts from $6. Mugs, coffee appliances and Garfield the cat merchandise are also sold here.

Flying Saucers
www.flyingsaucers.com
This site is a must for sci-fi-loving coffee-drinkers. Technically it's rather poor with text obscured by graphics, but somehow you don't really care as there are "70 flavors and varieties of coffee (in space ship packaging)". And as if this wasn't enough, there's a "community" section (for sightings etc) and the selection of alien merchandise is unrivalled – in this solar system, anyway.

Peet's Coffee & Tea
www.peets.com
You have to hunt for the teas on what seems at first to be a site exclusively for coffees, but you can search their extensive catalog by type, best-sellers or

specific name. Categories include green, oolong and Indian Black teas, and Dark, Americas and Pacific coffees. Prices vary but even the cheapest variety is given a lengthy description alongside staff and customer reviews.

St Helena

www.st-helena-coffee.sh

The Island of St Helena coffee company's site offers some stunning images of this remote South Atlantic island. If you can draw yourself away, the simple navigation system reveals a limited range but delivery is included in the price.

Starbucks

www.starbucks.com

Starbucks has put some of its riches into this stylish, easy-to-use website, offering as broad a selection of bean flavors and tea strains as you'll find in their stores. Since coffee is also a fashion statement these days, the site will also find you the coffee most suited to your tastes via a few simple questions (eg "what does coffee do for you?"). Tea drinkers can avoid this scrutiny.

Stash Tea

www.stashtea.com

The tea shop for those who want to know which finger to raise when sipping their Earl Grey, and how to adopt the English way of dipping cookies in tea. (You wouldn't want to dip a wafer if biscotti is more appropriate.) Apart from providing quotes and news for tea fans, Stash also sells hundreds of varieties, from green and black to herbal or medicinal teas for stress, sleep and dieting.

Ever wondered who put the bucks into Starbucks? You did. Coffe is now the ultimate fashion statement: just ask the Crane boys

Eating in Because staying in is the new going out

Dining out can be a pain. You have to dress and behave appropriately and shell out tips on top of inflated prices. Okay, so it's not all bad, but why bother when so many companies are willing to bring restaurant-standard food direct to your door? (If pizza is more your style, try www.dominos.com or www.orderpizzahut.com to locate your nearest local delivery man.)

Food.com
www.food.com
Take-out and restaurant food delivery service, with entertaining guides to help you create the perfect menu from the restaurants in your area.

Meals to Go
www.mealstogo.com
Meals to Go currently only operates in the Bay area, but it's one good reason to live in San Francisco. Select your neighborhood to view online menus from participating restaurants, from Thai and Mandarin to Mexican and traditional American delights. Menu prices apply, with $8 per restaurant delivery charge and a suggested 12 per cent gratuity. No online orders, telephone only.

Royal Palate Foods
www.ethnicepicure.com
Dine through Royal Palate and you'll literally be eating as well as you would in the Ritz or the Four Seasons, since you'll be selecting from the same menu of entrées, hors d'oeuvres and desserts. Browse and create your own 3-course menu or simply select your main option and with their superior knowledge they'll select whether cabbage or hen goes best with salmon. Prices are based on parties of 6.

Waiter.com
www.waiter.com
Waiter.com is another all rounder. A professional looking site, it offers you the choice to reserve tables, or order simple pizza take-out or restaurant standard delicacies in your own home. The list of restaurants is comprehensive, and all you have to do is simply click through the menu ordering your favorite dishes. Delivery charges and times vary. Best of all, ordering for a group (eg for lunch) is made easier by sharing your shopping cart with a friend.

Waiters on Wheels
www.waitersonwheels.com
Usual system with online ordering, but only applies to those within certain specified Bay area or Washington state zip codes.

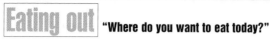

Eating out "Where do you want to eat today?"

I Seatz
www.iseatz.com
Rather than wasting time browsing restaurants only to find they have no tables free, iSeatz operates a quick and simple system whereby you tell them when and in which city you want to dine, and they come up with tables that are free. Comprehensive information about each restaurant is available, including atmosphere and any dress code. Reservations are guaranteed – if not iSeatz will compensate you with money off your next dinner.

Open Table
www.opentable.com
Open Table can reserve you a table in more than 1,100 top restaurants in America. For somewhere like New York, you can scroll through the list of restaurants or make an advanced search specifying region, price and cuisine. Unless you have a lot of time on your hands, opt for the latter. Each find offers descriptions, dress code, walk-in policy and other important details. Simply register a few simple details and make your reservation free of charge.

Reservation Source
www.reservationsource.com
This site is for those who like to have every detail of their vacation planned, right down to where they're eating each night. It only covers a small number of states, but make your selection, specify cuisine, price and even a specific restaurant, and they'll get to work. Information is limited to contact details, directions and the typical price of a meal, but if you join their club, you can use their online reservation system. It's free, and they promise no junk mail.

Savvy Diner
www.savvydiner.com
Simply select a savvy city, anywhere from New York to Scottsdale, Arizona, followed by the category of dining experience you'd like to have – upscale, casual, ethnic, Italian, steak & chops and so forth. You won't be blown away by the choice in some cities, but the information on each is comprehensive with maps and directions, sampler menus, images and descriptions. There's a useful event schedule too. If you see something you like, click to reserve a table, but remember most restaurants need 24 hours' notice to guarantee it.

Yahoo Restaurants
http://restaurants.yahoo.com
Fantastically useful search engine which, for example, can tell you the names and specialty of 210 restaurants within 50 miles of Tupelo, Mississippi (and that's not including 99 fast food joints and 57 sandwich shops).

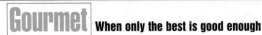

Gourmet — When only the best is good enough

Chef Shop
www.chefshop.com

If you're going to take this cooking malarkey seriously you really have to work with the finest ingredients. All the necessary ingredients to complete any kitchen are available, but you won't find the common or garden varieties here. If it's rice it's not simply long-grain, it's scented with jasmine; if it's oil it's not just olive, it's roasted hazelnut or mushroom-flavored; and we just don't know where to start with the chocolate and cookies. Prices are above average, but then you're paying for quality and exclusivity.

Dean & Deluca
www.deandeluca.com

Based in Soho, exclusive Dean & Deluca pride themselves on introducing good food to New York City, and their ultra-stylish site now hopes to extend their business to the farthest reaches of the country. It's beautifully laid out: simply select a category – anything from beans and grains to truffles and cakes – and the descriptions and images of each product will have your mouth watering in no time. If you're worried that you won't do their fabulous ingredients justice, a recipe section is on hand to help you create gourmet meals. The word cheap is not in their vocabulary, but if you're looking for delicacies that little bit special, this is the perfect store to shop.

Epicurious
www.epicurious.com

More of a general gourmet directory than a store, Epicurious aims to immerse you in a world of gourmet cooking, dining and drinking. It's hard to suggest where to start with so much to read and view, including field reports, recipe swaps, a report on the wonder of chervil, and etiquette hints. More enticing than such in-depth reports are the gourmet recipes from around the world. The full range of goods in the shopping section can be difficult to find (you have to browse the categories of their linked partner sites, including Dean & Deluca, above), but even the most inept cook should be able to produce a gourmet meal for 2 with the handy meal kits sold by Impromptu Gourmet.

Family Farms Direct
www.familyfarms-direct.com

Wholesome goodies from America's family farms (although America seems to have expanded to include countries like Chile and Australia). The site is easy to use: select a product type from the navigation bar (everything from organic foods and fresh pies to seafood and chocolates) to view a limited selection of goods. Meats, grains, vegetables, sweets and organic goods feature heavily, and there are gift baskets too. Prices are average, with no extra taxes to pay.

Gift baskets Cookies, gumbo, muffins

The Internet is groaning under the cyberweight of sites that will send a basket of goodies wherever it's needed, and that can mean anything from sausages to muffins. The following sites have a wide selection across a range of prices.

Cajun Shop
www.cajun-shop.com
If you're wondering what a Cajun gift basket would entail, it's in the shape of a New Orleans steamboat and contains gumbo and jambalaya mix, Creole shrimp, hot sauce and pralines, and hot coffee. Ordering is simple and each basket is described in full so you know just what you're getting or sending.

Dan the Sausage Man
www.danthesausageman.com
Despite Dan looking like an extra from *I Love Lucy*, the sausages are fresher than his hairstyle. Gift baskets include a variety of flavors along with other delicacies, pretzels, cheeses and breads. Prices range from $30 to $80, but you can get an individual slab of sausage for just $8.

Harry & David
www.harry-david.com
The owners of this comprehensive site have been selling food and fruit baskets since the 1930s and have it down to a fine art now. Popular items include the banana and chocolate, and strawberry and chocolate baskets, and even the healthy treat box looked appetizing. Prices are good.

Just Gift Baskets
http://justgiftbaskets.com
Baskets for those with a sweet tooth or who just like to kick back and relax. Prices for gourmet baskets for cookie, chocolate, coffee and tea-lovers range from $30 to $150, and there's a $6 delivery charge.

Gaucho Gourmet
www.gauchogourmet.com
With its selection of fine produce from Spain, Italy and South America, Gaucho Gourmet is the perfect store to visit if you've just returned from vacation and want to prolong the escape, if only from a dining point of view. The selection may not be huge but it's certainly interesting. The more unusual items include sweet potato jam, bruschetta olive paste and a wide selection of traditional Spanish and Italian pastries. And for once you're not paying over the odds. Ordering is simple, although shipping isn't calculated until you order.

Food

Gourmet Underground
www.gourmetunderground.com
Plain colors and simple layouts characterize Gourmet Underground's site, but
what impresses is just what you get for your time. You may just be looking
for your favorite granola but what you get are product descriptions, enlarged
pictures, reviews and customer ratings. The 1,600 products are a cut above
the usual but not over-the-top (eg clicking on cereals will bring you enticing
apple-cinnamon granolas and crispy maple-date mueslis rather than standard
cornflakes), and the reasonable prices and hundreds of discounts mean you
could do your weekly shop here no problem. Registration is needed, however.
Shipping (to mainland US only) costs vary: you get an estimate at check-out.

IGourmet.com
www.igourmet.com
Yet more sweet and savory delicacies (cheeses are a specialty), ideal as gifts
or just a treat for yourself. Prices are good at around $8 for the stickiest of
desserts or the smoothest of patés, depending on your palate. The site is
professional in look and to use, with order-tracking and extras such as recipe
suggestions, gift ideas, party planning advice and "Of The Month" sampling
clubs. You can also search for food by country of origin.

International Gourmet
www.intlgourmet.com
You'll probably be able to find most of the hundreds of products featured here
at other gourmet food stores, but it's more fun creating your own international
menu if you know where they came from. Try French escargots or Lebanese
hommus, followed by pomegranate soup from Persia, candies from Jordan
and finally coffee from New Orleans. A more interesting way to shop and eat.

Ottomanelli Gourmet Food
www.sals.com
Unlike a number of gourmet sites, Ottomanelli sells the basic ingredients.
If you want to add spices to your crab-filled shrimp that's up to you – they
just sell the shrimp. There are plenty of tantalizing images of their products,
including meats, seafood, sauces, cheeses and desserts. The site is simple to
use and order from. Some items can be pricey ($14 for 2 loaves of bread), so
think carefully about your menu, but generally you get what you pay for.

Pearl's Pantry
www.foodstuff.com
This virtual food mall offers products from vendors specializing in virtually
every food. Beef, cheese, salad dressings… even tea. It all sounds great,
but the site itself is laborious to search with a limited choice of items from
every vendor, and the pages are too wide for any normal monitor. Scrolling
up and down is tiresome enough, but scrolling across as well is not exactly
user-friendly. Prices and shipping are also on the wrong side of expensive.

Purveyors of fine truffles to Richard Nixon and Sophia Loren, Urbani's site is not for those who can resist anything but temptation

Robert Rothschild

www.robertrothschild.com

If good food is all about the added extras, then the dips, sauces, salsas, preserves and toppings at Rothschild's should see you in good stead at your next dinner party. The site is all too easy to use, and you have to struggle to stop yourself from buying too much. Some of the more unusual flavors include margarita mustard, ginger peach salsa and onion dill vegetable dip. Useful added extras include the salsa thermometer to separate the men from the boys, and recipes you can try with your new pineapple mustard.

Urbani

www.urbani.com

Stylishly simple in design, Urbani's site aims for those with the most refined of palettes. Beluga caviar and porcini mushrooms will taste like pizza when you've tried their more exotic meats: kangaroo, zebra and buffalo. Ordering is simple, although delivery charges aren't given until you begin your order. Just to emphasise their upper class status, Paul Urbani once presented a 3lb white truffle to President Nixon (don't worry Democrats, he must have presented one to one of your guys too). Sophia Loren and Anthony Quinn are both fans.

Zingermans

www.zingermans.com

Zingermans have spent the past 18 years searching out the most flavorful, traditionally made foods, and this bright, cheery, well-organized site offers breads, cheeses, oils and kitchen-cupboard essentials from around the world. Using this as your regular grocer could work out quite pricey, particularly if you opt for $40 cheeses to top off your burger, but there are cheaper options. Breads are particularly good value, with everything from Jewish and European to sweet specialty breads at under $4. Shipping is a standard $8 charge.

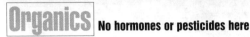 **No hormones or pesticides here**

Blue Sky
www.websitefoods.com

Quality Assurance International has stamped the cookies and muffins at Blue Sky as organic through and through, with brownies and breads soon to be added to the catalog. The site is fairly rudimentary with a simple order form, but they've taken into account that we like to know everything that's in our food these days, so each muffin's ingredient list and nutritional information is listed for inspection. Prices are expensive, particularly when you add an extra $11.50 shipping on top of $30 per dozen muffins, but sometimes, as Oscar Wilde so sagely noted, the only way to get rid of temptation is to yield to it.

Diamond Organics
www.diamondorganics.com

Hugely impressive site from a long-established company that guarantees overnight delivery to any address in mainland America, though shipping by FedEx air delivery works out pretty steep at approximately $11 plus $1 per lb of total package weight. There are cheaper, slower options, however, and you can ask for a quote. Try out their wares by ordering an organic sampler pack (delivery is free on these to most areas), or just jump straight in and select a grocery delivery from their delicious range of fresh fruit and vegetables, dried goods, bakery items and much more. Everything is guaranteed organic, so you know there are no pesticides or other chemicals lurking in your food.

Eco-Organics USA
www.eco-organics.com

One look at the homepage and you'll think you've been misdirected to a travel site, but despite their odd choice of site design, Eco-Organics sells organic groceries and fresh produce (fruit, vegetables, breads), along with juicers, diet programs and "eco-sensitive" fashion – cotton and hemp clothes and accessories. The choice can be limited, but you could still do your weekly food shop without problems. Prices are good (only slightly more than non-organic goods). Shipping is reasonable at $4 for the UPS ground service.

Health E Food
www.healthefood.com

If you're bothered about how many heads the cow had before it was turned into your burger, order from this organic, chemical-free meat company. (If you're not , read the Scary Facts section about the cancer-linked growth-hormone, steroid and antibiotic injections given to many cattle.) Then scroll down the list of every cut and variety of beef imaginable (strips, ground, roasts etc). Prices are good – $24 for half a dozen 8oz steaks – but everything is sold in multiples. Pork and chicken coming soon.

No diamonds, just lots of organic food on this site and overnight delivery in mainland US... if you're prepared to pay the steep delivery charges

Organic RX
www.organicrx.com
If you've gone completely organic, you can stock your kitchen cupboards by shopping at Organic RX. The limited but interesting selection of products includes organic peppercorns, garlic juice and (going for the prize of most arcane organic foodstuff) catnip tea, said to be an excellent form of sedative.

Village Organics
www.villageorganics.com
This quaint site is divided into 6 individual stores, including a coffee and tea shop, a gift shop and the main market. It's pretty obvious from the start that searches will be time-consuming. Select a category to view wordy lists of products, which you then have to call up individually for information and pricing. Prices are average for organic produce, with shipping charges calculated by weight, and a minimum order of $10 to use the site. A competent effort.

Wood Prairie Farm
www.woodprairie.com
Online Maine farmyard selling organic potatoes, and not just your common or garden French fries varieties. Choose from Elba, Butte, Reddale, Caribe and many more in 2lb, 5lb or 10lb bags. Seed potatoes for gardeners, organic vegetables and whole grain for baking are also on sale.

Food

Special diets — When tolerance is not an option

Cecilia's Gluten-Free Grocery
www.glutenfreegrocery.com
The tapioca hamburger buns may not be a particularly tantalizing selling point, but this comprehensive, if staid, site offers a good selection of gluten-free products to cover every meal of the day. Simply select a category from cereals and snacks to pizza bases and pasta. Each category holds a variety of brand names – Authentic Foods, Gifts of Nature and Gluten-Free Pantry included – but prices are generally high.

Diabetic Emporium & Confectioner
www.diabeticemporium.com
A catalog of over 1,000 specialty foods for diabetics, including normally forbidden items like cakes and sweets. There are nutritional facts for each and although the site is not very inspiring in its presentation, it's a boon for those struggling with a sugar-free diet. You don't have to have diabetes to shop at this site: the foods available here are healthier for everyone.

Dining By Design
www.diningbydesign.com
Great site for busy vegetarians and vegans who need a stock of top class, healthy meals for the fridge. The food is prepared fresh, frozen and shipped overnight in re-usable chill-packs and microwave-ready containers. The menus are split into such categories as Comfort Food and Asian Specialities, so you can choose the meal to suit your mood, and everything is guaranteed free of animal, dairy, wheat, yeast and other common allergens. Shipping costs 21 per cent of your order and all items are sent via 2-day air.

eDiet Shop
www.edietshop.com
Don't be put off by the name: you're not going to be pressurized into counting your calorie intake. eDiet is an easy-to-use site selling delicious yet sugar-free desserts. Each item (from fudgie rolls to choc-chip cheesecakes via blueberry muffins) has its ingredients listed in full, alongside fat and calorie counters. You are however, buying the cake mix rather than the finished product, so it's up to your own conscience whether you stick to skimmed milk or use full fat.

Food 4 Thought
www.food4tht.com
This site specializes in gift baskets of gourmet goodies for any occasion, and all food is 100 per cent kosher. There's a wide variety of choices and themes (sympathy, congratulations etc), or you can customise a basket to suit. The online order form is not secure and shipping costs are not detailed on the site,

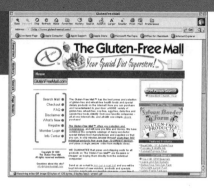

Gluten is, you will probably admit, somewhat overrated as a foodstuff especially if you're one of those unfortunate souls who happen to be allergic to it

which makes ordering a little precarious and aggravating, but there are some interesting treats to be had and the presentation of the baskets is great.

Gluten-Free Mall
www.glutenfreemall.com
Bread, pasta, muffins and a host of other grocery products for people on a wheat- or gluten-free diet are available from this comprehensive, easy-to-use food site. The Mall is set up for you to buy directly from manufacturers, so the prices are as good as you'll find and, on the whole, most of the vendors' shipping charges are reasonable. Check each store for excellent bulk-buy deals too, as this makes things even more cost-effective.

Kosher Club
www.kosherclub.com
Simple yet well organized site selling all manner of kosher food, from meats and dairy products to meals for vegetarians and those on lactose and sugar-free diets. It's more of a grocery stop than anything else – descriptions are limited to the name of the product – but the prices are competitive, and your shopping basket is displayed at all times so you know exactly what you've got in it. If you have queries, you can ask the rabbi, or e-mail him anyway.

Kosher Supermarket
www.kosersupermarket.com
Everything here, be it meats or vitamins, is guaranteed 100 per cent kosher, taking a big headache out of the weekly shop for many. There's even a range of ready-prepared meals for when you haven't the time or energy to cook. A 20lb box of non-perishable groceries costs a flat $6.99 to ship via UPS ground, but if your order contains perishables you're charged the actual shipping cost.

Supermarkets
From abalone to zucchini

Online shopping and home-delivery services vary from area to area. Visit
www.excite.com/guide/business/companies/retail_trade/grocery_chains
for a fuller list of regional operations, but here are some of the better ones:

Albertsons
www.albertsons.com
Delivery to home or office in Texas and Seattle (the latter offers perishables
and the option of in-store collection from a local store). Delivery is free for
orders over $60 (otherwise $5.95), and by UPS ground for Texas outside the
Dallas/Fort Worth area. Extras include quick recipes and cookery questions.

Homeruns
www.homeruns.com
Frill-free site (part of the Shop 'N Save group) delivering general produce in
Boston and Washington DC. Minimum order is $50 plus $5.95 delivery, though
this is waived if delivery is not within the specified time. Coupons accepted.

Pick n Save
www.picknsave.com
Browse, place your order and schedule a collection time (no delivery, but you
can save your shopping list for future reference), and the staff at your nearest
store will do the hard work for you at a charge of $4.95. WI zip codes only
(with a couple of IL, IN and OH exceptions). Extras include competitions,
recipes and even freebies (8oz bottles of salad dressing when we checked).

Safeway
www.safeway.com
This chain has 1,680 stores across the
country but fill in your zip code to see if
delivery is available in your area (it's
strongest in the West, Mid-West and
South). There's no delivery charge with a
minimum order of $60; coupons accepted.

Stop & Shop
www.stopandshop.com/peapod
Online shopping for home delivery if you live in
the Boston, Long Island or Connecticut areas.
Coupons are accepted, and you don't have to
sign up as a member first. Extras include recipes.

Low Carb Grocery

www.lowcarbgrocery.com

The breaking news at Low Carb Grocery on our last visit was new soy-free pizza kits. If you're not struck by Luigi's delicacies, the cyber shelves are stocked with low-carbohydrate grocery items from soups and breakfast cereals to jams, chocolate and tortillas. Their own Aunt Pearl brand products are made without artificials, preservatives and "all the other words no one can pronounce". Prices are better than average for such speciality goods, and shipping is free if you stock up and spend more than $100.

Low Sodium Food

www.lowsodiumfood.com

Just been put on a low-sodium diet and convinced it's the end of the world for your tastebuds? Don't despair, this isn't the end of snack foods as you know them. There are plenty of yummy low-sodium substitutes to be found here, including kettle chips, cream desserts, hot sauces and salad dressings, plus general grocery items to stock up on. Details of sodium content are helpfully listed alongside the general nutritional facts. Shipping is not cheap, however – $8.57 on our $11.69 sample order of 6 items to New York state.

Lumen Foods

www.lumenfds.com

Selling "animal replacement products" may make this site sound a bit scary, but in fact it's a good place to buy soy-protein products for those who follow any kind of meat-free diet. There are grains and legumes as well as meatless meats, and Lumen is also the manufacturer so prices are very competitive. You're charged exact mail or UPS rates for delivery, but you have to work out what this will be from links provided, which is annoying and time-consuming.

Macrobiotics Online

www.macrobiotics.org

Operated by the Massachusetts-based Kushi Institute (which offers a holistic, natural approach to health), this is the place to come for organic wholefoods, cookware and recipe books if you're interested in a macrobiotic diet. There are impressive testimonials from grateful followers of the super-healthy (if somewhat dull) diet, along with articles and a variety of Kushi programs. The shopping part of the site can be very slow to load: if you have problems, try accessing it from www.kushiinstitute.org which is sometimes a better bet.

Sugarless Shop

www.sugarlessshop.com

Suppliers of a wide range of sugar-free foods – including candy, cake mixes, syrups, desserts, snacks and spreads – for diabetics and anyone else on a restricted-sugar diet. There are even boxes of Valentine's, Christmas and Easter chocolates to send as gifts. Most orders are sent out within 48 hours, and shipping is via UPS and AirBorne Express.

Sweet things | A moment on the lips...

Heavenly Cheesecakes
www.heavenlycheesecakesinc.com
Plenty of heavenly flavors including white chocolate brownie, caramel and raspberry white chocolate.
Descriptions are tantalizing, images are juicy and at $30 per cake, prices are affordable. Ordering is simple but shipping times and charges are unclear till you begin to order.

Jeryl's Jems
www.jerylsjems.com
The choice is limited, but if it's traditional chocolate-laden sweets or the more original banana-cake truffles and almond Brickle brownies you're after, you're in luck. $20 will get you a slab of 16 brownies, and for just $5 you can be tucking into a half-pound bag of cookies. What does need improvement is the site itself: the system is slow, the order form rudimentary and the shipping details illegible.

Mary of Puddinhill
www.puddinhill.com
Having been in the business of desserts for 50 years now, Mary knows what she's doing. The simple site is easy to use, with a side navigation bar leading to cookies, chocolates, pies, cakes and candies. There are enough shots of delicious-looking pecan pies and chocolate-dunked Oreo cookies to make your sweet tooth cry out, and the prices won't control your appetite: $45 for a 2lb praline pecan pie is surely worth it, especially as delivery is free.

New York, Texas Cheesecake Company
www.nytxccc.com
The professional-looking site of this Texas-based cheesecake enterprise sells everything from guilt-free to guilt-ridden flavors, including Turtle Praline, Amaretto and Key Lime. Prices range from $25 to $40, and servings range between 6 and 30 hungry people. You do, however, have to take their word for it that the cakes look as good as they sound, as they currently use the same picture alongside each different description.

Sukhadia
www.sukhadia.com
Specializing in Indian sweets and snacks, Sukhadia has taken minimalism to new limits with its online store. There's a wide range of halva, chikki and ganthia, but precious little information as to what these treats actually are. Only those accustomed to Indian delicacies should shop here. Site comes complete with its own lush, slightly corny, soundtrack.

It's hard to find fault with a site which allows you to order your favorite chocolate bar as a great big, lovely, lipsmacking cake

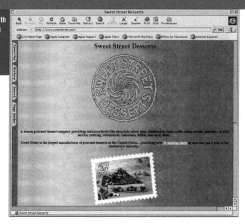

Sweet Street
www.sweetstreet.com
What a fabulous idea: now you can order your favorite chocolate bars in the form of a cake. With the Snickers Big Blitz, the Reeses Chocolate Butter Pie and the Oreo Chocolate Bash to choose from, even the sweetest palate should be catered for. Certainly more expensive than your average candy bar at $30 to $40 including delivery, but fun for special occasions.

Twinkies
www.twinkies.com
Where would we be without the Hostess Cup Cake, Twinkie, Ding Dong and Ho Ho to get us through life's crises? The cartoon-inspired site, complete with Hanna-Barbera noises is full of useless facts but it also offers recipes for the Tropical Twinkie Lasagna, the Ho Ho Surprise and Death by Twinkies.

 But no longer hard to find

Amish Pleasures - The Breakfast Shop
www.thebreakfastshop.com/
This site could completely change your perception of the Amish, especially if your only mental image of them is from the barn-raising scene in the Harrison Ford movie *Witness*. You can buy almost everything you need for a kingsize

Food

www.hometownfavorites. com

Even if you're too young to get all nostalgic about seeing such 50s icons as King Vitamin cereal and Drakes cakes again, the names and packages are amusing enough to keep your attention. You can search for the particular food that sums up your childhood (some may have new names: Bubs Daddy Bubble Gum is now Super Bubble Long Lasting, you'll be pleased to know) or simply browse through the multiple categories.

Old favorites include Chef Boyardee Pizza sauce, Betty Crocker cake mixes, Bre'r Rabbit Molasses and Moxie soda. The products may be from the past, present prices apply (eg $5 for a box of Count Chocula cereal). Still, it's cheaper than a trip to a therapist to regain your youth. Your only worry is the goods' sell-by date.

breakfast here from Makers Mark bourbon–flavored coffee to Biscotti shoofly pie. And if you need a pick me up after you've eaten all this, try the Amish made Vim and Vigor for just $24.

Food Locker

www.foodlocker.com

A stickler about the brand of ketchup or ice cream you want? Food Locker specializes in regional, local and hard-to-find brands you thought didn't exist anymore but still do (except only in Kentucky). Search by brands, products from meats to cookies, or restaurant foods (including Downey's soups and H & H bagels). As these items are aimed at diehards, bulk-buying is your only option, still, 2 dozen bagels should go down well at work.

GGHawaii

www.gghawaii.com

If your cornbreads, jams and cookies have to come from Hawaii, look no further. The selection is limited but the site is easy to use and prices are standard. And where else will you find Kauai Kookies?

Indian Harvest

www.indianharvest.com

Minnesota minestrone soup was not what we expected to find on the menu, but Indian Harvest specializes in selling beans, grains and rices to cooks. Other more general gourmet delicacies can be found here too, though chutneys are about as close as it gets to India. If you're not sure what to do once you've bought your Himalayan red rice and your Fiesta dip, online tips and recipes are on hand.

Mama Rose's

www.mamaroses.com

Prickly pear cactus, raspberry margarita, cranberry walnut crunch… and that's only the jams and jellies. Mama Rose offers a comprehensive catalog of salsas, con quesos, hot sauces and drinks from the Old West and South West. All items use quality ingredients and are additive-free. Prices are good – most items are between $5 and $8, with a discount for orders over $25 – but hefty shipping charges of $6.75 (and upwards) make it a pricey place to shop.

Free stuff

Yes, there really is free stuff on the Net (even if it doesn't yet extend to lunch). Whether it's worth having is another matter. Besides, as in the real world, there's a catch...

General Gateways to the giveaways

Free Stuff Net
www.free-stuff-net.com

If the flashing neon freebie sign doesn't trigger your brain into having an epileptic fit, this site is proof positive that the Internet is awash with junk. You'll find nothing as exciting as a free lunch here, and the free cash turns out to mean registering to get paid 50 cents a hour while you're online. Otherwise what's on offer includes such desirable items as free fonts, screensavers, catalog offers, coupons, contests, jokes, horoscopes and free chat. But then if you're actually paying for chat you probably need help, not freebies.

Free Vault
www.freevault.com

The name implies that this site may hold the key to some pretty valuable items, and it's true that movie and airline tickets are better swag than most freebie sites. You still come across the usual barrage of useless stuff, however, and there are lots of links to other freebie sites (including The Chocolate Page). Yet despite the 46 listings in the travel section, the idea seems to be that rather than offering instant wins, you read all the free information listed, get a job as a tour operator and enjoy free trips that way.

J Freebies
www.jfreebies.com/main.php3

Among the categories listed on this combined listing of US and UK sites is, intriguingly, "toys and babies". This turns out not to be part of a government drive to speed up adoption, but a link to free Pampers coupons, cassette tapes of kiddie songs, catalogs etc. Many of the freebies pointed-to here are hi-tech, but there are the usual competitions for the lucky and gullible.

Free stuff

MyFree.com
www.MyFree.com
The essential gateway for the aspiring American freeloader. Not all the offers are as tantalizing as a free issue of *Quiltmaker* magazine, and certainly not as genuinely useful as free movie tickets and *Star Wars* books, but you have to take the rough with the smooth. The rough here is generally in the form of the usual free software and "offers", including a free satellite system – as long as you pay $140 first. Call us pernickety, but that doesn't seem very free to us.

No Junk
www.nojunk.com
You won't necessarily all agree with the name of this site, but it does offer one of the more useful selections of free samples. You can find everything from lipsticks and cat food to clothing and voice-coaching lessons here.

 Hmm. Now why would this stuff be free?

The Book Cart
www.thebookcart.com
Just as online shops can put bricks-and-mortar operations out of business, could The Book Cart bring about the end of some libraries? All the previously read paperbacks here are free. Just register to list the titles you're finished with, or choose from the lists posted (browse by category). Reader sends to

Helping to feed the hungry by just clicking sounds too good to be true but, for once on the Internet, it isn't

reader, and a standard postage rate is credited or debited to your account. The only catch we could find is that you have to open this account with $10.

Casinos

www.24hourscasino.com
Just in case you're a bit of a skeptic and don't believe you can win thousands of dollars from the comfort of your own office, a winners' list (top prize money of $7,335) is listed before you turn around and head for your usual investment manager. The software is free, and of course you can play for free in the beginning – and we'll wager you'll win right up until you place a real bet.

Charities

www.thehungersite.com
Free food for the hungry! Sounds too good to be true but for once it isn't. You can make the world a better place at no cost to yourself. Just visit the site, make a couple of clicks and someone in need gets a cup of staple food from one of the site's sponsors. (See also www.feedyourworld.com). There are 6 charities in all at this site, including ones for breast cancer and landmine victims. Bookmark it now!

Mouse Pads

www.hotmat.com/index.htm
Not as good as a free lunch, but this site offers you a free mouse pad in exchange for your address. In fact, if you're really keen they'll give you a mouse pad every year for free, wherever you live in the world or solar system. Desperate or charitable? It's your call.

Sheet music

www.mysheetmusic.com
Probably the one and only time you'll find that Lobo "classic" *Me And You And A Dog Named Boo* just above Will Smith and his *Men in Black*. If you're not overly enthusiastic about playing either of these at your piano recital, they also offer a wealthy catalog of hymns, classical compositions and ragtime tunes.

Students

www.collegefreestuff.com
Students are the ultimate freeloaders. They now have their own site, offering all they need to support their college lives. There's everything from beauty products and food to phone cards (to stay in touch with their money-giving parents) and lecture notes (in case the free beer and condoms went down a little too well).

POETRY FOR NOTHING

As always, there's a catch and this time the catch is that the poet in question happens to be William McGonagall. Infamous, indomitable and, so unfeeling critics have said, poetically illiterate, the 19th century clerk-cum-poet from Dundee, Scotland, wrote these immortal words: "A chicken is a noble beast/The cow is much forlorner/Standing in the pouring rain/With a leg at every corner."

For more in the same vein (but thankfully a different arm) you can log on to *www. dundee22.freeserve. co.uk* where you'll also find a great portrait of the great man himself, looking uncannily like somebody's grandmother.

Gadgets

Online shopping is never more fun than when you're looking for something utterly ephemeral – like a robot dog, a talking backseat-driver toy or a pair of aspirin cufflinks…

General "I gotta have one of those!"

007 Gadget Lab

www.geocities.com/Hollywood/5727/q_lab.html

The mere mention of the word gadget brings to mind one man. Who else merits the title of gadget supremo than James Bond's sidekick, Q? Although you can't buy replicas of Q's wacky yet obviously effective gadgets here, the site is still full of quirky facts about talcum-powder tear gas bombs, razor-sharp knife umbrellas and submarine crocodiles, among other things.

21 Store

www.21store.com

21store was the first British website to accept an order over the Internet, way back in 1996. It has recently been bought by another UK company, Expansys, but prices are available in US dollars. There are a few gadgets here, but most of the site is dedicated to electronic gizmos, from mobile phones and MP3 players to digital cameras and pocket computers. Clicking through brings all the technical specs you could need. Prices are high, however, and shipping costs are near-prohibitive (they start at $36.64 for 5-8 day delivery). But if time and money are no object, it's still worth browsing for the kind of gadget, like a Casio wristwatch camera, you may not readily find elsewhere.

Brands Place

www.brandsplace.com

You can forgive the owners of Brands Place for their jumbled and text-laden homepage once you explore the site and see that they can pretty much cover any mad gadget master's fantasy. Sport equals roller hockey and paintball. Electronics equals state-of-the-art MP3 players and radar detectors. Or for the kids, how about a remote-controlled car or their own laser show? And everyone needs a weather station. Descriptions are concise, you can shop by category or brand name, and ordering is your standard Yahoo system.

Buy Choice

www.buychoice.com

A general site also offering furniture, clothing and cookware, Buy Choice may not be everyone's idea of a gadget paradise but they do stock the very latest in digital recorders, global positioning systems, and a nifty video traveller, ideal for keeping your kids amused on long trips. In the executive gift section the Waikiki Beach and Rainbow Falls hanging fountains may take your fancy, though the prices – $1,550 and $800 respectively – may not. All the prices are discounted and the site is stylish yet customer-friendly.

Gadget Universe

www.gadgetuniverse.com

If you feel that anything without a battery or an instruction manual is not worth having, Gadget Universe is a must-search. If you already have all the talking watches, radio torch lamps and planet remote controls you're likely to need, the kitscher items include an interactive penguin bank (it sings! it snores!), or for the serious techie, how about a Sony Glasstron viewer (makes a TV look like a 52-inch screen)? Shipping prices depend on how much you spend.

Gizmo City

www.electronicgizmos.com

Not a site to be mocked, everything within these cyberwalls means serious business and may one day save your life. You'll be kicking yourself for not buying the Smart Car Pager next time you're in Paris and you need to unlock your car in Baltimore. Everyone likes screening calls and for $80 we can all do it with the Telephone Privacy Monitor. The products verge on the terminally serious, and the site design reflects it. There are laughs to be had though – the motion-activated door chime could be a laugh, as long as it's not your door…

Golf Gadgets

www.golf-gadgets.com

Golf is now one of the biggest sporting industries in the world, so naturally you can buy almost anything associated with bad trousers online. Only $30 to improve your swing with the Electronic Birdie Putting Centers, or if the object of your affection treats his/her clubs like a baby, how about furry gopher or alligator-head covers? Ordering can be slow and there is no indication of shipping costs, so opt for next-day delivery at your financial peril.

Guy Toys

www.guytoys.com

Micro scooters and Sony robots are old hat to the serious gadget-collector. True to the site's name, these are true guy's toys – only men could see the

Gadgets

More acronyms than the US Army can't obscure the fact that this site is a must visit for the true gadget freak

worth in having a weather-alert contraption or the very latest GPS system. There's also a limited range of more traditional gadgets, including the latest digital cameras and sci-fi-inspired speakers. The images are poor quality, but the descriptions make sense of even the most unusual items and buying is user-friendly even for a novice. Particularly good for a more unusual gift.

Radio Shack
www.radioshack.com
No points for originality in design terms, but the site is comprehensive and easy to navigate. More importantly, their catalog of everything from toys to hardware gadgets has something for every budget. If Star Search has inspired you to invest in a karaoke machine, Radio Shack offers a portable version for $40, or a super-deluxe $400 version (which may or may not transform you into the next Whitney Houston or George Michael. Alternatively, if you're lacking in hidden talents, why not try a metal detector to help swell your bank account? Prices range from $50 to $500. Something for everyone.

Sharper Image
www.sharperimage.com
The gadget freak's favorite store, Sharper Image has produced a stylish yet customer-friendly online catalog of a few gadgets – some you may need, and a few more that you probably never will. Aside from the standard home, toy, personal and electronic categories, you can also opt to search for that micro scooter in the best-sellers, special offers or even auction sections. Best sellers include the Sony AIBO robot dog and the Palm Vx, alongside a host of more obscure items such as the Gyro FX (an electronic spinning contraption) or the Laser Ball – ideal for catch and throw speed times. Prices vary but you should be able to find something in your budget, whether it's a power tie-rack for $60 or a CD shower companion for $180.

Go on, your colleagues deserve a free laugh

Buddhas Belly
www.buddhasbelly.com
This site deserves a mention for its name alone, but the contents are equally wacky. Way-out categories include smokes, detox and dessert, and the items are equally extraordinary – whip cream dispensers, tools for the budding graffiti artist (entirely legal of course) and home marijuana-testing kits to catch out any sneaky children. Not your standard gadgets, you'll agree. Ordering is via the standard Yahoo system (the site is a winner of the Yahoo Top Service award) and prices are cheap. Great for more novel gifts.

Fridge Door
www.fridgedoor.com
Apart from infuriating your mom by ruining her stylish, color-co-ordinated kitchen, magnets are the ultimate in useless kitsch. This site has them all. Select a category from music, movie, celebrity to view endless images of colorful bits of plastic. Prices vary according to collectablility, but for $20 you should be able to cover the fridge and really annoy mom.

Fun-damental
www.fun-damental.com
This wacky site tries to put the "fun" into fundamental, although you may decide that the emphasis is on the "mental". Amid the frat humor of farting teddy bears and burping beer mugs, there's a toy backseat driver which you can set to say amusing things like, "Yo Sherlock! Since when are stop signs optional?" We can even forgive the e-mail-only ordering system.

Twisted Gifts
www.twistedgifts.com
The most sophisticated gadget you're likely to find here is a glitter lava-lamp. Twisted at its best includes the shot glass basketball (you sink it and drink it), the remote-control fart machine and the electric-shock cigarette-lighter. The site looks wonderfully bright and jazzy but, as the banner says, you'd be sane not to shop here. Prices are cheap, but this won't work out in your favor as they specify a minimum order of $15.

THE GADGETEER
www.the-gadgeteer.com/
new_gizmos.html

You won't be able to get your hands on most of the gizmos and gadgets featured here (seemingly inspired by a host of comic strip creations) for possibly years to come, but technology is always a good conversation starter or stopper, depending on your view. In the future we'll all be modelling our very own wristwatch phone, camera and even a TV. Combining two gadgets into one is perhaps predictable, but there are a few wildcards to be found. The iTag, for example, is for those who love adverts. It will grab and tag that radio advert for you to listen to at your leisure. Click on an item to read the full spec sheet, view prototypes and see for yourself whether the Internet radio is really the must-have of the future or merely today's fad.

Gardens

Your garden may be any-thing from a windowbox to a huge ranch, but with a little TLC, it can become a veritable oasis of natural beauty. Just click here for details

American Meadows
www.americanmeadows.com
If you're one of those folks who hates cutting the grass, why not turn your yard (or at least a section of it) into a wildflower meadow with the help of a few packets of seeds from this wildflower gardening site? There are all sorts of seed mixes to choose from, with something appropriate for all regions. There's even a Salsa Garden mix containing Cilantro, Tomato, Onion, Jalapeno, and Parsley seeds. Bulk orders are also catered for, with discounts offered if you buy more. Standard shipping costs between $3.95 and $9.95 (orders over $100 are carriage-free), or you can pay extra for a FedEx service.

Amish Outdoor Furniture
www.amishoutdoorfurniture.net
Yes, we too are a little confused about what the technology-shunning Amish are doing hawking their wares on the Internet, but this is a terrific site, selling wooden yard furniture and decorative items such as windmills and bird tables. All are made by Amish craftsmen, and from the photos on the site, the quality looks to be outstanding. Helpfully, each product description includes how much it will cost to ship the item to your door.

Equinox Nursery Inc.
www.equinoxnursery.com
There's an emphasis on natural gardening on this site (which has been set up jointly with Home Harvest, if you're confused by the banner). Products such as organic fertilizer and natural pest control are on offer here for gardeners who like to avoid chemicals where possible. There's also an impressive range of specialist equipment for hobbies, such as hydroponics or raising bonsai or orchids. Most orders are shipped within 2 days of receipt and charges depend on the speed of service you choose.

ESeeds

www.eseeds.com

Well-designed and absorbing garden site based in Canada, offering fully grown plants, bulbs and seeds from an extensive range. There are excellent photos of most plants and seed packs, so you know what you're getting, and there is also a wide range of books and links to information on plant care. Shipping costs and time depend greatly on whether you've ordered any live plants, and do remember that all prices shown are in Canadian dollars.

Gardener's Supply Company

www.gardener.com

Whether you're just browsing for inspiration or using the search facility to find exactly what you want, this is an easy-to-use site. It's stronger on selling equipment and decorative yard and patio items than actual plants, but the level of expertise displayed throughout the site shows that this is somewhere run by real gardeners who know how to get the best out of your back yard. There's also a clearance section where you can make some excellent savings on out-of-season items. Costs do vary as some of the items are shipped directly from the manufacturer, but most in-stock items are sent via UPS and should arrive within 5 days.

Gardens Etc

www.gardensetc.com

Simply laid-out site that can deliver a wide range of perennials direct to your door. There are good descriptions of most of the plants (although some are missing photos) along with clear instructions on what they need to thrive. A hardiness map is included on the site if you're unsure about which plants will suit your climate. You can browse the different categories, such as Border Plants or Ground Cover, or, if you're more of an expert, use the search facility to go to exactly what you're looking for. Prices are keen, shipping is free and gift certificates are available.

GroGro

www.grogro.com

They say that the British like gardening better than sex, and you can see exactly what it is that gets them so excited on this official shopping site from the Royal Horticultural Society. It sells a huge range of unusual garden supplies, decorations and tools, as well as books and garden-themed gifts. Delivery

Bad case of mildew, thrips or carrot fly? Draw the screens round the affected plant and call in Dr G

time and costs vary since many items are shipped direct from the manufacturer, but all larger items have this information included in their description. Not all products are available for delivery outside the UK so check before you buy.

High Country Gardens

www.highcountrygardens.com

Online catalogue from a Santa Fe, New Mexico-based nursery specializing in easy-to-grow, hardy plants that will thrive in temperature extremes, especially on the arid high plateaux of the western states. You can use the plant-finder facility to help you track down, say, a summer-blooming, rabbit-resistant shrub for your shady bed, and there's even a set of useful irrigation tips to minimize the time you have to spend looking after your yard. Plants are sent in specially-designed boxes (delivery and costs depend on weight and time of year) and come complete with planting instructions.

Hortus Ornamenti

www.hortusornamenti.co.uk

Get an authentic English country garden look with this glorious selection of handmade tools, planters and other garden accessories, all made by British craftsmen from the finest materials to the highest specifications. Most items are available for shipping to the US, although for a few of the larger products you have to contact the site separately for full details. The site also offers gift-wrapping and engraving services if you're looking for that chic gift for a gardening friend. Delivery charges depend on the weight of your order and will be calculated when you get to the checkout.

I Can Dig it

www.icandigit.net

Once you're past the cutesy opening graphics, this is actually a refreshingly simple and well-designed site. There's a great range of decorative items such as birdbaths, planters and fountains available here, along with more everyday items such as yard tools, furniture and seed kits. There is a shopping cart facility, but little information about delivery costs and times, although you can e-mail the company if you have any specific questions.

Park Seed Company

www.parkseed.com

Online version of the popular and well-established garden catalog. There are more than 2,500 varieties of top quality seeds and plants to choose from here, so you're bound to find something to suit that bare patch of ground. The zone calculator will help you decide which plants are suitable for your area. There's even a recipe section for produce-growers, for when you run out of ideas for what to do with all that squash you've grown. Delivery options and time depend on what live plants you have ordered, seasonal restrictions, and where in the country you live, but you should be able to get full information about all this on the site before you order.

Shepherd's Garden Seeds

www.shepherdseeds.com

If you're after the tastiest varieties of vegetables, herbs and fruits, this is the site to visit. Shepherd's can supply you with year-round culinary bounty, as well as plants and tubers for flowers and shrubs, and you can find tips for successful planting in the Growing Guide section of the site. Since many plants can only be shipped at certain times of year so that they are ready to plant out, the delivery options are varied, but standard shipping starts at $2.95 and costs are reasonable, even on larger orders.

White Flower Farm

www.whiteflowerfarm.com

Expert advice is on offer along with an outstanding range of plants and seeds from this Connecticut nursery which has been in business since 1950. There's a selection of tools and plant gifts available online year round, or you can browse the stunning selection of plants and bulbs for Spring and Fall planting. Customer service is excellent, and most orders are shipped via UPS.

Wild Flowers

www.wild-flowers.com

Good site to check for wildflower information, with links to the database, directory and shopping sites on GardenWeb (www.gardenweb.com). It also lists native plant societies and collections, and there's a glossary of botanical terms plus forums, a calendar of events, and links to nurseries who specialize in wildflowers so you can grow your own.

Windowbox.com

www.windowbox.com

Fabulous resource for city-dwellers who still hanker for their own patch of green. This is the place to come for realistic ideas to brighten up the smallest of outdoor spaces, even if you only have a porch, terrace or even a windowsill to play with. There are windowbox kits containing everything you need to get started, plus containers, tools and even products to involve the kids. Shipping is via UPS and orders should arrive in around 7 days. Express shipping can be arranged via phone or e-mail.

GARDENING ADVICE

All these sites are terrific resources for garden planning and plant care, with useful features for gardeners of all abilities and backyard layouts.

Garden.com
www.garden.com
Despite closing its retail arm due to lack of funds, this outstanding site is still full of great ideas and tips for creating a gorgeous outdoor display, plus articles on subjects such as which birds you can expect to attract to your yard.

Garden Bazaar
www.gardenbazaar.com
Portal site with links to nurseries and retailers of the complete spectrum of yard design, equipment and plant requirements. Browse by categories or search for specific items.

Virtual Garden
www.vg.com
Join the Garden Club for news and reviews about gardening developments and trends. The monthly To Do list is a boon for novices still learning the seasonal workload and there are searchable discussion forums if you're looking for info you can't find elsewhere on the site.

Gifts & flowers

You can say it with flowers, a star, or a pair of skull-shaped maracas. Call us fuddy-duddies, but we'd advise you to think hard before saying it with maracas

 Cards **Digital sentiments for that special occasion**

American Greetings
www.americangreetings.com
All bases covered with this slick site. If you have a few days to spare, you can opt for a paper card. Head for the suitable occasion, browse, select and either have it sent to you to add your own personal note, or have it sent direct and they'll add a suitable message. If it's too late for that, check out the cyber greeting section, complete with animated and musical cards for all occasions. The cards themselves are cheap but don't forget the shipping charges.

Hallmark
www.hallmark.com
A huge selection of traditional paper and e-cards for all occasions. They're generally priced at $2, plus a little extra to personalize your card and send it to your intended. Although most famous for their cards, they also sell gifts through RedEnvelope, flowers, gift certificates and the usual selection of branded novelty items, Harry Potter and the Grinch featuring strongly.

USA Greetings
www.usagreetings.com
Online and offline cards for all occasions, and we do mean all. If you thought Mother's and Father's Days were exploitative, how about Arbor Day, Save the Rhino Day or Teacher Appreciation Week? Your friends probably never knew you cared so much. You can also buy regular birthday and Christmas greetings, and add a suitable quotation from hundreds listed for that personalized touch.

Flowers — Roses, posies, sprays and bouquets

Angels Flowers
www.angelsflowers.com
You can guess the design: cherubs with the odd flower thrown in. The catalog of arrangements is immense, but you can search by product type, price or occasion. Prices range from $20 to $150, and if a simple bunch of carnations or roses is not enough, they offer teddies and chocolate gifts for bulk or tropical selections. They could use detailed descriptions, though.

Bobs Tropical Flowers
www.bobs-tropicals.com
For something a little more unusual, poipu, wailua and flower leis can be found at this site. Each variety has a brief description and clear image, although it would be nice to know a little more about them. Best of all, none of the tropical flower arrangements, plants or Hawaiian hula items costs more than your average bouquet.

Great American Rose Company
www.garoses.com
Despite the name, roses aren't the only flowers here. Select a category from mixed bouquets, lilies, plants and of course, roses to view clear images of beautiful bouquets, generally priced around $35. Next day delivery is available, with prices stating from $9.95.

Great Flowers
www.greatflowers.com
One-stop shop offering bouquets according to occasion or your favorite flowers. Apart from roses, there are some more novel bouquets, including daisies and lilies. Prices start at around $20 but there's an extra $10 for delivery ($20 for Saturdays).

Jungle Roses
www.jungleroses.com
Your selection of South American blooms is delivered in a stylish Bengal Tiger box, from a site with a huge celebrity client list including Julia Roberts, Jim Carrey and Mickey Rourke. You'll also have celebrity prices to contend with, however – anything over $100 possible.

FLOOZ

Men! If you can't quite decide between the latest Britney album and a Prada purse for your beloved, maybe you should send her Flooz instead. No, they're not fashion accessories but gift e-vouchers for shopping in cyberspace.

This Flooz e-currency can be spent in more than 60 online stores, from Cigar.com to Art.com and BarnesandNoble.com. Most people, interests and items are covered in the selection of outlets.

All you have to do is give the Flooz people the e-mail details of the lucky one, precisely how generous you want to be and any message you wish to add. (There's a selection of electronic greetings cards too.) It's then up to the recipient as to how they spend your e-vouchers.

The Flooz site itself is clear and concise, and they have enlisted Whoopi Goldberg to help guide you through the system step by step.

---

www.flooz.com

Snack tins, model guillotines, or 200lb of pork rind?

1-800 Flowers
www.1800flowers.com
Despite the name, 1-800 Flowers is dominated by gifts of the edible variety.
Search by brand, occasion or budget, or simply browse through the extensive
collection. Each item comes with a complete description, picture and delivery
details on one page so you know exactly what you're buying. Novel items
include the Movie Snack Tin ($26) and Mrs Beasleys Thankyou Basket ($43).

Ashlane Gift Baskets
www.ashlanegiftbaskets.com
You know the deal. A catalog of baskets filled to the brim to suit every
occasion, from celebrating a new baby to sincerest gratitude or even college
survival. Each basket is specifically tailored for different people, with plenty
of cuddly toys for babies or chocolate for students. Prices range from around
$30 up to $60, and shipping is calculated according to your whereabouts.

Bubble Bodywear
www.bubblebodywear.com
This site has to be seen to be believed. It won't provide you with the perfect
gift if you're looking to impress, but every item of clothing here – from bikinis
to blouses and suits to wedding dresses – is made from bubble wrap. The
"world famous" women's business suit can be yours for $125, but we kid you
not, they need to know your exact measurements to process the order.

City Morgue
www.citymorguegiftshop.com
"Welcome to the best place for gothic, mortuary, forensic and death-related
gifts" is the cheery greeting from this site. Guide your cursor past the flying
skulls and head straight for the gift shop. Click here to enter a strange world
of skull maracas, model guillotines and celebrity death certificates.

Exotic Gifts For You
www.exoticgifts4you.com
Not a vast stock but owners Lance and Yaffa are confident that they can fulfil
the gift and accessory needs of any woman. Choose from beaded jewelry,
velvet shawls, ornate perfume bottles (minus the perfume) and giraffe-print
handbags. Prices are cheap – starting at $7 – and ordering is simple.

Gifts.com
www.gifts.com
A *Reader's Digest* site, Gifts.com is well-thought out with options to search by
him, her, kids or even pet-owners, browse their best-seller list, or stick to

classic favorites – flowers, gourmet food and jewelry. Items vary from portable DVD players and cakes to travel irons and sushi-making kits. Click on the item to read a full description, price and shipping details. A brilliant site both in terms of ideas and layout.

Perfect for tracking down just the right gift for your 13-year-old kid brother, Gift Crap is sure to please

Gift Crap

www.giftcrap.com

This weird and wacky site sells inexpensive, fun and sometimes tacky gifts. You can select the personality most suited to the recipient, with ball-breakers, couch potatoes, geeks and many more catered for. Top items include caffeine gum for the couch potato who can't be bothered to make a brew, a 200lb pork rind for the glutton, and a combined telephone/kitchen blender "for people who like to hear: 'Where in the **** did you get this?'." Delivery costs and times vary. A great, fun site.

My Freaky Family

www.myfreakyfamily.com

Advertised as offering "eclectic gifts for students and hip professionals", this site offers a comprehensive catalogue of funky items, displaying a little more imagination than just the usual lava lamps and beanbag chairs. These are of course included, as every student and hip professional should have one, but alternative suggestions are useful gifts such as yoga accessories and suitcases in faux fur. Not so useful is the Guiding Goddess Fortune Teller. Ordering follows the standard Yahoo system, with a price for every pocket.

Perfect Giftshop

www.theperfectgiftshop.com

You know you're on to a winner when the category list exceeds the usual choice of 10. Our advice is to search according to your price range, rather than wade through the vast range of categories featuring everything from the African Heritage Collection to Whimsical Fairies. At under $20, each item is at a knockdown price – even the mini tool kits are reduced from 79 cents to 59 cents. Not every item is gift material, but there are useful bargains, such as cameras for $50 and body-massage tools for under $10. Ordering is easy too.

Red Envelope

www.redenvelope.com

There's a stylish homepage with clear images and useful search categories with options for occasion, recipient, lifestyle or shop. The catalog offers something for everyone, with interesting items including a mohair necklace at $95, a monogrammed, silver-plated PC mouse (with black mouse pad) at $30, and a whole host of cigar and wine accessories for the connoisseur. Click on the item for an enlarged image and adequate description, then click to buy.

Star Wishing
www.starwishing.com

Hollywood not interested? Then how about being immortalized in space? This site enables you to name a star for yourself, or a friend, in your constellation of choice. The stars are registered with the Millennium Chronicle, a catalog of over 10,000 stars numerically designated by the Smithsonian Astrophysical Observatory. For $40 you receive a customized map, scientific data and a certificate to prove your star status. Celebrities who will be keeping you company include Leonard Nimoy, Naomi Campbell and Elvis Presley.

Ten Dollars
www.tendollars.com

All items here cost $10, shipping is free, and their warehouse offers everything from candles and jukebox radios to cocktail shakers and cigar-cutters. We're not sure if everything is actually worth $10 – the cheesy made-for-TV films are not very appealing – but it's fun (a Wash Your Sins Away bubble bath was on offer when we visited) and mostly it's worth it just for the hassle-free search.

Tickles
www.tickles.com

Tickles offers a selection of funky, pop-culture gifts and novelty items. The categories include the World of Dr Seuss (the good doctor's best accessories) and the Zany Bin, which offers anything from a plastic Buddha cell phone to a Parking Space Goddess. Spiritual guidance for under $5! Best of all are the funky retro 50s nightlights, a bargain at $5.99.

Tickles offers great stuff cheap. This site also promises a free gift with each order – a Bendy Frog anyone?

Treegivers
www.treegivers.com

Buying a star is so common these days. Why not honor your loved one on that special occasion with an entire tree? Don't worry – Treegivers are tree-lovers so they won't be uprooting a 1,000-year-old oak and shipping it to any old living room. Just select the occasion and they'll send the recipient a certificate to prove they own the tree and then plant it in the state of your choice. All trees are planted on public land, and the type depends on what suits the climate best. $30 gets you a tree and unframed certificate, and $50 a framed variety. It couldn't be much simpler, and it benefits the environment.

Wireless Too
www.wirelesstoo.com
Wireless Too calls itself "a celebration of American popular culture past and present". Its male-oriented gifts range from a Bowling Bunnies game ($30) to classic radios (from $200) to a signed Pete Rose jersey ($995), but you should find something for everyone: the most popular item is the Champion Pedal Car ($400). Each item is displayed complete with description and image, and shipping is relatively cheap at $15 for a standard 7-10 days.

Celebrity gifts Megastar merchandise

Kenny Loggins and Barry Manilow (to name but 2) may have their own cyberstores, but will they last? Here are some of the true icons online:

The Beatles
www.beatlemaniashoppe.com
Familiar images of the Fab Four emblazoned on every piece of merchandise possible, from mouse pads and mugs to ties and tote bags.

Betty Boop
www.bettyboopcandy.com
An unusual choice for an icon? Yahoo has an entire section devoted to the animated sex goddess, so who are we to argue. Candy gifts for all occasions.

Elvis
www.doghaus.com
King cologne, *Love Me Tender* shampoo and Elvis tattoos are just a few of the more imaginative Elvis gifts to be found.

I Love Lucy
www.destinysfavorites.com
TV classics from yesteryear immortalized. *I Love Lucy* fans just won't be able to say no to the 50th anniversary commemorative cake plate, a snip at $45.

Madonna
http://madonnadirect.com
Fitness is Religion book with an introduction by the Queen of Pop for just $24.

Golf

From links to hyperlinks, the Net is the place to buy that club, those pants or get advice on improving your swing. But can it make you into the new Tiger Woods? Sadly, for that you need his dad, Earl

Bad Golf Monthly

www.badgolfmonthly.com

This online magazine is for those who can't quite grasp the difference between a bogey and a birdie, or those who do but can't quite make it round a course without losing a dozen balls. Serious news plus humor and commiserations from fellow golf-lovers who've never completed a course anywhere near par.

Golf Ball Zone

www.golfballzone.com

Keep losing your balls into the rough? Then check out this store devoted to just one thing: used golf balls. The brand selection is large, the condition is nearly new (there's a no-quibble guarantee) and you can buy in bulk (flat rate delivery via UPS is $4.95), so start lining up your practice shots now.

Golf Circuit

www.golfcircuit.com

This site allows you to post an advert for those clubs that you bought your 18-year-old in the hope he would love the sport as much as you do. Buy, sell, receive help from a teaching professional on your technique, answer a poll question or look up a rule of the game – it's all here, plus a pro shop for when you decide that maybe your 14-year-old may share your obsession…

Golf Club Trader

www.golfclubtrader.com

You want to get your hands on a set of clubs without remortgaging the house? Start your search here. You can buy, sell, or trade clubs, and if you're selling, the good bit is that you don't have to wait for a buyer – the company will buy your clubs then list them on the site. If you're buying, there's a money-back guarantee on the used stuff. This site was undergoing a revamp as part of http://cbs.sportsline.com as we went to press, so the "new improved" version may prove slightly different to the above.

Golf Digest
www.golfdigest.com
Another green site with a how, what and where to play listing, plus more unusual articles such as how Bush and Gore stacked up when it came to wooing the golf vote. An instructional archive will help you to perfect your swing and the pro shop will provide all the equipment you need.

Golf Etiquette
www.mrgolf.com
This site offers lots of advice on golf etiquette, from the practice area to the green. Books are available to buy – as a subtle hint to your golfing buddy?

Golf Insight
www.golfinsight.net
This subscription program tracks your stats and spotlights your strengths and faults with a "shot summary" and "tendency report", and suggests corrective actions. Exhaustive game and course analyses and golfing news are also provided. At $79.95 for 12 months of unlimited visits, it's a great gift idea too.

Golf Link
www.golflink.com
Directory that links you to just about anything to do with the wonderful world of golf – merchandise, resorts, real estate and travel packages to name a few.

Golf Serve
www.golfserv.com
The definitive online resource for golfers, now owned by golf shop Chipshot (www.chipshot.com). Free membership brings you advice on everything from your swing to first-tee jitters, a booking facility for many US golf courses, and details of golfing holidays. If you must win at all costs, there's also a multimedia golf trainer where you can watch lessons online to refine your technique. Plus discounts with GolfPass.

North American Golf Directory
www.golfdirect.com
Comprehensive guide to not just courses and schools, but also to resorts and even real estate golf communities. Par, distance and slope info is available at a click of your mouse, plus web links.

Golf is not just a sport – it's a lifestyle. And Golf Link can help you live, eat and breathe your favourite game

Health & drugs

The quest for the perfect body, on the inside and on the outside, continues online. Whether you're looking for extra energy, clearer skin or regular bowels, you'll find something to cure whatever ails you. Or so they claim…

 No substitute for a qualified doctor

Doctor George
www.doctorgeorge.com
Unfortunately you're not face to face with Mr Clooney in his *ER* get-up, but with another, mysterious Dr George, making it nearly as exciting. Despite the pros of having a doctor on call 24 hours a day with no waiting time and no need to search for a parking space, Dr George is adamant in pointing out he is simply a source of information and advice. This aside, the advice is useful, with clinics covering diabetes and asthma, and stories and studies on a host of illnesses. Consultations are only available once you've registered.

Familymeds.com
www.familymeds.com
Seeking medical advice from a source other than your doctor can always be dangerous, particularly with the possibility that the hypochondriac element of your personality will take over and consume your every thought. If you think you can still keep a grip, Familymeds is a comprehensive reference tool for partial self-diagnosis, with an online store to sell you everything from contact lenses and diabetics' supplies to beauty products and shaving accessories. The health clinics cover every ailment from depression to poison ivy, including details of symptoms you can expect, and both natural and proven medicinal remedies. They do, however, suggest that you always consult a real, live doctor. The reference library of vitamins, supplements, food and herbal remedies provides essential information (so you know exactly what you're putting into your body) and ideas on how to stop illnesses in their tracks.

Alternative therapies To be well healed

Alaska Northern Lights
www.alaskanorthernlights.com
Light therapy has long been used in treating Seasonal Affective Disorder (SAD) and you can now use this technology to help fight fatigue and jet lag in your own home (and maybe even get your insurance provider to pay for it). This site sells a broad-spectrum light box, with a price-match guarantee.

Association of Reflexologists
www.reflexology.org
Click on a link on this surprisingly primitive site to learn a little about how the natural healing process can be stimulated by reflexology, or to find the contact details for your local association. A few have websites that adequately explain the practice of reflexology and where to become a reflexologist, but most are offline associations. Nothing for sale, and only really useful as a directory.

Aster
www.asterinc.com
Babies are particularly in tune with their sense of smell, to the point of being able to recognize their mother just by smelling her. Bearing this in mind, introducing your baby or small child to the healing powers of essential oils seems all the more natural. Aster has selected oils and scented toys which should help you and your child get through those early teething problems, coughs, colds and colic, and even help your baby to sleep or wake up in a better mood. It's just a pity they can't guarantee the same result for adults.

Avalon Crystals
www.neatstuff.net/avalon
Skeptics beware. Kellie and her dreamy site promoting and selling the healing properties of stones and crystals is likely to make your blood boil. Those who remain open-minded will find a comprehensive, if amateurish, site packed with information about various gemstone chunks and jewelry, all infused with healing properties. According to Kellie, these simple rocks can be used to heal anger, backache and even alcoholism. Prices range from $5 to $200 (cleansing and activating with Reiki energy upon request).

Ayurveda
http://ayurvedahc.com
This latest holistic therapy has dozens of sites trying to convert you to this ancient Indian "healing science". This remarkably far-reaching site (it even has a Wall Street section) gives you plenty of info about the practice, and sells a few interesting products, from herbal supplements to a portable sauna. This site is one of the more convincing, as it keeps you firmly in the Western world.

Ayurveda, the ancient "healing science", has embraced the Internet with many sites spreading the word. This one does it better than most

Colon Health Network
http://colonhealth.net
Detoxifying seems to be the answer to many illnesses, according to this site, but the accompanying articles are not much more than extended promotions for the products on offer. Ear candling (irrigation for the ears) is also covered, and there's a therapists' directory. The products featured (categories include heart health and weight loss) have no ingredients lists or even much to tell you what they do. If you are interested, consult a qualified practitioner first.

Holistic Channel
www.101AlternativeMedicine.com
Link live to Dr Liu, Debra J and many more for expert advice on Reiki, emotional release therapy or whatever their specialty may be, or e-mail your questions for immediate response. The health notes will help explain symptoms or provide straightforward explanations. There's a comprehensive herbal remedy dictionary and herbal and homeopathic remedies are on hand to be explored. Nothing to buy, but a useful starting point.

Human Growth Hormones
www.lifespandynamics.com
This site specializes in selling human growth hormones (the latest in anti-ageing treatments), but has lots of other health articles. There's plenty of information about the hormones, though it could be put in terms that are easier to grasp. The prices are reasonable, the claims quite astounding. You be the judge.

Infant Massage with Lasting Impressions
www.lastingi.com
Infant and pediatric massage has been shown to help babies gain weight, improve their sleep patterns and promote better digestion. It also helps with child-parent bonding. This site offers a kit including a book, with instructions for children with special needs, plus a video and massage oil.

Just Relax Me
www.justrelaxme.com
More traditional methods of relieving stress – and no, that's not quitting your job or asking for a divorce, but essential oils, healing herbs and a bit of pampering. Glide through soothing pastel pages selling both old and modern forms of stress relief, some of the more unusual being infra-red heat massages, eye pillows and audio tapes of selected sounds and music. Prices are good and shipping is a flat $2.95.

Life Aromatherapy
www.lifearoma.com
You can reduce stress, improve your mood or set the scene for a romantic evening with these products made from concentrated oil extracts. The Egyptians thought they were a good thing, and here you can find everything from hair-growth oil to headache oil. If all else fails, at least you're sure to smell better.

Mindgrowth
www.mindgrowth.com
A simple site selling one product line: a behavioral management system (ie stress control). A palm-sized monitor can be used just about anywhere to detect minute changes in the skin's sweat glands, which can help you monitor your stress triggers and reactions. A series of cassette tapes can help you to manage the stress and encourage relaxation, and even help to control specific problems such as a fear of flying.

ReikiOne
www.tamoore.com/reiki/msgctr.htm
Reiki, which channels the energy of the universe to help heal and regenerate, has recently become more mainstream. This site offers brief information about the practice, a chat forum, newsletter and practitioner listings. The products for sale include books, music, cards and candles. As soothing as the treatment.

QUACK WATCH
www.quackwatch.com

Questionable marketing, fraudulent claims, bad side-effects and general health scams are investigated by this site run by alternative health scourge, Stephen Barrett, MD.

Dr Barrett sides firmly with Western conventional medicine (that's where he gets his income from, after all) and the site would be improved by a slightly more open mind, but there are some very good investigations here, along with excellent advice on what should ring warning bells in a practitioner or product.

Particular scorn is heaped on some cancer therapies and badly trained chiropractors.

From aspirin to Viagra (and probably back again)

Aspirin
www.aspirin.com
No online buying but you can read the history of the little white pill that Neil Armstrong took to the moon. You can also read how pain passes around the body so you can speak fluent medicalese: "It's like this, doc – I've got these sensor tissues, right? I know they're only a millionth of a millimeter in diameter on average, but they're hurting like hell... can you give me something?"

Direct Prescriptions
www.direct-prescriptions.com
If you're using the Net in a public place and don't want passers-by to know you're seeking help with weight-loss, sexual dysfunction or hair-loss problems, this site's vibrant, attention-grabbing colours are best avoided. If you can bear to continue, the order form includes patient-responsibility statements to read and sign, and a medical questionnaire. In terms of price, 10 Viagra tablets will cost you a hefty $140, plus $18 postage. Not the cheapest solution on offer.

On-Line Medical Center
www.on-linemedicalcenter.com
This site sells a limited range of prescription-only "lifestyle" medicines, including Viagra, Propecia and weight-loss pills. You need to fill in a medical-history form and a disclaimer, which will be reviewed by a doctor (licensed in the US, a claim they can document on request) before your order is approved, and an adult's signature is required. Delivery is included in the prices, which are not exactly cheap ($140 for 10 Viagra tablets).

On Rx.com you can search by symptoms to find the best drug. Shipping free if you buy own-brand

Rx.com
www.rx.com
Rx.com sells both prescription and non-prescription drugs, and you can search for specific products or symptoms to find exactly what you need. Additional information (the kind you read on the side of the box) is available for each product, next to links to buy. The selection on offer will beat that found in your corner drugstore, but shipping at $3.95 makes it advisable to buy in bulk. Shipping is free, however, if you buy any Rx.com own-brand products as part of your order.

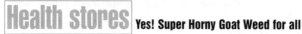

Health stores Yes! Super Horny Goat Weed for all

Alternative Healthy Stores
www.healthestores.com
This site sells magnetic products, supplements and other natural remedies including carcinogen-free products. Their parasite-prevention program is a thought-provoking idea. Shipping is $5 no matter how much you order and there's a 10 per cent discount when you e-mail a friend about the site.

Condomania
www.condomania.com
Top of the list of modern health and safety products has to be the humble condom, but keeping stocked up can be pricey, not to mention the potential embarrassment of buying them in public. Solve both problems with this straightforward yet fun site. Search for the most suitable condom among 11 categories from extra-strength to non-latex (female condoms too), or novelty gift, or read the "road test" reviews and fun features. Prices are good – about $9 a dozen (the minimum quantity) – and delivery is cheap – $3 unless you request courier service. And every order arrives in a discreet brown envelope.

CVS/pharmacy
www.cvs.com
This is a great site that reflects the offline store. CVS sells 12 per cent of the nation's prescriptions, and you can send in yours, which it will verify before filling. As well as shopping from its vast selection of products, you can search for counter-indications to your Rx, get the facts about illnesses from ADHD to Sudden Cardiac Arrest, and find legal and insurance information. When in one section you have to return to the homepage before accessing another, but this site covers it all, from finding a doctor to researching health plans. A good resource for all things health-related.

Drugstore.com
www.drugstore.com
This well-organized general health store sells everything from vitamins and supplements to beauty products and general medicines. Simply click on a category and browse. Prices are average, with the bonus of discounts and "buy one get one free" offers to encourage you to fill your medicine cabinet. There's also an online pharmacy, with free shipping on most prescriptions.

Earth's Pharmacy
www.earthspharmacy.com
Manufacturers of own-brand vitamins and supplements. The categories are helpfully broken down into men's and women's health, with individual sections including heart, vision, digestion, weight-loss, sport, arthritis, anti-oxidants,

stress, sleep and brain supplements. There's an extensive resource library and the biographies of the advisory staff are reassuring. Shipping is a flat $4.95.

General Nutrition Centers
www.gnc.com

There seems to be one of these stores in every mall and now you can access its vast library online. Pick your concern, from brittle nails to night blindness to photosensitivity, and you'll get a summary of the problem, suggested dietary and lifestyle changes, and recommended nutritional supplements. These all have links to pages that explain their properties in more detail. Side effects are set out and homeopathic remedies are also given if appropriate. The site also has a very comprehensive drug directory, with prices up front. Other health and personal care items are also available, and prescriptions can be filled.

Healthy Back
http://healthyback.com

Anyone who has suffered from a bad back knows how it affects everything you do. Concentrating on prevention, this site has everything to keep you sitting up straight. It's scanty on shipping and return policies, though, and the Educational Information page was disappointingly blank.

The Health Store
www.thstore.com

The Health Store has four departments: water purification, air purification, healthy home and healthy body. You can buy anything from magnetic therapy necklaces and portable hot tubs to heart-rate monitors and tanning lamps. There is plenty of information on the products on offer, along with news and technology sections. Some products ship for free, and many prices are discounted (though 5 cents is not much to crow about).

Longs Drugs
www.longs.com

If you just want to fill or re-fill your pre-scription, then Longs is an online pharmacy possibility. You can also e-mail the pharmacist a question, or browse answers to earlier questions. There's a fitness cen-

Healthy Back wants to keep yours in good shape, so advocates preventive care. Good, but could be better

ter for sports, training and nutrition information, while the "Health Connection" section is an archive of health-related articles. A bit bare-bones, but it does the job.

Natural Life
www.paincarestore.com
A source for drug-free pain control, this site focuses on massage, supplements, magnetic therapy and aromatherapy. Shipping is included in the price, but you must register for the site to recognize your cart, an annoying detail that does not appear until you try to add another item or check out.

Nutripeak
www.nutripeak.com
This is a very professional-looking enterprise, easy to navigate with a wide selection of vitamins, sports nutrition, food supplements and drugs to select from. The additional notes on each product are particularly useful, with most items available at discount prices. Head for the herb section for alternative nutritional advice and aids. Our favorites include Super Horny Goat Weed to help support sexual function, and Artichoke Extract for improved digestion.

Sangster's
www.sangsters.com
A minimal site that lets you select your ailment, then gives you a brief description of what supplements to take. It is fond of lists – click on Women's Health and you get a very long one, but click on the individual item and it only gives you slightly more information. However, Sangster's *Natural Living Magazine* has an online archive with informative articles.

Savon Drugs
www.sav-ondrugs.com
Fill or refill your prescription at this site, and either have it delivered (free if you can wait 7-9 days, or pay for UPS delivery) or collect it from an offline store associated with parent company Albertsons. A variety of other goods are available, much like any major drug store. You can e-mail the pharmacist with your questions and get advice about diet and other health matters from the Health Awareness section, though many of the pages were not recognized and some were not particularly helpful beyond providing term definitions.

ONLINE EYE OPENER
Lens Express
www.lensexpress.com

Glasses and contact lenses at about 50 per cent less than you would pay at an optician. Simply select the brand or type of lens you would prefer and send them your eye prescription via their online order form. Don't worry if you don't know your prescription – they will obtain your details, free of charge if you can give them the name and address of your doctor.

Cut-price designer frames are also on offer here: Calvin Klein, Ralph Lauren and many more. Lens solutions, including Ciba Vision and Bausch & Lomb, can also be ordered direct. Delivery costs $5.95 and your order will be with you within 7 business days.

Virtual Health Store

www.vhs.com

This lovely site has been around since 1994, and it shows. The categories are
all there for you to access on the homepage, along with company information.
Health articles are available to download, and the recipes for smoothies will
make your mouth water. Shipping information only comes up when you hit an
order button, but they have zip code specific shipping charges, rather than a
flat fee. Pity about the steep $3 handling charge on all orders, though.

Vitamin Shoppe

www.vitaminshoppe.com

Vitamin junkies can save a fortune on their supplements at this comprehensive
site. All the usual health-helpers are here, along with some you won't have
heard of yet, at prices far lower than retail. The site also provides a newsletter,
health articles and a dietary Q&A if you're really interested in keeping in tiptop
shape. Tiny type, but information and customer support are readily available.

Walgreens

www.walgreens.com

Another nationally respected pharmacy, and a well thought out site that aims
to offer its complete store online (complete with neighborhood specials and
printable coupons). Like CVS, you can have your prescription filled, or just
browse the store for many other everyday-living items, from cameras to toys.
The health library by the Mayo Clinic gives advice on nutrition and fitness, as
well as other health-related issues. There's also a fascinating, inspiring history
of the store and its founder, Charles Walgreen. A great, reliable resource.

Vitamins & supplements | Health helpers

Affordable Supplements

www.affordablesupplements.com

Before heading to this site take a quick look at your body. If you're more on
the puny side of weedy, even the strongest supplements found here aren't
going to have much of an effect. The majority of products listed are for body
builders, as you'll realize from the jargon-filled homepage that only the truly
obsessed will be able to decipher. However the categories here also include
joint pain, vitamins and tanning products, along with the likes of weight-loss
specials and energy formulae. And, as the name suggests, the supplements
are indeed affordable, with discounts galore.

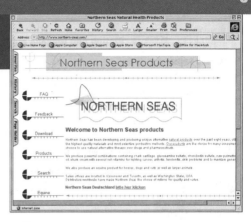

Northern Seas brings you a unique blend of shark cartilage to cure what ails you

Northern Seas

www.northern-seas.com

One of a number of sites promoting the healing properties of shark cartilage. You may have thought these sea predators were only interested in gnawing on your cartilage, but combined with certain herbs or vitamins, shark cartilage can, it's claimed, have healing effects on those suffering from arthritis, tendonitis, skin problems and cancer. Northern Seas have been developing their supplements for nearly a decade and these can now be bought online at around $20 a bottle. Ingredients and additional information are displayed.

Web Vitamins

www.webvitamins.com

This useful site is simple to use: select a brand or the particular boost you feel your body needs – everything from male and female specific items and sports nutrition to general A, B and C vitamins. There's no additional information about the products, so this is really a place to restock supplies rather than experiment, but the prices are good, with most items listed at a discount.

Whole Health Discount Center

www.wholehealthdiscountcenter.com

Not exactly the snappiest of web addresses, but this fairly rudimentary site is worth a look. A, simply click on a category (men's health, vitamins, pain relief and so on) to view extensive yet concise information about each item and find links to buy. The order form itself is basic, but prices are good, with both discounts and offers. Orders should be with you the following day.

Weight loss
Dieting and lifestyle guidance

The Atkins Center
www.atkinscenter.com

The Atkins Diet, famous for being high protein and low in carbohydrates, has many detractors, but it has been around since the 70s, with many devotees. The Center itself offers alternative treatment for many conditions such as heart disorders and allergies. This informative site is a vehicle for selling the Atkins lifestyle, but overall there's plenty of information and guidance. Weight-loss products on offer include bars, shakes, supplements and other foodstuffs (including prepared foods), books, videos and more.

THE BRACE CENTER
www.bracecenter.com

A bandage is seen, by men at least, as a sign of sporting grit. You're only serious about your game if you've got the injuries to prove it. So why not cut out the middle man – just get yourself a top of the range back brace, knee sleeve or ankle brace.

This site is crammed with probably the most extensive range of fitness supports you'll find on the Internet, and enough additional information about each for you to be able to bore your friends to tears with details of your latest mishap.

On the downside, we had problems with the search facility, which made searching through over 200 products a very tedious task. Otherwise this is a good site to head for, and gentler than a physiotherapist.

Beverly Hills Weight Loss and Wellness
www.beverlyhillsintl.com

This site is a back-up to the nationwide operation. It sells itself as a "professionally supervised individually counseled program", but the constant push to sell you a franchise seems to undermine the professional bit. The "success" stories have a "results not typical" disclaimer, further eroding confidence. With its dull design and uninspiring photos, the impression is that they want to sell you a franchise, not a program.

Physicians' Weight Loss Center Online
www.pwlc.com

This great site will really get you motivated. You begin with an interactive analysis of your current lifestyle and goals, after which the site recommends a program to buy. Your progress is then monitored weekly. Buying membership also allows you access to offline centers, and food products and supplements are also on offer. Games, chat rooms and articles will keep you on track.

The Zone
www.zoneperfect.com

This diet may sound like a fad, but the nutritional basis behind it is nothing new. Advocating the proper ratio of fats, carbohydrates and protein, this site maintains that you can keep your body in the "zone" of proper insulin balance. There's not much in the way of extra nutritional or health information, and even less on exercise: this site is there to sell Zone products – food and supplements. It takes the guessing out of dieting.

Hi-fi

Whether you just want a steam-powered radio, the latest in MP3 technology or the racks of silver boxes so beloved of hi-fi "enthusiasts", the Net is ready to separate you from your money

---

 Separates, personals and portables

800.com

www.800.com

Despite advertising everything from CD players to CDs, the choice of systems is generally limited to just a few models. Not the ideal site to buy from, but they do offer useful advice sections including buying and hook-up tips, and what kind of system is best suited toward your own particular needs.

Abes of Maine

www.abesofmaine.com

Abes specializes in photography equipment but stocks a considerable range of electronics, from Discman and CD players to accessories for the serious audio enthusiast (including top-of-the-range speakers and equalizers). With brand names and prices to suit all, plus store specials, you should be able to find a bargain (the Panasonic Jogger Discman was on offer at only a little over $100 when we visited). Ordering is simple and shipping charges are listed.

Best Buy

www.bestbuy.com

Despite the bland design and poor organization, this site has one of the most comprehensive selections of audio equipment online. Extensive descriptions and features charts lead you toward making an informed purchase, while the numerous camera angles mean you even know what the rear of your purchase looks like – handy for planning your wiring. Ordering is standard, although you have to set up a password account. UPS ground shipping takes 3-10 days.

Circuit City

www.circuitcity.com

This general electrical store offers home and car audio as well as the latest in MP3 technology. Select a section to browse their entire catalog, or narrow your search down by brand or preferred features. The additional information is extensive, and if you're not an expert, a glossary of technical jargon is on hand to help you make an informed purchase. Circuit City also offers a handy service whereby you order online but pick your gear up from one of their stores, thus doing away with shipping costs.

Egghead

www.egghead.com

Online auction site with a limited, but potentially bargain-filled audio section. Sharp hi-fi systems were going for $70 when we visited.

Good Guys

www.goodguys.com

The suitable steely-gray design complements an easy-to-use store that's full of general electrical goods. There are several ways to search – we suggest you head for audio equipment to choose from speakers, CD and mini-disc players and cassette decks. Prices are good – top of the range CD players for less than $200 – but if looks are high on your list of priorities, Good Guys offer only distant and sometimes blurry images. In terms of information, however, they're spot on. With free shipping and no sales tax, this is a pretty good site.

Enough is enough It's the music that matters

While we'd all like megamoney systems composed of fancy electronics and speakers with 5-figure price tags, the whole purpose of buying a system is to listen to the music, right? If you're constantly worrying whether a new amplifier or that piece of black sponge you put under a CD player would make all the difference, you're not enjoying the music – just indulging in electronic masochism. So what's the answer? A large part of it is to buy right in the first place. When you're auditioning a system component, only get something that blows your socks off with the improvement it makes to the music. (Audition with a favourite CD so you can compare the sound of music you already love.) What's the best single upgrade anyone can make to their system? The answer is invariably: more music. Music is relatively cheap – especially if you buy online – and the thrill of discovering something new via that system on which you spent all that money is hard to convey. But one thing's for sure: it beats hearing a CD player that may be a tad better than your current one any day.

HiFi
www.hifi.com
Not a great site if you want a quick but informed purchase. Best-sellers are easy to find, but if you want to look at their entire range of MP3 players, for example, there isn't a huge choice and just a few lines of description. If you know the model you must have, great – otherwise you need to click on each model for more detail and images. But the spec sheets are comprehensive, and there's a hi-fi dictionary and library of articles. The prices listed promise savings of anywhere between $50 and $150.

Outpost
www.outpost.com
This comprehensive site sells everything from your average Panasonic CD player to the not-so-average Henry Kloss classic tabletop radio. Search by brand or product, with top names including Sony, Technics, and Denon. The product pages contain more than enough information, alongside a variety of alternate models for quick and easy comparisons. Prices vary: top-of-the-range Denon CD players start at $200, with free overnight shipping.

Radio Shack
www.radioshack.com
Reputable chain with an average site that's searchable by category (home entertainment, computers and security devices etc). The initial information is limited, but they do offer handy links to product manuals for the definitive account, and ordering is simple. Delivery prices start at $2.50. Worth a look.

The Wiz
www.thewiz.com
If you know what you want and just need somewhere to buy it, The Wiz is as good a place as any to start. Otherwise we suggest you look elsewhere, as searching is limited to brands rather than products, information is limited to a few lines and the pictures are poor. Ordering is a piece of cake, however.

In-car audio Radio, cassette and CD systems

Audio Wizard
www.theaudiowizard.com
In-car cassette players rub shoulders with top-of-the-range Blaupunkt speakers on this site. If cost is your main consideration, head for the closeout section for knockdown prices; otherwise select your favorite brand, with Sony, Pioneer and JVC mingling with less notable brands such as Hollywood and Phoenix Gold. Images are clear and they provide loads of jargon-filled descriptions alongside the more practical warranty and delivery information.

Car Discount Stereos

www.cardiscountstereos.com

A dull-looking site, but strong on price and variety. With a comprehensive range of in-car stereo systems, and a wealth of accessories to turn your existing system into a demon player, it's easy to let the dreary design slide by. Any category will lead you to a host of top names including Pioneer, Blaupunkt and Audiobahn. Prices range from the sublime to the ridiculous.

Original Car Radios

www.originalcarradios.com

If you feel your brand new Blaupunkt stereo doesn't quite blend with the ambience of your 1968 Cadillac, Original Radios offer their comprehensive selection of car radios. Select your car make to view concise descriptions and enlarged images of original-issue car radios dating from the 50s to the 70s. Prices generally range from $150 to anything up to $400, with additional shipping to be calculated later. No online ordering – e-mail only.

 The brave new world of music on the Internet

Elite Gizmos

www.elitegizmos.com

Limited to Sony, Diamond and Samsung models, but what they lack in range, they make up for with prices – more than $100 off the RRP in every case.

MP3 Player Store

www.mp3playerstore.com

If you're tired of being one step behind the rest of the group when it comes to technology, the MP3 Player Store offers what might be termed "My First MP3 Player". You won't see a Sony, Creative Labs or even a Pine, because what you are dealing with are the lower ranges of the MP3 market: Avex, Lenoxx and the creatively titled Disco Trip. The prices are cheap, generally less than $100, but where they scrimp on price, they don't on images, information and performance. Worth a look if budget rather than brand is your main priority.

MP3 Shopping

www.mp3shopping.com

Every brand of high-tech music equipment, plus news and reviews so you know your Diamond Rio from your Iomega Hip Zip and Philips Rush. Each product page has all the information you're likely to need to make an informed purchase, full features lists, software compatibility and shipping times. Prices range from $100 to $500, with free US shipping. The site may lack even a hint of imagination, but it's easy to use, comprehensive and you'll struggle to find a better selection of MP3 players. An excellent all-round MP3 universe.

MP3 Solutions
www.mp3solutions.com
An apt name for a site low on products but high on information. If you're a bit of an MP3 novice/general technology-phobe, this site offers handy guides to the differences between say, a Flash MP3 player and a CD/MP3 player, and useful comparison charts for the models on offer here to buy. In-store prices range from $65 to $200 with free shipping. Not bad, if not the best.

 Still alive and kicking, despite the video

Radio Attic
www.radioattic.com
Radio Attic is a fairly amateurish offering in terms of site design and technology, but those behind this antique radio den are true enthusiasts. If you're new to the game, the experts provide articles offering a brief history of radio, and how to tell your Philco from your Granco. Otherwise, if you just want something a little bit different to your current Sony offering, there are hundreds of models available, from a Beatles CD/Radio Stereo player for $320 to more traditional Cathedral models. Ordering is via e-mail, with payment made through PayPal.

Windup Radios
www.windupradio.com
Emergency-preparation products (quake-alert systems, solar-power lanterns etc) are this site's business, though radios are the big sell. Top brands Sangean and Freeplay take pride of place, with prices from $20 to $300. Ordering is simple – mark the box by the item you want and fill in your details – but check shipping charges first, as a single radio will set you back anywhere up to $40. Worth it for that stylish blue Perspex wind-up model with flashlight, though.

Get ready for the apocalypse with the emergency-preparation products available at Windup Radios... or just a new portable

Home

Interior design is the new rock 'n' roll, or something like that.
If your pad isn't up to scratch, you can surf the Web to find that new look you're after, or maybe you just need a new dish-drainer for the kitchen

---

Home improvement  **An extension in a day**

The Home Depot
www.homedepot.com
The online version of this offline store is full of great home improvement and gardening ideas. It has illustrated instructions on such projects as laying a brick edging to your lawn. You can even use the site to design your kitchen. You have to type in your zip code and the availability of the products you select depends on the store in your area. It will tell you where the nearest offline stop is, and provide a map on how to get there. This site takes helpfulness to new levels.

Corner Hardware
http://shop.cornerhardware.com
This site really is the online equivalent of your local hardware store – only better. Clearly laid out (that gives it an edge over the offline version for starters) the site is easy to find your way around and important details like shipping charges are posted up front. Customer service is available 24/7 online and by phone. The site takes you through such projects as installing a kitchen sink step by step. If you don't have the skills to do the improvement or repair you have in mind (and be honest, not many do) there is a directory to help you find the right professionals. A great resource.

Lowe's Home Improvement Warehouse
www.lowes.com
Lowe's online store sells appliances, tools grills and patio furniture. Once again, availability is tied to the store nearest your zip code. The range of items

available is impressive, for example, well over 50 side-by-side refrigerators were listed when checked. Product descriptions are limited to manufacturer specifications. There's also an authoritative project library and advice center. Orders can be picked up at a local store or delivered to your home. Lowe's tries to serve the community through charitable organizations and its own foundation. You can request funds through the site.

Our House
www.ourhouse.com
This site is not so user-friendly – it took quite a few clicks and a lot of searching to find the refrigerators, which were quite a bit more expensive than on other sites. Less irrelevant illustrations and a clearer contents list would be more helpful. The "Bestselling" selection at the top of each section is not particularly useful either as the items are so diverse you'll end up wasting a lot of time. As you might expect, a contractor directory is available, but other sites just seem to do it all much better.

 From futons to Harley Davidson barstools

Abracadabra Furniture
www.a-furniture.com
This site has a lot of furniture to sell whether you want entry benches or toilet toppers. You are not getting anything special, there is definitely a mass-produced quality at work here, and the low prices reflect that. Shipping is a steep 15 per cent of the order, rising to 45 per cent if shipping to Alaska, a trend with which Alaskans must be drearily familiar.

Antique Arts
www.antiquearts.com
There are almost too many antique goods on sale here. But then this site acts as a host for many individual antique dealers and shops, displaying the goods under one "roof" in the same format. Because the Antique Arts site doesn't sell the items (it just handles the setting up of the catalogs) you must trust the individual store for authenticity and quality. The consistency of presentation makes it easy to browse and compare. If you see something you like, click on it and you'll either go to the dealer's online catalog or visit the individual store's homepage. An e-mail system allows you to ask the dealers questions, a wise idea as many of these antiques cost $10,000 or more.

The Atrium Furniture Mall
www.theatrium.com
You can't actually order online through this site, but it deserves inclusion simply because of the effort it has made to get you to visit the offline mall. The mall houses several furniture shops, and this site links you to each one,

This site acts as an online mall – the vast selection means you are sure to find that special something to fill that awkward corner

several of which are e-commerce sites. But the purpose here is to get you to come in person, so a 'Shop 'n' Stay' feature lets you plan a weekend visit. The only downside: the hopelessly old-fashioned design and colors – a livelier appearance would work wonders.

Baby Max Company
www.babymaxcompany.com
A lot of sites sell custom-painted furniture, but this is one of the few that allows you to order online. There are many designs to choose from, and a variety of furniture, from step stools to storage shelves. The site is well designed and ordering is easy with shipping costs displayed beside the prices. A bit pricey, but then nothing's too good for junior, right?

Baik Designs
www.baikdesigns.com
What does a shop do that sells a lot of one-off designs and handmade furniture and is based offshore (in this case Hawaii)? Well, it is a bit complicated, but you display your stock online, have a price request form, and then items can be ordered through the site after a reply. Shipping rates and delivery methods are even more complex, but you could get something unusual here. Baik, in case you were wondering, is Indonesian for "fine".

Batvia Interiors
www.balistyle.com
You can't order through this site but browse through and then call in your order. The Bali furniture is very tempting and though a tad pricey, is competitive with offline stores. Shipping can add up 20 per cent to your order.

Benchmark BeHome
www.behome.com
This online version of the family-run offline store offers middle-of-the-road furniture from recognisable brand names, nothing adventurous but sure to appeal to most and not date. User-friendly and informative.

D'Avignon
www.davignonstore.com
If you've always wanted to recreate the atmosphere of Provence in your home here's your chance. This importer has a limited range of furniture from the region and some accessories. The site design is poor – you have to type in the item category, but beds turned up a side table, while tables resulted in a "no items found" response. Because the pix aren't great, it is hard to tell how a collection would work together. The stuff ain't cheap, but the shipping is free.

Decor Creations
www.decorcreations.com
This site has some lovely furniture and accessories made by artists in Boise, Idaho. A bit sparse on details like shipping, returns etc, making it a bit of a gamble but one you might decide is worth taking.

Fran's Wicker and Rattan Furniture
www.franswicker.com
Here you will find a wide selection of modern wicker. Everything from complete dining and bed sets to rockers and all-weather furniture is easily viewed and ordered. No design masterpieces and wicker is never cheap but if it's wicker you want, look no further.

Salton
www.saltoninc.com
From the people who brought you the Breadman, the Juicemaster and the George Foreman grill comes a homepage with a certain hometown charm. Just click on the door and enter a world of famous home brand names and, er, Marilyn Monroe. (The connection being that the late star has her own line of massage chairs, hair dryers and travel irons.)

Sofa.com
www.sofa.com
The wonderful world of leather – tactile, hardwearing, and easy to clean. A good selection of sofas in a rainbow of colors and styles are available here with free shipping in the continental US.

KITCHENS BY DESIGN

The kitchen really is the heart of the home, and the one room that could cost you many thousands to remodel and still end up not meeting the needs of the family. What to do? Check out this elegant, interactive site to explore endless virtual possibilities to help you create the kitchen of your dreams – whether you cook daily or just pass through on your way out the back door.

Lots of photos, info and ideas, a practical budget planner and advice as to what to expect when the workmen arrive. The site also provides links to local suppliers.

www.kitchens.com

Catalogs Stuff you might want to find some room for

Blackwelders
www.blackwelder.com
Not everything from the print catalog is featured here, but there is still a pretty wide selection. The clear layout allows you to see the collections rather than having to scroll through a list of brands that don't mean much to the general public. Prices are below retail. As this book went to press, the site was being revamped for 2001/2.

Bombay Company
www.bombayco.com
Fans of dark colonial furniture will be familiar with this company. It has many offline stores, but most customers know it through the catalog. Here is the same stock, focusing on accessories to get that British Empire look.

Pottery Barn
www.potterybarn.com
Lovers of this contemporary country look will drool over this site, which only sells a selection from the printed catalog. The "see in a room" option will not only convince you to buy the original item, but probably make you want everything else displayed. The site is simple but gorgeous, reflecting the bright, calm, crisp style of the catalogs.

Kitchens & bath Pots and pans

BathClick
www.bathclick.com
All your bathroom needs are addressed (well, not *quite* all, you understand) by this site, which sells a large range of products from glass sinks for over $3,000 to one in ceramic for $56. Items come in various colors and finishes, and they estimate the lead time for each item. Shipping is free within continental US.

Bodum
www.bodum.com
You can buy this famous brand's products directly from this site, but don't expect discounts. As clean as its famous cafétieres, this site will convince you never to make instant again. Luscious range of other sleek kitchen items too.

Buy Bathware
www.buybathware.com
No frills with this site – just a straightforward list of items which you can

browse by style. If co-ordinating your toothbrush holder to your tissue dispenser to your shower curtain is your idea of decorating bliss, then a) get a life and b) this site is your virtual paradise. Shipping is very reasonable.

Chadder and Co USA
www.chadderusa.com
This site offers a limited range of antique-look bathrooms. The sinks alone will set you back thousands of dollars but if only the best will do, check it out.

Emily's Originals
www.emilysoriginals.com
If you are the kind of person who likes to disguise your toilet roll under a hoop-skirted dolly, suffice to say you've come to the right place. Lace-edged bath towel sets with matching toilet roll holders dominate, and some of the color combinations are something to behold: black lace on beige towels, white on plum or navy, and enough peach and other froth to please the girliest of tastes. Custom orders are welcome, but are they advisable?

Fieldcrest Cannon Outlet
www.fieldcrestcannonoutlet.com
The advantage of buying from well-known brand Fieldcrest is quality assurance and a vast range of colors. This may be called an outlet store but the discounts are fairly minimal. When visited, the clearance sale proved mildly disappointing with a grand total of two products heavily discounted. Shipping is free if you spend $50 or more.

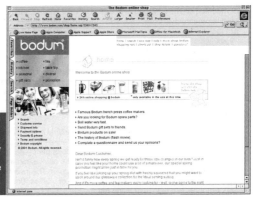

Bodum's site has those gorgeous accessories that any modern interior cries out for – just don't expect it to be any cheaper by buying direct

Health For You
http://healthforyouministry.com
This site has everything from the field to table in terms of breadmaking. The breadmaker here is you, and you will find equipment to mill the flour, flake the grains and grind the spices needed. This site will give you very definite instructions on what brand of equipment and which ingredients to use to make the perfect loaf, and remember, as the site says, Jesus is the bread of life! A steep 15 per cent restocking fee applies to all returns.

Kitchens Unlimited
www.kitchensunlimited.com
Serious kitchen equipment like lazy susans, recycle bins, roll racks and stemware racks, and all the essential paraphernalia of the modern kitchen are available here. Shipping is a percentage of your order and there's a very steep per cent restocking fee on returns, so be sure to order carefully.

Ming Tsai
www.mingspantry.com
Here you'll find not only Ming's recipes, but the ingredients, the methods and the equipment needed to do the culinary business. It's all tried and tested by the Food Network star himself, so if the result is not as mouthwatering as if it came from his kitchen, you only have yourself to blame.

Pot Racks Online
www.pot-racks-online.com
Need a pot rack? Well, this site sells nothing but (with the exception of a couple of wine racks). Rectangular or round, hanging from the ceiling or mounted on the wall, and available in several finishes and colors, Mediterranean-style or modelled on those used by butchers – this site is to pot racks what Elvis is to rock 'n' roll. Shipping is about 12 per cent of order.

Snicker Doodles Kitchen Shop
www.neatkitchenstuff.com
This shop appears to have just about everything – gadgets, cookbooks, seasonal items, food, ceramics and cookware. And if you don't find what you are looking for, call them up and they will not only check out the offline store, but send you a picture of the item to be sure it's what you want. To offset shipping charges you get a $5 certificate against your next order over $25.

Vieco Kitchen
www.viecokitchen.com
Serious cooks will delight in the range of goods of offer here. More than 9 rice-cookers were for sale when visited, and the cookie, tart and sweet molds would not be out of place in a professional kitchen. The inventory is vast: with what's on sale you can make espresso, ravioli or waffles. Shipping is free over $50, but there is a high restocking fee.

Contemporary design   It's the new retro

Cosmopolitan Home

www.cosmopolitanhome.com

Lots of funky yet functional products are available on this easy-to-use site. There are many fabric options to choose from, but you will be buying blind as there are no swatches. Prices are not for the faint-hearted. Delivery is free, though, so take that into account if comparison shopping. When visited, the candles and soap section was all out of soap.

Crate & Barrel

www.crateandbarrel.com

Crate & Barrel's site has the same feel as its shops – clean and modern. You can buy products featured here as well as many items from the printed catalog, though some furniture is not yet available online. The selection of dinnerware and flatware is extensive but anyone familiar with the offline stores will know the quality. Easy to use but full product availability would be better.

Modern Home

www.modernhome.com

This site may be called Modern Home but it has a funky 60s early 70s feel, right on the mark designwise. Lots of groovy furniture in that top textile: velvet. All this and lots more accessories to get your home feeling gooood. Shipping is 10 per cent of your total order, a saving compared to many sites.

Pure Design

www.pure-design.com

This is another beautiful site mirroring the streamlined funky furniture and accessories for sale. The site design can be a bit too precious for its own good, though: the gray type can be hard to read, and having to place the cursor on numbers or bars to see what they refer to gets tedious. The shipping and returns policies are a bit buried, but shipping is a flat 10 per cent of the order. Not bad.

Modern Home features items with that retro 60s and 70s feel – perfect for outfitting your funky bachelor or bachelorette groove-time pad

Slate Design

www.slatedesign.com

This site has a limited product range, but you won't find these products anywhere else. Each piece is made to order, and can be customized to fit your dimensions. Payment is through I-Escrow, which holds on to your money and releases it to the site after you receive the goods.

Totem Design

www.totemdesign.com

Designer sites usually look great but they don't always make using them as simple as it ought to be. Once you've hit the skip intro button, you come to a neat-looking homepage where, alas, it is all too easy to miss the product list, the virtual showroom and, indeed, the gift shop. And where is the shipping or return policy? Shopping is secure and there are some lovely things to buy, but more clarity in navigation would help enormously. The online catalog was being updated when we dropped in to pay our respects.

Accessories From Czech chandeliers to Greek rugs

Americana from the Heart

www.americanafromtheheart.com

Fans of handmade Americana crafts will love this site, which is heavy on that apple/angel/bear/flag/cherry imagery synonymous with this style. There are lots of items that can be customized; you can even have an object you already own painted in one of the designs. Some products are available in limited quantities only. Shipping is free, and prices are pretty competitive. If you're not a fan and you end up here by some virtual detour, you may find the products affect your digestion rather than your heart.

Andy Designs

www.andydesigns.com

You can buy the award-winning Flex Vase (if you don't know, you have to see it to get it) through this site, as well as several other unique takes on everyday objects such as letter-openers and CD racks. The selection is small, but each object has an explanation of its origins and the Flex Vase has complete instructions and design ideas. Prices and shipping are reasonable.

Angela Adams

www.angelaadams.com

Capitalizing on the current trend for retro graphics in muted shades of beige and grey from the 50s and 60s, this site offers rugs, accessories and furniture in this style. Prices are high, but each piece is made with care. Shipping info was a bit scant, but the site looked fabulous.

Blue Ridge Gypsy Studio
www.blueridgegypsy.com
A small product range that features handmade goods, most of which are decorated with decoupage, painted or hand-embroidered. Fire screens, pillows, plates, trays etc can also be customized to suit your décor. The site's design could use some attention, but otherwise the navigation and ordering is quite straightforward.

Bordure
www.bordure.com
You will find a fine collection of high-quality handcrafted work on offer here. Ordering information is clearly explained, and the biography of the artists is an interesting read, if a bit eye-straining due to the small white type. Some lovely items are available, but as most are made to order, you might have to wait 8 weeks for delivery.

Bottaro-Skolnick
www.bottaro-skolnickonline.com
This site features a small selection of traditional accessories and lamps plus some furniture from its offline store. An eclectic mix of items is offered at below list price. Sale items may be discounted by as much as 30 per cent.

Brass'n'More
www.aimhi.com/~mca
The "more" certainly doesn't refer to site design. The ultimate "what you see is what you get" site, this opens with a list of products which runs all the way from bookends to hurricane lamps. You can't order directly through the site: you have to phone, so take that opportunity to reconsider.

Angela Adams taps into the trend for 50s and 60s retro. If you want to be big in beige, look no further

Buybuzz

www.buybuzz.com

Another community site bringing together many e-tailers in a one-stop format. Specializing in an Asian theme, you can search either by country of origin or category. Cart contents are displayed continuously. Other features include articles are on decorating and an "Ask the expert" section. Unlike some similar sites, Buybuzz handles the financial transactions, taking the risk out of dealing with different merchants, and ordering couldn't be easier.

Carlson Bay

www.carlsonbay.com

Here you can combine decorating your home with a creative project to keep the kids occupied on a rainy day. The pots, urns, bowls and candle holders are lovely in themselves and come in several styles, from classic to southwestern. But they are also suitable for decorating, and this site provides plenty of step-by-step projects such as painting and decoupage to turn the items into personalized objets d'art. Prices are low and shipping free.

Chiasso

www.chiasso.com

Not a massive product range for the home, but these designer goods should look at home in any loft or contemporary house. Clean, spare and simple, the prices aren't bad, nor are the shipping costs. You can even register for your wedding list here. A word of warning: the procession of products across the middle of the homepage can have a powerfully hypnotic effect.

Danforth Pewterers

www.danforthpewter.com

If your image of pewter is of the tarnished tankard engraved with your initials you got when you were a babe – well, this site will surprise you. Pewter can be gorgeous and elegant but you probably have to see it to believe it. The shiny bowls, pepper mills and napkin rings will convince you that you were meant to have pewter in your home. As far as we know, the site has nothing to do with J Danforth Quayle.

Earth Spirits

https://earthspirits.safeserver.com

Creating harmony in your house is the principle here, with furniture, accessories and artwork to improve the flow of energy throughout your home. For example,

How lucid are your dreams? How lucid are you when you're not dreaming? You need a Zen alarm clock from Earth Spirits

the intriguing Zen alarm clock will gently wake you, allowing you to develop something called "lucid dreaming", especially desirable for those of us who aren't lucid even when awake. Shipping is free in the continental US.

E-clectics
http://store.yahoo.com/eclectics2000
This much-improved site has some interesting and unusual items that you never knew you needed. Kids and pets get their own section and if you have both, the Feng Shui section will get your house back in balance. Shipping costs can be steep and is not calculated until the very latest stage of ordering.

El Paso Rug and Import
http://elpasorug.com
There are so many great southwestern products available here that with just a bit more effort this site would be a real winner. You can find your way around easily enough and the photos are clear, but there is minimal description of the products and of the craftspeople that make them. The functional stuff (shipping costs) isn't worked out until you start to order. You could always call, but that kind of defeats the convenience of ordering online.

Fuzzy Pink
www.fuzzypink.com
Despite its name and girlie homepage, this site has a number of normal accessories as well as a few that definitely fall under the kitsch label. Not a huge selection, but items are added every couple of weeks to encourage repeat visits. Worth a look for something a little bit off the wall.

Gorgeous Interior Designs
www.gorgeousdesigns.com
This site has plenty of lovely things to decorate your home, from unusual salt shakers to Asian lanterns, and items like silk flowers and garlands that you

can use to make your own decorations. Decorating themes and hints are available. Links to other sites that sell complementary items are helpfully illustrated with the actual product, a very generous feature for the shark infested world that is commercial cyberspace these days.

Home and Dreams

www.homeandreams.com

This unusual site has some unique features which make ordering fun. The products for sale are different in themselves – plaster architectural wall accessories. The screen shows a photo of a decorated room: move the cursor over the picture and click on the items you are interested in. There is also a mix and match section, allowing you to see, for example, various mirrors on different fireplaces. The room settings really make the products come alive.

Home Comforts

www.homecomfortshop.com

This site could win an award for clarity in displaying its merchandise, offering a straightforward scroll down page with the items displayed one after the other. There's a decorating ideas page full of common sense advice. Less clear is some of the type (tiny grey type on a grey and white marble background – hmmm) and info on delivery costs and returns.

Do your bit for the environment and create a natural, calming atmosphere in your home with products made entirely from reclaimed materials, sold by Natural Spaces

Hudson Home
www.hudsonhome.com
This clean-looking site has a limited selection of quality Americana-style accessories, rather than the usual homemade-looking stuff. Clear instructions make this site a breeze to use and shipping is free.

Natural Spaces
http://store.yahoo.com/naturalspaces
All the objects from this site are made from recycled glass, reclaimed wood, reused industrial parts and many other discarded items. Bed linens are made with untreated cotton and natural dyes. The glass products look fantastic. Buy from here and feel you're doing your bit to save the world.

Pierre Deux
www.pierredeux.com
This gorgeous online site is as elegant as the well-known offline shops. Using many old fabric patterns from Provence, this shop has built a lovely collection of desk accessories, pillows and bags. Also on offer are a selection of French dinnerware and other accent pieces. One of the few e-commerce sites which will pass on your details to other companies, as well as get in touch with you by phone or e-mail, unless you expressly tell them not to.

Roots Home and Garden
www.rootshomeandgarden.com
Provincetown, on the tip of Cape Cod in Massachusetts, has a long history of attracting artists and craftspeople. This online shop sells home accessories handcrafted by local artists. The site design is rather sterile considering the homey items for sale and it doesn't bring across the funky atmosphere of P'town, but it's well worth a visit for some authentic New England goods.

Sea Level Online
www.sealevelonline.com
The lovingly crafted homepage should probably be understood as an exercise in post-modern irony. Among the nautical bric-a-brac on show here are bellpulls, dolphins (statues of), lighthouses and papier maché angel fish. You wouldn't exactly call this quality art, but the colorful items may just fulfil that gift need. Shipping and return policies are not easily accessed.

Widerview Village
www.widerview.com
This umbrella site is host to several themed specialty stops making up a virtual village selling cottagey accessories and furniture. A brief description on the homepage lets you know what's inside each store, and a click will get you in. Similar design keeps the shops cohesive, and descriptive product entries and good photography is always reassuring. Lots of desirable items to tempt you. Shipping is free on orders over $100.

Jewelry & watches

Easier than trudging the streets, but can any computer screen stir the soul like a jeweler's window?

Body jewelry

More holes than Swiss cheese

Amber Moon

www.amber-moon.com

Based in Australia, Amber Moon holds an extensive collection of body jewelry. You could have anything from a dolphin to a butterfly or an UV glitter-ball sprouting from your navel. Prices range from $9 to $20 depending on how ornate your choice is, and worldwide shipping is set at $3. Each picture can be enlarged, but most useful are the dimensions alongside each item so you should manage to get the perfect-fitting banana bell. If you don't know what that is, you shouldn't be reading this review.

Body Jewelry

www.bodyjewelry.com

This site's gothic backdrop and busy homepage may have you thinking of looking elsewhere for your body-piercing needs but persevere. The imaginatively titled Body Jewelry has a huge selection of studs, barbells, chains, rings and banana bells, jeweled, gold and titanium to choose from. Prices start at around $15 up to $150 for your deluxe gold number. Pictures can be enlarged and although the descriptions are limited there's only so much you can say about filling holes in your body.

Sozra

www.sozra.com

Gold too common for you? Silver too flimsy and platinum too expensive? Then try niobium. Sozra currently sells a limited, if unusual selection of ear-cuffs and other jewelry items, in one of the world's newest precious metals. Prices range from $5 to $30 and shipping is a bargain at $3.

Got it? Flaunt it. Not got it? Browse for it

A Bird Named Dog
www.abirdnameddog.com
You don't get any more novel than jewelry made from bones. Whether these belonged to dog or bird isn't specified. Easy to navigate, the site includes bohemian glass, freshwater pearls and turquoise as well as bone items. Each image can be enlarged, and prices range from $20 for earrings to $500 for a glass leaf necklace. The descriptions are poor for such novel accessories, however, especially the reasoning behind such extravagance for glass, but if you want something a bit unusual, A Bird Named Dog should assist.

Art de Corps
www.ArtdeCorps.com
Art de Corps sells a range of fun, handcrafted jewelry. The site may be rudimentary but the hand-patterned range – made of the finest metals, antique and contemporary glass, gemstones and pearls – is well designed and reasonably priced around the $60-$80 mark. Ordering is simple, shipping is cheap at $5 and they point out sales tax where applicable. A useful site for something a little funky.

Art Wild
www.artwild.com
Make your own jewelry from Art Wild's selection of funky beads. Choose from giraffe and leopard animal prints, floral patterns and even nautical designs. Beads are priced at 25 to 50 cents; they also sell complete kits. Discounts apply with bulk buys, and shipping is $3.60. The site is easy to navigate with clear pictures, but the design lacks inspiration. Worth a look.

Ashford
www.ashford.com
Search for jewelry by brand (including Whitney Boin, Catherine Iskiw and Bojangles), price, item and even gender. Enlarged images and detailed descriptions are available and you seem to get value for money. Some of the more unusual items on sale here include vintage Rolex watches from the 20s to the 70s – great if you can afford them.

ANDREA RENEE

If you think celebrities only wore jewelry they were given by Harry Winston and the like, you are wrong. Thanks to this Soho-based store, you can look like your favorite celebrity, or at least have matching jewelry. Designer Andrea Renee is particularly proud of her celebrity customers with a wall of Hollywood thanks and autographs to prove it, and each piece of jewelry is identified according to who's worn it this season.

You could match necklaces and hair accessories to Liv Tyler, Madonna, or even Lenny Kravitz. The jewelry is unusual, rhinestones and flowers everywhere, and considering the star status, prices aren't bad at $50 to $150. So keep it a secret and make your friends jealous.

---

www.andrearenee.com

Christian Bernard
www.christian-bernard.com
Christian Bernard of Paris sells globe-trotting jewelry, with Tanzanite from Tanzania, Colombian emeralds, and pink and yellow sapphires. Considering their unusual nature, prices are competitive (between $150 and $1,000 plus).

De Beers
www.adiamondisforever.com
Although you can't buy online here, if you are thinking of buying a diamond engagement ring, this is an essential stop. You can design your own ring, and De Beers will help you plan that perfect surprise (for your bank manager).

Jewelryland
www.jewelry-land.com
Jewelryland buys from pawnshops and estate sales, with up to 70 per cent discounts on many items. It's stylish and easy to search by product or price, but they could use more items on offer. Descriptions are limited, but images can be enlarged. Good for the more traditional designs.

 Watches **Don't be seen with a naked wrist in public**

G Shock
www.gshock.com
The flash graphics and skaters soundtrack suit the makers of the toughest watch in the world very well. Select from G-Shock, Baby G, Pathfinders and limited editions, priced from between $99 and $250 for your unbreakable, water-resistant, James Bond-style gadget watches. Ordering is simple.

Storm
www.storm-watches.com
This site appears to feature the entire Storm collection. Costing anything from $100 to $200, they're not cheap but you may pick up something more unusual than from your local department store. The site is relatively dull compared to the stainless steel sci-fi watches to be found inside.

Techno Marine
www.technomarine.com
Buying a Techno Marine watch is buying a lifestyle, or so their website would have you believe. The extensive range of sturdy watches for sturdy men and women has something for every occasion and offers guidance about what to do when as you can't possibly wear an evening watch to the gym. Prices range from $200 to $2,500 for the Techno Millennium White Diamond watch, containing a 1.1 carat revolving diamond bezel. Not sure about the pink strap though. Ordering is simple. Allow up to 6 days for shipping.

Magazines

Whether you're looking
for a publication about
crochet or something more
obscure, you'll find it on the Net

1000 Magazines.com

www.1000magazines.com

1000Magazines claims its prices are so low, the publishers won't let them sell
their titles any cheaper. This plain and simple site is justly proud of its low
overheads ("You won't see our commercials during the Super Bowl,"
it says) and its homepage instantly shows how it passes the fruits of its
frugality on to customers with 84 per cent off a subscription to *Newsweek*, for
instance. Eight titles in the database had something to do with crochet.

Dr Mag

www.drmag.com

According to Dr Mag there are 11 magazines dedicated to knitting and
crochet. And they're all available from the good doctor, whose specialty is
magazines from around the world. It's great for gift subscriptions (go on, treat
your aunt to 12 issues of *Hooked on Crochet* or maybe the racier
Crochet Fantasy) and each magazine carries clear information beside it on
pricing and the availability of delivery to various countries. If you can't find the
international oddity you're looking for, e-mail Dr Mag and he'll try to find it.

FreeBizMag

www.freebizmag.com

The idea is that you tell the site what business you're in and what you do,
and it comes back and tells you which free business magazines you can,
potentially, receive. We told it we were involved in an editorial capacity in the
IT/Internet and publishing sector and it threw up a disappointing four choices,
one of which was *Travelocity* (the online travel agent's mag) – interesting, but
less than relevant. We then told it we were involved in agriculture and farming
as a therapist and it recommended one magazine: *Travelocity*. Worth a look
to see what freebies you're entitled to. Alas, no free crochet mags on offer.

Magazine City

www.magazinecity.net

The site claims to have the lowest "legitimate" prices on the Web with savings
of up to 90 per cent – and if you find a magazine cheaper elsewhere, it will

MAGAZINES ON THE NET

Some magazines make all or some of their content available online, while others generate new material. Try keying in your favorite magazine after www. followed by .com and there's a fair chance it will take you to the online incarnation. The magazine's own site will nearly always give details of subscriptions and sometimes let you subscribe direct from the site.

There is also a virtual stack of e-zines on the Internet that don't exist in printed form. Here are a couple of the best:

Salon is justly famous. Although it has fallen on harder times of late, it's still the nearest thing we have to an online *Vanity Fair*. Its range is astonishing – from the minutiae of technology to compulsive vignettes of life. Recommended. *www.salon.com*

The Onion is famous for the sharpness of its wit and satirical send-ups, and it will hopefully again reach the amusing heights that it did following Clinton's impeachment. *www.theonion.com*

match it. A good cross-section of titles grace the homepage. It also attempts to package sets of magazines to cater for a specific lifestyle. The Fashion Plate, for instance, comprises a packaged subscription to *Vogue*, *Elle* and *Harper's Bazaar* for $42, while It's A Guy Thing nets you *Maxim*, *Stuff* and *Gear* for just $36. Clever marketing it may be, but it's also pretty good value. Database includes 6 of the best titles about crochet.

Magazine Zone
www.magazine.com
At the Magazine Zone "it's twilight on high subscription prices". If you can bear to get past its opening gambit, there are bargains to be had here with more "lowest prices". You can search by category or browse a simulated newsstand. The latter takes a while to download. A staggering 18 mentions of crochet here, including the niche publication for fans of classic crochet, *Old Time Crochet*.

Mags To Go
www.magstogo.com
The discounts on offer here are not as dramatic as at some of the other sites, but with up to 50 per cent off newsstand prices it's still worth visiting. It certainly has one of the fastest magazine search facilities. Click MagResource to be taken to its rare or special interest magazine finder. Only two crochet mags to go, though.

Yahoo Auctions
http://list.auctions.yahoo.com/21884-category.html?alocale=0us
There were around 900 magazines up for auction when we visited, the highlight being a New Zealand issue of the *Listener* attracting a bid of $26 with three days to go, thanks to an interview with Russell Crowe. You have to register to take part (this will only take a few minutes) and be sure to read the terms and conditions before you dive in with your bid. Timeless classics up for grabs as this review went to press included a 1962 copy of *Life* with Lucille Ball on the cover and a 1977 *TV Guide* featuring "The Farrah Phenomenon" – going, going but not quite gone for $9.99. To cap it all, there was a copy of the seminal *Danish Petite Crochet*, on the market for just $1.

Motorbikes

Head out on the information superhighway and you can do everything from browse for gear to buy a bike or book an on-road vacation

Accessories — Helmets, parts, people to ride pillion

Motorcycle Superstore
www.motorcycle-superstore.com
This site is a biker's dream. You're unlikely to find a more comprehensive store anywhere else, as it stocks everything for dirt, street and even snow biking. Prices for jackets, footwear and helmets – and also for more casual wear when the bike's in the garage – depend upon the brand. Jackets, for example, are priced between $200 and $500. Brands include Alpinestars, Answer and No Fear. The women's section is fairly limited, and the images could certainly be improved, but overall this is a great starting point for your biking essentials, even down to radiator water bottles.

Motorcycle USA
www.motorcycleusa.com
Exhausts, handlebars, stands, ramps and even fuel cans are sold on this site. If your bike is lacking a few essential items, or you're just not happy with the top of the range Kawasaki fish-tail exhaust you bought last month, Motorcycle USA offers an extensive collection to suit most needs and tastes. If your own appearance is a higher priority than what you are riding, this site holds dirt and street apparel, including goggles, helmets and jackets. Ordering is easy, with shipping charges based on how much and where the items are going.

MotorSport Warehouse
www.sdmsw.com
Browse through the collection of tires, exhausts and clothing, or simply type in what you're looking for. All the information you'll need is included on the same page, with images, brief descriptions, shipping times and charges, although most items are shipped for free. There's also a parts service and a technical bulletin board; add the bonus of discounts on all products, and this site adds up to a very useful stopping point.

HARLEY-DAVIDSON

Orange County
Harley-Davidson

Don't get too excited. Although this Irvine, California site has an impressive array of genuine Harley bikes, you can't as yet buy them online. You'll have to make do with browsing the collection and sending an e-mail enquiry.

What you can buy here, however, are Harley gifts and collectibles, clothing (including steel-toe-capped boots for $150), parts and accessories to customize your tired old Suzuki. You can also enquire about renting a late-model bike from this approved dealership.

---

www.ocharleydavidson.com

 Bikes Before you empty your wallet...

Boss Hoss Direct
www.bosshossdirect.com
Despite the fabulous name, Boss Hoss can only muster a limited range of both new and used motorcycles. The information is on an e-mail basis, with only images and prices to work from. On the plus side, if you do find something and can already feel the wind in your hair, only a standard set of questions stand between you and that $35,000 bike.

Britalia
www.britalia.com
This California-based site offers both new and used motorcycles, accessories and apparel by all the usual top names. The catalog is extensive but the amount of info provided is superficial to say the least. The best you can say about this site is the pictures are clear.

Power Sports
www.epowersports.com
One of the few sites that sells motorbikes online, Power Sports boasts a selection of sport, dirt and street bikes, watercrafts and scooters that any offline store would be envious of. Full descriptions are available, complete with financing options, and there are shipping quotations to anywhere in the world.

 **On and off the road**

Edelweiss Bike Travel
www.edelweissbiketravel.com
Edelweiss runs an international operation, but the American tours should keep you amused for a few summers yet. The adventures offered include the Grand Canyon, Yellowstone Park, Royal California and Smoky Mountain Scouting. Before you book you can read up on the sights to see, the prices and the day-by-day itinerary. You can book online, right down to the BMW bike you would like to ride the open road on, plus the biker T-shirt of your choice. There's also a useful section providing heaps of information about the company itself as well as the CVs of the tour guides.

Movies & DVD

Let the Web help you buy cult horror classics (*Stuart Little*), top documentaries (*Dr Goldfoot And The Girl Bombs*) or the big blockbusters (*Howard The Duck*)

General Mainstream movies and a cast of thousands

AV Bandit
www.avbandit.com
Excellent and easy-to-use site with terrific prices and outstanding specials. Set up a wish list for future purchases or be really mercenary and alert your nearest and dearest of your entertainment wants. The films come with a star rating, review and cast list plus info about the key stars. A Shipping Calculator can be accessed from your shopping cart page, and there are 7 different methods of delivery. One of them is bound to work.

Big Star
www.bigstar.com
Big Star bills itself as The Superstar Moviestore and for once the hyperbole is deserved. There's a huge selection of old and new movies to buy on video and DVD and prices are excellent, with many videos at under $10 and DVDs under $20. There's also plenty of movie news, interviews with film stars and savvy reviews of the latest releases. A choice of standard (3-7 business days) or the slightly misleading overnight (2-3 business days) shipping, with costs depending on whether you are ordering videos or DVDs. Check the incredibly thorough customer service pages for current rates.

Critics Choice Video
www.ccvideo.com
More than 61,000 movie titles are available here, from the rare (check out the Hard To Find section for some truly obscure titles) to the latest blockbuster

Movies & DVD

releases. There's even a section on British video for all you Monty Python fans (we know you're out there). The site runs regular specials and prices on most items are keen. Parcel Post delivery to the 48 contiguous states is free or you can pay $13.95 for overnight FedEx. For the good folk of Alaska and Hawaii, there's the usual penalty ($6.95 in this case).

Film International
www.filminternational.com
One of those sites which has a blank outer homepage whose only purpose seems to be that it adds a few seconds onto the average time spent on the site by every visitor. But don't be put off. This is a fantastic site and a wonderful resource. When you get to the real homepage, it's refreshing to see a couple of foreign language films featured on the homepage alongside the usual blockbusters, if only as a reminder that there is a film industry beyond Hollywood. Search by keywords, full title or country (although we wouldn't advise the latter). Even the "If you like this, you'll like…" option isn't utterly fatuous (as it is on most sites). Shipping charges are reasonable but there are so many options that you'll have to check the help section for full details.

Mr. Benson's World of Home Entertainment
www.bensonsworld.co.uk
You can search through the 25,000 or so titles on this entertaining site, or just browse the categories to see what takes your fancy. There are some interesting film choices highlighted on the homepage – when visited it featured the 1922 Inuit documentary *Nanook of the North*, and the World Cinema category has films in Mandarin, Farsi, Bengali and Welsh. There's plenty for the blockbuster fan, too. The site is based in the UK so you need to contact them direct for international shipping costs. Remember that videos bought abroad often have a different format and may well not work on your system, and that DVD has gotta be code-free.

Reel.com
www.reel.com
Much more than just a place to buy videos and DVDs, this site contains extensive and well-informed articles and reviews about movies in particular and the film industry in general. The Advanced Search facility is terrific if you sort of know the film you're looking for but can't quite remember the title, and you can subscribe to a newsletter if you want to be kept up to date with new releases. The prices are average, but they do have regular specials that can

really help you save some money. The shipping charges are calculated for you at the checkout and will, of course, depend on the size of your order.

Used Movies
www.usedmovies.com
If you're looking to save some serious money, this will be the site for you, with its huge range of "previously viewed" movies on sale at prices starting at just $3.25. All tapes are guaranteed to be genuine copies, clean and free from defects, and the site also stocks brand new tapes if you don't like the idea of secondhand. There's flat rate of $4.95 for shipping up to 9 videos, but if you order 10 or more, delivery is free.

Video Varieties
www.videovarieties.com
Despite the hectic homepage, this is a good place to search for DVDs and videos at good prices. Browsing is made more fun by the selection of movie-related articles (when we looked they had a great list of the stupidest movie lines ever) and lively message boards. A variety of shipping options are available and the cost is calculated for you at the checkout.

And there's more...
All the websites below sell a range of films on video and DVD, as well as other items like books and CDs. Their catalogs may not be as extensive as the above sites (although they will still offer more than the usual mainstream fare), but these well-known names are worth checking out. You may, for example, feel that you're better off dealing with an online store you've already bought other goods from.

Amazon	www.amazon.com
Blockbuster	www.blockbuster.com
Tower Records	www.towerrecords.com
Videomatica	www.videomatica.com

 For the "cognoscenti"

The American Film Foundation
www.americanfilmfoundation.com
The Foundation creates and sells videos of independent features and shorts, plus documentaries on a wide range of subjects which often pop up as Oscar nominations. It's a great site to find stuff you'd never see down at your local video store, and the Foundation itself is worth supporting for its work with up-and-coming filmmakers. Shipping costs start at $5.

Christian Cinema

www.christiancinema.com

Wide selection of movies on video dealing with Christian themes, with thrillers and high drama included alongside the more obvious titles about teens trying to preserve their virginity. You can order online or by phone or fax and there's a flat $5 charge per order, no matter what the size. Goods should arrive within 3-5 business days.

Creepy Classics Video

www.abulsme.com/creepy

Tucked in among the US horror convention information and gruesome movie trivia, there is a charming little store selling copies of cult classics like *Gamma People* from 1958 and *Macabre Serenade* from 1968. If you buy 5 titles, you'll get the 6th one free. There's no shopping cart, just an online order form to fill out, so you may prefer to phone your card details through. Priority mail shipping costs $5 no matter what the size of your order and takes 2-4 days.

Family Wonder

www.familywonder.com

No slasher flicks or full-frontal nudity here, just good wholesome entertainment you can enjoy with everyone from your three-year-old nephew to Grandma. The site's store is usefully split into appropriate age categories, and there is even a Movie Mom reviewer who rates theater releases for kid-viewing suitability. But it's not all adorable talking animals and mushy stuff – there are genuine classics here like *12 Angry Men*, as well as great adventure movies like the Indiana Jones series. Shipping is via FedEx 3-day service and costs $3.85 per order plus 99 cents per item, or for last-minute shoppers there's a Premium service for $8 per order plus $2.95 per item.

The rating system can be misleading, so for mom-approved movies check out Family Wonder and sit back and enjoy

Rare Reels
www.rarereels.com
This site specializes in hard-to-find movies on tape and DVD, either new or used. The catalog is not extensive (the silent movies section only listed 2 titles) but you can e-mail them for a specific title and they will do their best to track a (legal) copy down.

Science Fiction Continuum
www.sfcontinuum.com
"Where reality hits the road" is the tag line of this site, and it's not wrong. *Dr Goldfoot and the Girl Bombs* is just one of the joys to be found in the fab B-movies area after you've perused the usual sci-fi fare and UFO documentaries. Standard shipping costs $4.50 for the first item, plus $1.50 for each subsequent title.

TLA Video
www.tlavideo.com
This Philadelphia-based store sells all the usual titles, plus a hefty section of gay and lesbian film and video (including a page of lesbian vampire films). Classics like *Desert Hearts* are here, along with more up-to-date issue movies like *If These Walls Could Talk*.

Viaduc Video
www.viaducvideo.com
If you want to dazzle your peers with your knowledge of Euro culture, visit this European documentary video site with films in English, German or French. Check very carefully that the format you buy works on your VCR or life could turn ugly. Prices are in French francs and Euros, but your credit card can do the math. Shipping charges are calculated before you buy.

Vintage Video
www.vintagevideocanada.com
Canada's other great contribution to cinematic history (after Mike Myers and Dan Aykroyd). Among the movie memorabilia, you'll also find lists of long deleted titles like *Night of the Creeps*, at only slightly inflated prices.

Westerns
www.westerns.com
Roy Rogers and Tex Ritter feature heavily in the Trading Post section of this tribute site for classic Westerns. Many of the titles are pretty obscure, so if you've been hunting a copy of *The Gay Amigo*, you're going to be very happy.

COLLECTING

Building a movie collection is a serious business that can take over your life, not to mention your living room. What you need is some friendly guidance on which movies are worth buying to keep and which are only good for the occasional viewing on TV. So before you rush out to buy an expensive DVD, check out the websites below for a bit of movie fan advice and insider gossip. There are also some great links that can take you straight to movie shopping sites.

Ain't It Cool News
www.aintitcoolnews.com

Film.com
www.film.com

The Internet Movie Database
www.imdb.com

Movies.go.com
www.movies.go.com

My Movies
www.mymovies.net

Museum shops

Desperately seeking an Egyptian
hippopotamus (ornament, that is)?
Some freeze-dried astronaut food?
Or maybe a thermowave wireless
weather station (only $129)? What
luck! You've come to the right place...

Adler Planetarium

www.adlerplanetarium.org

All the standard categories are covered here: clothing, jewelry, books and
novelty items. The selection is limited but does include some fab star-gazing
equipment, such as the Tabletop 76 telescope for $150. If this is a little out
of your price range, the *Star & Planet Guide* will guide you through the stars
for only $13 and that's just one of a whole range of educational books being
offered here. If you're looking for something for the kids other than the latest
Pokémon kit, you could always opt for the Climbatron robot or a pair of funky
space slippers. Something for all ages.

Guggenheim New York

www.guggenheim.org

Thanks to the Guggenheim store you can turn your own home into a work
of modern art. Suitably sophisticated, the site itself is enjoyable to search
with clear categories and customer service area, enlarged images and easy
ordering facilities. Best buys include art books and prints, but the store also
holds more unusual collectible items such as Venetian masks for $175 and
jewelry from the Van Gogh collection (including earrings!) starting at $15.

Metropolitan Museum of Modern Art

www.metmuseum.org

Slightly pricier than your average tourist haven, the Met offers a host of
beautiful accessories for yourself and your home. Tasteful ornaments range
from an Egyptian hippopotamus, or William to his friends, for $50 or a Degas
dancer for a little short of $300. Jewelry-wise you can choose to go down
the Roman decadence route with a garnet ring for around $250, or the less
ornate Cypriot-style items for around $350. Discounts are available if you
become a member, ranging from associate status for $45 to a patron for
a mere $6,000. The 10 per cent discount applies to both.

Museum Shop
www.museumshop.com
The Museum Shop is designed to both provide you with a larger array of cultural items, and provide extra funds to museum exhibitions around the world. The store currently has 40 museums working with the scheme, from the Corcoran in Washington DC to the British Museum in London. The catalog contains more than 3,500 items, with prices ranging from around $35 for a replica Staffordshire plate to $700 for a Head of Aphrodite. You can search by museum, artist or period. A perfect overview of the cultural world.

Rock And Roll Hall of Fame
www.rockhall.com
You obviously can't buy any of the immortalized guitars and drum kits on display in the Hall of Fame, so you'll just have to make do with the usual array of tourist souvenirs. Choose from rock 'n' roll sweatshirts for $50 or that essential rock item, the denim jacket for $85. The best items can be found in the novelty section with harmonicas and CD wallets at under 10 bucks.

Smithsonian Store
www.smithsonianstore.com
From here you can browse the stores of the National Air & Space Museum, the National Museum of Natural History, and the National Museum of American History. Each store is tailored to represent the respective collections, and we're not just talking about mugs and T-shirts. Top finds include kites, model aircraft and walking robots, and a thermowave wireless weather station, whatever that may be, for $129.

Taos Museums
www.taosmuseums.org
You should be able to find some thing from the Taos organization to suit your taste, as their list of contributors ranges from La Hacienda de Los Martinez to the Millicent Rogers museum. Choose from southwest artifacts, such as handmade red willow baskets for $200, or functional art in the form of mosaic Kleenex boxes for $90. Each item comes with a full description of the artist and their inspiration. Prices are quite steep and delivery could take as long as three weeks, but you're paying for art and handmade artifacts rather than run-of-the-mill Perspex numbers.

The Tech Museum of Innovation
www.thetech.org
If the museum is half as good as the online store, it must be brilliant. Choose from techie gifts to robot kits and educational toys for all ages. Worth a look simply for the novelty aspect as you're not likely to find crystal-growing kits, Intel Bunny People, freeze-dried astronaut food or a Super Sonic Slinger in your local Toys R Us. Ordering is simple, prices are good considering what you're getting, and only the very brief descriptions let the site down.

Music

From guitars to zithers, from
Rachmaninov to Roy Rogers,
from mikes to Moogs, it's all here

Instruments Born to play the noseflute?

Guitar Xpress
www.guitarxpress.com
Acoustic and electric guitars and basses, plus amps and other accessories
from top manufacturers are all here at a discount. Some items tell you to call
for the price as the manufacturers will not let the lowest price be advertised
on the Net, and you need to speak to them for the best deals. There are also
playing tips on the site so you can instantly start to play like a pro. Possibly.

House of Musical Traditions
www.hmtrad.com
Lovely Washington DC-based online store offering great selection of unusual
musical instruments from around the world. Decorated mandolins and zithers
rub shoulders with noseflutes and panpipes. DC area residents can also sign
up for lessons in their chosen instrument. There's a secure order form, with
a shopping cart system promised. Shipping is via UPS and starts at $7, but
the cost will depend on whether you're after some bagpipes or a harmonica.

Lone Star Percussion
www.lonestarpercussion.com
Buy yourself a drum kit and be the lone star in your bedroom. Whether you're
looking for a set of timpani or a triangle, this is the place to come for things
to hit with sticks (they sell the sticks too). The site is on the sparse side – you
could have crossed Texas in the time it took to download for us and the order
form is basic – but the selection and prices are worth checking out. Shipping
starts at $8 plus the obligatory surcharge for Alaska and Hawaii.

Music 123.com
www.music123.com
Great authorized-dealer site to browse, whether you're looking for electric,
electronic or good old-fashioned acoustic instruments. Prices are excellent –
we found a Yamaha Marching Mellophone discounted by around $800 – and

the site is easy to find your way around with a good help and advice section (including a live online chat facility). Most items, barring such things as mouthpieces and sheet music, come with a 30-day return policy, and shipping costs are calculated for you before you order.

Nova Musik
www.novamusik.com
This vast electronic musical equipment site has everything from recorders to software, mikes to Moogs. There are some real bargains to be had in the used equipment section too. Shipping charges are based on the actual product weight and all items are returnable as new within 7 days for a full refund.

Plowsharing Crafts
www.plowsharing.org
This site also features craft items from all over the world but the music section is a treasure trove, with a selection of African and Indian drums, pan flutes from Peru and gongs from Cameroon. You also get the pleasure of knowing your purchase is directly helping Third World artisans. No shopping cart yet.

Sam Ash
www.samash.com
This online arm of "The World's Favorite Music Store" offers not only a huge range of instruments and music equipment, but also comprehensive advice and tips on getting the best out of your purchase. The call center is staffed by fellow musicians, music producers and DJs, and a classified section will help you hook up with likeminded music-makers. There are some serious deals to be had and you can choose an express delivery to speed things up.

Yamaha
www.yamaha.com
Not an online store, more a fancy sales brochure for Yamaha's acoustic and electronic musical instruments from portable keyboards to euphoniums. E-mail for further details, look up the nearest dealer, or just check out prices to compare with your local retailer.

 **You can download this too**

All Music
www.a-zmusic.com
If you're looking for something different, or you play an unusual instrument, this is *the* place for sheet music. Specialising in ethnic and folk tunes, you'll definitely find something to add to your repertoire. When we checked, there were 693 folk pieces suitable to play on the balalaika, for example. Shipping is via US mail (regular or priority) and starts at $2.45.

G&S Works Inc.

www.gsworks.com

If you have a deep-seated yearning to be a Pirate of Penzance but lack the resources of the D'Oyly Carte Opera Company, this site can provide scaled-down scores of Gilbert and Sullivan classics for small theatre companies and bands. You can attempt *HMS Pinafore* with just 7 musicians (and presumably even fewer sailors), and there's a list of companies who have successfully used the scores. At present only 4 of the operettas are available, but the plan is to have all 12 within the next couple of years. E-mail through the site for rates and further details.

Music Mart, Inc.

www.musicmart.com

A couple of minutes' perusal of the slightly hectic homepage reveals that this site can supply you with pretty much anything you're after in the sheet music department, from the vocal score for Wagner's *Die Walkyrie*, or a handbell arrangement of *Greensleeves*. The site also sells a selection of cassettes and CDs of backing music for karaoke fans. Shipping costs depend on the size of your order and which service you choose, and are calculated at the checkout.

PIANOLA ROLLS

Proving again that the Net has everything, what about some new music rolls for your pianola? Check out The Keystone Music Roll Company at *www.keystonemusicroll.com* or *www.leedyrolls.com* with its links to The Automated Musical Instrument Collectors Association and The Pianola Institute in England. Other sites are:

Bam Bam Piano Rolls
members.aol.com/BamRolls

Meliora Music Rolls
members.aol.com/meliorarol

New England Music Rolls
members.aol.com/NEMRoll/home.html

QRS Music
www.qrsmusic.com

Sheet Music Now.com

www.sheetmusicnow.com

If you've got Adobe Acrobat you can buy and download sheet music directly from the site, cutting out any tedious waiting around for the mailman. Search by composer or instrument in categories such as classical, jazz, choral or standards, and then follow the step by step instructions and you'll have your music in a trice. Each piece also comes with notes from *Groves Dictionary of Music*. Prices depend on the piece, but there's quite a reasonable selection of freebies on offer too.

Sheet Music Plus

www.sheetmusicplus.com

Bach's greatest hits aren't the only highlights that you can teach yourself to play, badly. Sheet Music Plus boasts the largest collection of sheet music going, with a catalog of more than 350,000 titles, from REM and Bonnie Raitt to Roy Rogers and White Zombie. Prices vary, seemingly with popularity, from $4 to $25. Ordering is simple with numerous shipping and payment options from which to choose.

Net stuff

Thousands of websites say
they can make your surfing
more productive and enjoyable.
But few deliver on the promise

 **Save trees, handwriting and pandas**

Blue Mountain Arts

www.bluemountain.com
Missed someone's birthday? Quick, send an e-card as though that's what you
intended to do all along. Blue Mountain offers a huge range of cartoon cards
to personalize and send, from the silly to the soppy. They even have cards for
events you never knew you had to celebrate, like "Kiss and Make Up Day".

E-Cards

www.e-cards.com
Send an e-postcard to anyone with an Internet account. This site, run by
three Netheads in San Francisco, generates revenue for a variety of wildlife
and ethical charities and many of the cards feature stunning photos of the
natural world, including endangered species and rare flowers. You can also
send video cards if you're feeling really ambitious.

 Redecorate your desktop

Art Museum Screensavers

www.artmuseumscreensavers.com
Screensavers for those of you who are looking for a little sophistication.
Choose from the pre-Raphaelite collection, Klimt, Monet, Ansel Adams
and more. Free demos are available, otherwise it costs $20 for immediate
downloads, and $25 for your own CD.

Celebrity Desktop

www.celebritydesktop.com
Customize your desktop with a favorite screen or sports star. Wallpaper or full

screensavers available, as well as links to many other celebrity sites. It should make coming to work just that bit more bearable.

Screen Savers Bonanza
www.bonanzas.com
This site features in excess of 450 different screensavers for Macs and PCs, all arranged depending on your operating system. Anything you might possibly want, from a tribute to Frank Sinatra to a cube of Egyptian mummies bouncing around your screen, is here. You can also download a free version of WinZip to open the files.

ScreenSeek
www.topfile.com/ss/
The ultimate screensaver directory. Ideal if you prefer to look at a B-52 in the morning, rather than the more common Britney Spears or Brad Pitt.

Software Try, buy, download

Dave Central Shareware Archive
www.davecentral.com
This may sound like someone's dodgy homepage, but it's actually a brilliant portal for finding software downloads for Windows or Linux platforms. Whether you need conferencing software or a graphics package, you'll find something to link to here, with many downloads reviewed by techies.

DemoNet
www.demonet.com
Try before you buy. Many of the 47,000 items of software available here have demonstration versions you can play with before you take the plunge. To keep you informed while you browse, the site also contains updates on the Nasa mission to Mars, and it is planning a new venture, DemoNet TV, which will broadcast information and instructions for all kinds of software.

ZD Net Downloads
www.zdnet.com
Software downloads for Mac, PC and even Palm here. Some are free or costlier options to enhance your computer or just provide you with new games.

FLASH HARRIES

When you're surfing the Net, you'll doubtless find sites, even basic shopping sites, that say they are best viewed with Flash or Shockwave or any of the many video and graphics packages. This can be annoying if you don't have them, but basic versions are available for free. Or, if you're seriously into downloading video and graphics, you might want to buy an upgrade. You can often download the software through the site you're on, but these URLs might help too...

Flash
www.macromedia.com

QuickTime
www.apple.com/quicktime

RealPlayer
www.real.com

Shockwave
www.shockwave.com

Office supplies

Let the Internet be your
very own personal digital
assistant, even if all you really
need are some some padded
envelopes, a rubber stamp
and some more business forms

1-800-Buy-Rack

www.buyrack.com

Office furniture, shelving and other big ticket items at rock bottom prices.
Whether you need a conference table or an industrial workbench, you'll
probably find something here, although the design may not be exactly cutting
edge. There's a discount scheme in operation so the more you buy, the more
you save; orders over $500 are shipped free in 3-5 business days.

Ace Business Cards

www.acebusinesscards.com

Great prices and speedy service on full color business cards. You can e-mail
them your full design, or just some graphics and ask them to complete your
card for you. They also accept designs on disc, and can do postcards and
other printing projects too. There are full instructions on the site about how to
send your information through, as well as a UPS delivery tracker so you can
find out how long it will take to have your new cards ready to hand out.

Acro Office Supply

www.acroos.com

Frequent office-supply buyers will love the user account on this site which
remembers your favorite items so you don't have to search around for them
more than once. For other items there's a speedy search facility, or you can
just browse the 25,000 online products to help make your working life easier.
They can also arrange printing services all online and prices on all items are
usually at a discount to the manufacturer's list price. Orders over $50 are
shipped free via UPS ground.

All Ink

www.all-ink.com

Straightforward site capable of fulfilling all your printer ink cartridge needs

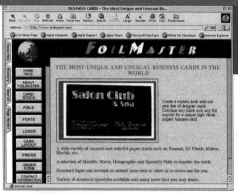

whether color or black and white, for Epson, Brother, Canon, Okidata or Xerox models. Simply select which manufacturer and model you want and you shouldn't be disappointed. Prices are good, up to 70 per cent off the RRP, with free priority delivery.

At Your Office
www.atyouroffice.com
You can stock up on everything from batteries and Post-it notes to break-time refreshments and Bic pens at this suitably well-organized site. Simply select a category to browse through thousands of well-documented items, complete with descriptions and images. The buying process is simple, and orders over $50 are shipped free, otherwise there's a $4.95 charge. Order by 2pm and your box of goodies will be with you the following day.

Dolphin Blue
www.dolphinblue.com
Through Dolphin Blue you can work to keep your business going, and do your bit for the environment. All the paper products here are recycled from a host of materials including denim, hemp and old money bills, and the printer toners and cartridges have been re-manufactured. Generally recycled items are slightly more expensive, but monthly discounts are available and all prices listed include postage and packaging.

Fax Superstore
www.faxsuperstore.com
Setting up any kind of office is an expensive business, so why not try and save by buying your fax machine or copier through this factory-direct, authorized

reseller, which guarantees the lowest price on everything it sells? There are big savings to be made on top brands like Brother, Ricoh and Okidata. Orders received before 2pm Pacific Time are shipped by FedEx the same day.

Foilmaster
www.foilmaster.com
If you think your business card lacks pizazz, why not go for one of Foilmaster's holographic or glitter options? The site contains a choice of layouts, card stock, foils, fonts and colors, so you can build your entire design online and have it printed straight away. You can also send them a copy of your logo for inclusion on your card. All orders cost a flat $5 to deliver within the US.

Home Office Association of America
www.hoaa.com
Nothing specifically to buy except membership, but if you're one of the rapidly growing number of people working from home, this site has a great newsletter with tips about setting up your own business and how to deal with the tax man. If you join the Association, you'll become eligible for their group healthcare plan, a boon if you no longer have an employer to do it for you.

iPrint.com
www.iprint.com
The key to success in business is to make sure you have your details brandished across every bit of paper and piece of cheap plastic you think the average Joe might glance at. Okay, so this isn't necessarily the soundest business advice you'll ever receive, but if you think it might work, iPrint can take care of you. As well as being an online copy and binding store, it can brand business cards, banners and plastic giveaways with your company logo and contact details. The site itself is easy to navigate, with clear instructions and good prices – 250 business cards for less than $20.

Mailing Supplies.com
www.mailingsupplies.com
If you send a lot of bulk mail or parcels, you'll know how enormously frustrating it is not to have the right packaging. Here, there are hundreds of specialist mailing items, from tiny padded bags to mailing list software. It's aimed at businesses so there's no shopping cart facility yet, but you can call them to place an order.

Office Depot
www.officedepot.com
Not only can you buy a vast range of office supplies, equipment and furniture here, you can also get tips on running a small business or managing your money. The Super Values section has some outstanding offers and there's a customer service facility to answer any question you might have about which particular product is best for you. Delivery is free on orders over $50.

SORT OUT YOUR HOME OFFICE

Your work space may currently be nothing more than a shabby, scuffed table in the corner of your living room, but these sites could help you devise a designer home office to be proud of.

Biomorph Interactive Desks
www.biomorphdesk.com
Very groovy, space-age computer and office furniture for the 21st century.

Body Bilt Chairs
www.bodybiltchairs.com
Custom-made ergonomic seating for aching backs.

Computer Furniture
www.computer-furniture.com
Great prices on a range of desks and chairs.

Desks by Design
www.desksbydesign.com
Hide the clutter of a modern office, including all the wires and computer peripherals, in a top-of-the-range, custom-built desk.

Soho
www.sohoaccess.com
Stylish, modular office furniture with a useful room-planning feature for awkward spaces.

Office Max

www.officemax.com

If you buy a lot of stuff it's worth registering with this site. It has regular offers and deals that are restricted to members only, and these could save you some cash and earn you frequent flyer miles. The stock list is extensive but mainstream, so if you're in a hurry, know what you want and it's not too obscure, this is as good a site as any.

Office Products

www.officeproducts.com

This portal site features links to websites for many leading manufacturers and sellers of top brand office supplies and equipment. The site also has articles on which products are best suited to your needs and a lively virtual business community forum for when you're feeling a bit lonely and want to start a lively conversation about paperclips.

Staples

www.staples.com

Online arm of the office-supply giant featuring all the usual great deals on everything under the sun for your office, whether it's a new battery pack for your PDA or a stack of paper towels for the restroom. The site has a useful zip code facility that lets you know if the item you're after is available for immediate delivery to your area, which saves waiting around if stuff is out of stock. As with most of the big guys, orders over $50 are shipped free.

Volume Buy

www.volumebuy.com

If you're in no particular rush to stock your office cupboards with new supplies, Volume Buy is the perfect way to keep your overheads to a minimum. Among other things, this group-buying site offers a large selection of office supplies and computer hardware at potentially knock-down prices. Once you've found what you're looking for, you simply decide whether you wish to enter the 5-day or the 7-day pool. In either case the discounts are impressive, with the potential to save hundreds of dollars. All in all, one of the more interesting ways to buy generally dull items.

Outdoors

From ice climbing to ice fishing, it's all happening in the great outdoors. All of which, thanks to the magic power of the Internet, you can access from the not quite so great indoors

Adventure Camping

www.adventure-camping.com

Staying dry and warm is a must when camping and here's the equipment to help you do just that. A good selection of tents, sleeping bags, apparel, backpacks and other equipment will make your campsite a home away from home. Shipping is free and this site couldn't be easier to use.

Arkatents

www.arkatents.com

Another site selling all you need for the outdoor life – sleeping bags and tents, plus bigger items such as boats and rafts. Not the prettiest site on the Web but you get to see what you are buying, and the friendly text is inspirational and fun. Shipping free over $25 within the mainland.

Back Country Experience

www.bcexp.com

This site sells a good selection of hiking equipment, with the benefit of free shipping on orders over $25. Boring design and an annoying catalog system that doesn't use thumbnail pics, but other than that the site is user-friendly.

Backpacker

www.backpacker.com

This online version of *Backpacker* magazine is really *the* site for the hiking and backpacking community. Not only is it jammed full of info about nutrition, technique and nature, but there are listings of trail clubs, events and even webcam links so you can keep tabs on what's happening in the wild even when you're stuck at your desk. The product review section is friendly and an invaluable resource. The site will link you to others that sell the items reviewed, but if it's reading matter you're after, then there's a large selection of nature, travel and adventure books available right here.

Be Outdoors

www.beoutdoors.com

Whether your passion is boating, camping, rowing, flying – or just about any outdoor activity really – this site has it covered. It can't sell you a plane, boat or gun, but it does just about everything else. In fact, it is phenomenal to see the list of things you need. If you thought a good pair of boots and a jacket were about it, think again…

Big Fish

www.bigfishtackle.com

If fly, deep sea, offshore or even ice fishing is your sport, this site will have the tackle and gear you need. A bit fussy and an age to navigate due to the many images on each page, but have patience and you will be rewarded. It is, though, best to have a fairly good idea of what you are looking for. Tips and forum pages are always worth a look.

Birdwatchers

www.birdwatchers.com

Feeders, houses, binoculars, seeds, software, videos and books are available here. The site is as plain and simple as could be. Shipping charges are a mystery, however, and there is a 15 per cent restocking charge on returns.

Blue Ridge Mountain Sports

www.brms.com

This site will link you to the homepages of such companies as Patagonia for outdoor apparel and Old Town Canoe for serious boating equipment. But not all are e-commerce sites. The Blue Mountain Ridge offline stores also rent out gear, and you can find out what and where on this site. It also acts as a resource for hikes within Virginia.

Camp and Ride

www.campandride.com

Bikers who camp have their own requirements, and this site is not only a source of the appropriate gear but an excellent resource for planning a trip. Bike events and clubs, campgrounds and state and national parks are all linked, and the current traffic and road conditions links are invaluable. The design could use some attention, especially the list of products which is hidden at the bottom of the page.

Campman

www.campman.com

This site sells more than just camping equipment. It also has a strong selection of rock and ice climbing and paddling products. It sets itself apart from other sites by choosing specialist items from smaller manufacturers, and keeping the product line updated with best equipment available. Shipping costs are pretty competitive.

Coastline Adventures
www.coastlineadventures.com
This well-organized site is not overflowing with products but they still manage to cover everything, from medical kits to water filters. There's a travel section with a featured adventure trip of the month, and a good section with articles and advice, plus the opportunity for you to add your own experiences.

Cold Spot Feeds
www.coldspotfeeds.com
Dog sledding may not be possible in most states, but if it's what you do in your free moments, then here's a handy site where you can pick up the latest gear. This is definitely a specialist sport, and you really have to know what you need, but there are practical items for any dog-owner here – the dog booties would be good for any dog that has to cope with snow and ice. Sleds and dog food are only shipped within Alaska.

Eastern Mountain Sports
www.emsonline.com
EMS sells mostly apparel associated with general outdoor activities, plus gear for camping and canoeing and a few accessories. Note the outlet section for online-only bargains and a good selection for kids. EMS runs day clinics in Massachusetts, Colorado, New Hampshire and New York, and there's also an ice climbing and mountaineering school. No detail is left out in explaining what the courses are about, how to get there and where to stay.

Fresh Track Maps
www.freshtracksmaps.com
You can't get there unless you know where you are going, and here is the resource that will minimize your chances of travelling in circles. From basic

EMS isn't content to just sell you outdoor gear; a range of activities puts the pressure on to put it all to proper use

compasses to sophisticated topographic software, you'll always know where you are with these tools. As it helps to be in touch with fellow hikers, there are also two-way radios to keep in contact with those who are out of sight.

MoJo's Gear

mojosgear.com

Paraglider enthusiasts will thoroughly enjoy browsing this site, packed full of equipment, kites, gliders and accessories. The equipment specs are comprehensive – a good thing considering it's just a few bits of equipment between you and a fatal freefall. Free ground shipping on orders over $30.

National Sports Center for the Disabled

www.nscd.org

This site specializes in events that allow special needs individuals to take part in activities such as skiing, rock climbing and kayaking. You can't actually book online, but all the information, dates, equipment requirements and directions are available. Well worth looking into.

ON THE UP

Not everyone has big hills on their doorstep but climbing is now open to everyone. Maybe not under blue skies with scurrying wildlife, but there are tons of sites promoting climbing centers. Even Nashville has one. Failing that, why not try one of Climbing Wall's mobile models...

Classic Rock Gym
www.classic-rock.com

Climbing Wall
www.climbingwall.com

Extra Vertical
www.extravertical.com

Outdoor Gear Exchange

www.gearx.com

This easy-to-use site features the usual outdoor gear and equipment, plus a section of used items. There's also an archive of articles from the newsletter, plus a discussion forum and reviews of the gear. There is also quite a selection aimed at those who wouldn't dream of leaving home without their best friend – all canine necessities are covered.

REI Outlet

rei-outlet.com

This user-friendly site boasts 20-70 per cent off retail prices for this camping and hiking brand. Illustrations and specifications are clear. The selection is good and shipping costs are reasonable.

Wilderness Mining Company

www.goldpan.com

This site appears pretty amateurish and the order form is a pain, but all the pans, sieves, tweezers, funnels, claws, picks and vials that you'll need if you're planning to join the gold rush are available here. You can end up spending quite a bit of that gold even before your first panning, but just think of all that fresh air and the fact that you are following in the footsteps of all those old-time prospectors (not many of whom retired rich). Shipping is a very steep 25 per cent.

Parties

Sort out that celebration
with a bouncy castle or
a murder mystery party
and post all the gory details
on your own personal website

 All you need for little kids... and big ones

Boxed Parties
www.boxedupparties.com
For those busy folks who want a ready-made kids' party in a box, look no
further. A complete party for 8, choosing from such popular themes as *Star
Wars* and Barbie, is available for $49.95. Everything but the food is included.
Activity kits like sand art are available separately.

Display & Costume
www.costumes-partysupplies.com
This site can provide all the costumes, supplies and materials to make your
event hum. It even has materials to build a float should you feel inspired in
that direction. They do encourage an instore visit as the inventory is too vast
to put online, but everything on view can be ordered through the site and
shipped UPS. Cheap and cheerful.

Fundways Theme Party Warehouse
www.fundways.com
Perhaps best suited to trade shows or fundraisers, this company will produce
a theme party of a quality, as befits a firm that has worked in the TV and
movie industry. Of more use to the average party-thrower are the celebrity
lifesize cut-outs – just $24.95 each and you can pretend to be mixing it with
members of Hollywood's A list.

Great Entertaining
www.greatentertaining.com
For those looking for first-class party accessories, this site is a winner. Items
are a bit pricey, but the quality shines through. Food and fine wines with
customized labels are also on offer. Many of the items available will become
a permanent part of your entertaining repertoire. Refreshing.

Parties

Little Favors
www.littlefavors.com
Party favors are a must, and this girlie site (lots of lace and ruffles) has treats that are sure to put a smile on the kiddies' faces. Cake tops are available for birthdays, weddings and christenings too.

Party Outfitters
www.partyoutfitters.com
Money no object? Then why not surprise Little Johnny with his own inflatable bouncy castle at his next birthday? For a cheaper option you can always rent.

Shindigz
www.shindigz.com
This discount party site has thousands of products to make your party truly memorable. Themes includes 60s and 70s, Cheerleading, Hanukkah and Casino Night. Free shipping on orders over $75 to the continental US.

The Plunge
www.thePlunge.com
This site lets you create your own website, complete with a map and after-the-event photos, with hundreds of site designs ranging from a Movie Night to a Bachelorette Party. Stacks of other ideas to make your party a success too.

 Best confined to the silver screen

All American Reunions
www.allamericanreunions.com
Do you face hosting a reunion with a degree of dread? Then why not hire professionals to do the work, leaving you to enjoy the fun? The cost is borne by ticket sales so you won't end up out of pocket. The organizers service the reunion, and with 10 years' experience should know what makes a party rock.

EZ Reunion Kit
www.ezreunionkit.com
If you want to do the whole shebang yourself, then you can order a kit to be sent to you or downloaded straight to your desk through this site. The kit includes all the info you need, plus sample documents, all from $24.95. Extra points to the staff for posting their own yearbook photos.

Family Reunion
www.family-reunion.com
Mr Spiffy will guide you through getting Uncle Joe and long-lost cousin Sam together for a big family bash. The advice is practical and there's plenty of it, with lots of links to cover food and entertainment. Useful and down to earth.

From partying aliens to a full-on mystery

Mad Science
www.madscience.org
Mad Science is a franchise organization providing science-based entertainment for children's parties and events. The idea is to "spark the imagination" of kids by showing them how much fun science can be. And despite offering to make "ooey, gooey slime", they absolutely guarantee no mess. Parties can be themed and customized by age group, and the entertainment lasts about an hour.

Murder Mystery Parties To Go
www.izad.com/mystery
Tired of the usual office banter and gossip at your annual do? Then turn your next private or corporate event into a party to remember with these Mystery Games. $7.95 per person may sound steep, but the organization that has gone into the game is worth it. Best suited for large parties.

Party 411
www.party411.com
This fun site is packed full of ideas for theme parties. Once you've picked a theme, it can sell you the stuff to make the whole shebang come together, plus menus, advice and activities. Themes are inventive – there's one for an Alien Christmas Party, for example. The site also offers a caricature service to make your celebration truly individual. There are also plenty of links to other sites for anything extra you might need.

This is a site that just screams "Party!" If you can't find a theme to suit here, you must have seriously off-the-wall tastes...

Pets & pet supplies

Herpers, lamb's ears, cat's kaviar:
there are times when the world
seems to have lost the plot...

Cat Claws
www.catclaws.com
Not a stylish site but then we're sure your cat doesn't mind as long as it's
being pampered. Cat Claws offers unusual cat pampering and exotic treats
with something for every pocket, from Kitty Kaviar at $4.95 to a Drinkwell Pet
Fountain for $80. There's even Peacock Feathers, the ultimate cat plaything,
for $12. The most extravagant items can be found in the bedding section,
with everything from a cat tent to a thermo kitty bed and a snuggle kitty. The
extensive catalog has images and brief descriptions, and ordering is standard.

Dogwise
www.dogwise.com
Dogwise has everything to help you understand your pet pooch better, and
all the tools and treats to help keep it fit, healthy and happy. What they don't
have is a decently designed site. Unless you know exactly what you're
looking for, you'll need to spend a considerable length of time browsing
page after page of books, treats, healthcare products and toys. This aside,
you'll eventually come across something suitable in their huge catalog
of everything from Tug 'n Talk toys to anti-ageing health items for your dog.
Prices are reasonable and buying is easy.

eHerp
www.eherp.com
This site features the banner "Run by herpers for herpers", and if you've no
idea what a herper is you're probably best sticking to pets of the fluffy variety.
eHerp has everything for the reptile enthusiast, from cages and feed for your
current slinky friend, to a zoo full of reptiles just waiting for a new home. You
can't order any of the albino rattlesnakes or bull snakes online – for this you
need to e-mail the experts, presumably so they can check you out. Prices
range from $65 for your common or garden variety of rattlesnake, to $850

for a supreme beast. What you can buy online are all the necessary supplies, from cages and heating appliances, to (gulp) sexing probes and incubators.

Foster Smith
www.drsfostersmith.com
Ponchos, denim jackets, ski sweaters, life preservers… yes, this *is* a pet site. Doctors Foster and Smith aren't just concerned with your pets' welfare, but are also keen to make them independent animals with no need for an owner. Not impressed by the wardrobe? How about automatic cat and dog feeders? Or if the dog's getting out of hand, how about a bark controller or vibration training collar? If only it worked on humans. Prices are cheap (unless you opt for ultra high-tech) and the site is easy to browse with full, useful descriptions.

Interplanetary Pet Products
shop.store.yahoo.com/ippi/natpetnut.html
Worried that your dog may be teased by the neighborhood hounds about the size of his hefty potbelly? Try putting him on a nutritional yet tasty diet. Interplanetary sells natural pet nutrition specially formulated by a team of vets, biochemists and scientists. Low-fat treats include Zukes Power Bones, high in protein and low in saturated fats and available in chicken, beef and peanut butter flavors (all $30 for a box of 20), and low-fat dog wafers for $7.95.

Jake's Dog House
www.jakesdoghouse.com
You could be forgiven for thinking this is for toy-lovers rather than dog-owners, but skip past the jokes, figurines and plush toys and you get to a limited but special collection of treats, toys and accessories. The novel, yet useful items include a doggie car seat for $50 and a Raised Health Diner to help minimize your dog's digestion and
bloating problems. Best of all are the mint-flavored tennis balls to stop your dog chewing you and prevent their breath having the power to stop traffic. Quite pricey shipping charges, however.

Being in the doghouse used to be a bad thing but a trip to Jake's Dog House would top any pooch's wish list

JB Pet
www.jbpet.com
If you're a total novice at this pet-owning lark, JB takes you through the essentials step by step – and then of course gets you to spend a bit of money in their store. Use the paw-fitting or

dog-measuring charts before you buy any clothing essentials, or read up on the importance of the water bowl before you buy. On the serious side, they do offer helpful advice on dog nutrition. Presumably they have opted for simple lists of products due to the size of their warehouse, but pictures would be useful, especially if you want to know the exact shade of the red cable-knit dog sweater. Prices are cheap and ordering is simple.

PET FOOD EXPRESS

www.petclick.com

Pet Click doesn't sell the ordinary run-of-the-mill, foul-smelling pet food. It deals in natural foods – free of preservatives, sweeteners, colorings and flavorings – for your cat, dog, bird, horse, fish or even your favorite reptile. Select your pet type and browse through the collection of top natural brands. Most items look (and probably smell) like your regular store variety, with the usual array of wet and dry food, but if your pet lizard likes a walk on the wild side, he can have the pleasure of live meal worms, fruit flies and crickets to munch on. Most items are quite pricey and most items are sold in bulk ($24 for 4lbs of dry food, for example), but there's also a handy weekly or fortnightly subscription system that you know that your cat's going to love that tuna-free fare.

Merrick Pet Delicatessen

www.merrick-deli.com

If you can bear to go beyond the lamb's ears and stuffed hoofers featured on this site, the Merrick Deli does also sell less stomach-turning items. You could probably make your pet its own three-course meal from this selection of snacks, which includes cheese and crackers, ostrich, venison or lamb and potato chips, and every variety of sausage. The deluxe boxes for $11 feature no description of what's inside but as long as it's meat your pet should be happy. A useful alternative site, if not for the faint-hearted.

Noah's Pet Supplies

www.noahspets.com

Having been doing this for thousands of years, Noah is obviously well clued up. As well as cats and dogs, the site also looks after fish, birds, hamsters, gerbils and ferrets. The site is clearly laid out with a section for each animal and a huge list of sub-categories with travel items, nutrition, houses and even a wardrobe selection. There are descriptions and close-up images, and shipping is free if you spend more than $30. Price-wise, you can be as cost effective or as frivolous as you like, with treats for every pocket.

Pig Stuff

www.pigstuff.com

George Clooney says a pot-belly pig is his best friend, instantly making them the in-thing in Hollywood, but if you haven't already rushed out to your local pet store to get your hands on one, why not adopt instead? Pigstuff has a (thankfully limited) selection of pigs in need of a good home. Pictures aren't currently available but the heart-wrenching stories of abuse do the selling trick. Simply select a Daphne or a Buddy Lee and use the e-mail address for more details. Once you've got your pig, you can then choose from the Pigstuff collection of harnesses, fleeces and treats.

Phones & pagers

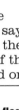

The phones, the phones, the phones... As Jerry Seinfeld says, haven't we gone crazy with the phones? For definitive proof that he's got a point, simply read on

 From freebies to a few flashier models

Beep Wear
www.beepwear.com
Sick of craning your neck to try to see your pager hanging off your pants or searching endlessly through your bag? Beep Wear has the answer. Timex and Motorola have teamed up to produce the pager-watch. Priced from $130 to $170, this sporty wristwear has all the features of your average watch and pager. Read the extensive spec sheet, view 3D images and then buy online.

Pro Page Communications
www.ehot.com/share/cgi-bin/site.cgi?site_id=propagepagers&page_id=home
A snappier address would be a help but this is just an aberration at an otherwise useful site. The selection is limited, but does include free models. Select the make, coverage area, additional regional needs and insurance, they'll tot up the costs and you simply buy. Additional information is pretty sparse, so this is probably the site for the communication savvy.

Also worth checking out:
Communications Group
www.radiopage.net
All the latest technology, though the site is lacking images and additional info.

Pager Wholesale
www.pagerwholesale.com
You'll be in and out in no time, with a brand new bargain pager.

Phones & pagers

Phones — Top brands and info to help you choose

123 Cellular
www.123cellular-phones.com
An authorized dealer for AT&T with monthly plans for all budgets and needs.
Phones from all the top names – Nokia, Ericsson, Motorola and Mitsubishi.

CellWest
www.cellwest.com
Useful if you're updating your current brick-sized model to the new pin-sized
ones. Brands include Nokia, Motorola and Samsung. Stylish but expensive.

Decide.com
www.decide.com
Info about each network and make of phone; good for the cautious type.

Let's Talk
www.letstalk.com
This site could sort you out with a state-of-the-art cell phone even if you were
living in remotest Alaska. Brilliant site for information.

Some other sites worth a look:
American Nokia Tips www.American-Nokia-Tips.com
Cellular Phones www.cellularphones.com
Everything Wireless www.everythingwireless.com
North Coast Phone Center www.phonecenter.net

Dead ringer — The secret life of Thomas Edison

This space was supposed to be full of vital info about Wireless Access Protocol
(WAP) and all the other ways that you can access the Net from your phone. But as
that scene is changing as fast as a very fast thing indeed, the usefulness of any
such info in a publication working on these deadlines would be summed up by that
fine American word "diddlysquat". So instead here's a snippet from *New Scientist*
about Thomas Edison's bid to lead a real communications revolution: "Did you know
that Thomas Edison attempted to construct a 'spirit communicator' in the 1920s?
He didn't get far but, undaunted, continued the work after his death, communicating
his progress through a medium called Sigrum Seuterman in 1967. Since Edison's
pioneering efforts, methods of communication with the 'living impaired' have come
on apace." For the rest of the story: www.newscientist.com/weird/theend.html

Property

Finding your new home
sweet home can be a breeze
if you take the online route

Buy & sell
Mr Blanding, your dream house awaits...

4 Sale by Owners
www.4sale-byowners.com
As you would expect from the web address, this is the place to come if you
want to cut out the expensive middleman and buy your home direct from the
people selling it. With over a million hits per month it's a popular site, with
clear listings and great advice for buyers and sellers alike. If you're selling, the
Featured Properties plan will cost you $99.95 for a year's listing complete with
10 photos of your home, a virtual tour, a 30-page neighborhood report and a
link from all the top search engines and directories.

AAA Timeshare Solutions
www.aaatimeshare.com
If you want to buy, sell or rent a timeshare, this is the site to check out first.
As there can be pitfalls associated with getting involved in timeshares, you're
best off doing really thorough research first and there's plenty here to consider
before you jump in to find the vacation home of your dreams. In the Hot Deals
there are some outstanding bargains to be had, and the site can guide you
step by step through the whole process.

All Real Estate
www.allre.com
Portal site stuffed with links to real estate agents and listings all over the
country. Search by City and State to find professional agents and relocators
to help with your move, or look up government info on buying property. There
are also articles and tips on making the whole process less of a headache.

Bates Foreclosure Report
www.brucebates.com
Presumably no relation to Norman. If you're looking for a real estate bargain,
check out this online listing for properties whose previous owners have
defaulted on their loan. The banks and mortgage companies are usually pretty

Property

GET YOUR ASTEROID HERE!

www.mindspring.com/~tluthman/stroids.htm

If you're wondering what the real estate business might look like in 100 or so years' time, this great spoof can give you a taste. The rich and famous will no longer be content with tracts of prime land near secluded beaches or stunning mountains; they'll want an extraterrestrial pad to reflect their full stellar glory. Crazy Andromeda will be offloading plots on Asteroid Ida 243 or Asteroid Gaspra 951, and if you can't afford to buy, you can always get a taste from a luxury cruise through the asteroid belt.

Judging by the rest of his homepage, Tom Luthman, creator of the site, loves outer space a lot – though we'd love to see him actually show what sort of properties you could build on these chunks of rock. Let's just hope he's still around to see some of his predictions come true.

keen to recoup their losses after foreclosing and you can snap up some great deals. When we looked there were 94 properties in Los Angeles alone waiting for a new buyer. You have to subscribe to the site ($19.95 per month) to get the detailed listings, but general information on the properties is available to everyone.

Econorealty
www.econorealty.com

Well-designed, "for sale by owner" listing site where you can list your property and add a photo for free. The search facility for buyers is speedy and there seems to be a good range of properties on offer. Once you have found something that catches your eye, the rest of the process is up to you, so make sure you've thoroughly researched the buying process before you start looking.

First American Real Estate Solutions
www.firstamres.com

Access the public records of real estate ownership and sales details in counties across the States. This information can be invaluable to anyone looking to make a real estate purchase but unsure if the price being asked is a reasonable one. The site also has a link to a valuation model where you can get informed feedback on any property purchase you are considering.

Guide to Retirement Living Online
www.retirement-living.com

Excellent news and information about real estate for retired folk, plus links to hundreds of company websites aimed at people looking to swap the daily grind for something a little more welcoming. Whether you're after a small condo in Florida, or a huge mansion on the edge of a terrific golf course, you're bound to find something here. There's also a useful savings planner so you can make sure your pension will cover everything you want and need in your new home.

HomeStore
www.homestore.com

Great fun site with much more than the usual links to realtors and property listings. There are channels on home design, both interior and exterior, and articles on subjects like buying a factory-built home, or a historic property. The site can also help you find a local professional to tackle those household chores and maintenance projects you just never seem to get around to.

Monster Moving

www.monstermoving.com

Once you've found the home of your dreams, how do you get all your stuff packed and shipped there? Monster can help you with its great directory of removal services, from full quotes to packing materials for those doing the whole thing themselves. The site also has tips on how to plan your move, reduce the stress of relocating and avoid some of the major house moving pitfalls.

Kelli Naegele can seriously improve your health – or at least minimize the headaches associated with moving

Neighborhood Reports

www.4neighborhoodreports.com

Not a property sales site, but a must-visit if you're planning a move away from your current neighborhood and want to know everything about where you're moving to. For $19.95 you can buy a detailed report on the environment, crime figures, school standards and all the essential services in your new area. It will also tell you the most recent property sales in the area so you can be sure you're not paying over the odds, and even give you a guide to the weather. It could save you a lot of hassle in the long run.

New Home Portfolio

www.newhomeportfolio.com

The very helpful Kelli Naegele has put together a hugely useful workbook to help people relocating, showing every step of their financial transaction and moving program. There are clear sections on all the elements of moving house that you will need to consider, and places to keep all the required paperwork so it's at your fingertips at all times. There are even new home design and remodelling sections. At $28.50, it's a headache-relieving bargain. The ordering process is a little temperamental as you are sent to a separate site to place your order, and even if you think you've put a copy in your cart you probably haven't, but do persevere – it works eventually.

Realtor.com

www.realtor.com

The official site for the National Association of Realtors is the place to look for the professional's take on moving house, as well as links to member realtors across the US. With access to more than 1.4 million properties for sale, you're bound to find something you like (and can afford). The site also boasts lots of useful information, such as recent property purchase prices so you can gauge how big an investment you're going to need to make.

Unusual homes
Psst... wanna buy a pyramid?

Buy Inn
www.buyinn.com

Looking for a change of pace and of career? What about running a bed and breakfast or maybe, for something completely different, a country inn? Buy Inn lists over 500 gorgeous and often historic properties for people looking for an alternative to the condo lifestyle. For $2.5m you could own a 15-room lodge on a tranquil lake in North Carolina, but there are cheaper options too. Subscribe to the mailing list for regular updates on available properties, and you can also check out some of the articles and books on becoming an innkeeper to see if it's the life for you.

International Realty Service
www.2ndhomerealty.com

Why bother working your way up the property ladder when you can jump straight to the top? Here's where you can buy a 13th-century chateau in France ($1.3m) or a 480-acre sporting estate in Ireland ($10.9m).
Trading in your townhouse might not raise the necessary cash for either of those, but there's always the possibility of buying a 14th-century thatched cottage in the English village of Woodbury Salterton for a rather more affordable $192,460. Either way, a change of pace is guaranteed.

Ken Lund's Islands for Sale
www.islandsforsale.com

Always dreamed of buying your own island? Ken Lund is your man, and he has plenty of dreams to chose from. He specializes in the stunning islands off the coast of British Columbia, but if you're after a slice of Caribbean or Pacific heaven, he can help there too. A 5-acre island just off Nassau will set you back a cool $259,000, but after a few rum punches, you're unlikely to care.

Own History
www.ownhistory.net

Online resource for buying and selling historic property across the US, whether it's a 1917 Arts and Crafts home in Athens, Alabama, or a Victorian Italianate villa in Vallejo, California. The site is regularly updated. In addition there are lots of articles on historic districts in featured cities (Savannah, Georgia was being profiled when we looked), plus outlines of what the various architectural styles entail and what a historic property can be like to run. Think "expensive" and you won't be too wrong.

Pavilions of Splendour
www.heritage.co.uk

If you're feeling really adventurous and long for a slice of Olde Englande, then

Pavilions of Splendour may be a good place to start. It specializes in selling unusual and historic properties in the UK, which often have preservation orders attached to them and are in need of a great deal of loving care and attention. You have to be prepared to fork out huge suitcases full of cash just to repair a window (no home improvement devotees need apply) but a look through the portfolio may just convince you it will be worth it. Besides, you can guarantee no one you know will have anything similar.

Phi Designs

www.phidesigns.com
Eco-architecture practice in Oregon specializing in the construction of hugely funky solar pyramid homes which are economic to run as well as kind to the environment. There are lots of pictures of completed pyramid homes, including interior shots so you can see how the insides work (a lot better than you might expect), plus there are details on energy conservation and the materials used. If you want to find out how to get one of your own, you can e-mail the architect through the site.

Tropical Islands

www.tropical-islands.com
If you're a wannabe 21st-century Robinson Crusoe, this is the website that will set your heart racing. Don't worry if you don't have $1.3m for 846 acres of paradise on an island near Costa Rica, you might stretch to the lease on an island near Nicaragua for 30 years at a mere $100,000. You'll still have to fork out to build a home though – oh, and dig a well – but that's not really much to ask for "your own kingdom in today's developed world", is it?

World of Private Islands

www.vladi-private-islands.de
Welcome to one of the most comprehensive island sites on the Net. While some sites offer you the island equivalent of a timeshare in Florida, this site has something for the more independently minded, like Gallinara Island off the east coast of Italy or, for the more hardy, the isle of Gigha off the west coast of Scotland which will set you back around $9m. Struggling to find the cash for this month's rent? Have a browse anyway – it's a lovely site to come and look at just to dream.

Some exclusive private islands are a lot less expensive to buy than you might. Some, of course, aren't...

Finance
Don't forget to read the small print

Finding the right mortgage can be a minefield of conflicting advice, terrifying interest rates and the prospect of getting into staggering debt. So we've picked out a few of the best and clearest housing finance sites for you…

A-Refinance
www.a-refinance.com
Online, low-cost, flexible home-loan packages, direct from the lenders.

Crestar Mortgage Corporation
www.crestarmortgage.com
Research tips and mortgage calculators among other things.

EZ Mortgage Loans
www.ezmtgloans.com
Real estate finance for property-market beginners. User-friendly too.

Fidelity Mortgage Corporation
www.americashome.com
Well worth checking out for the excellent Rent vs Buy Calculator.

Green Tree Home Improvement
www.homeimprovement.gtfc.com
Get advice and a loan on any remodelling project you have in mind.

Hartland Mortgage Centers
www.hartlandmortgage.com
Well designed and easy-to-use discount loan site.

How's Your Mortgage?
www.howsyourmortgage.com
Online consultation service to help you get the best deal on your home loan.

Just Found My Mortgage
www.mortgage-with-bad-credit-mortgages-home-loan-bad-credit.com
As the cumbersome site address suggests, this is the place to come for a home loan if your credit rating is on the fragile side.

Also worth checking out:

NovaStar Home Mortgage	www.novastarloans.bigstep.com
Quicken Loans	www.quicken.com
UC Lending	www.uclending.com

Records, CDs etc

The Net is a vast, virtual treasure trove of music, where you can find anything from obscure Sixties psychedelia to MP3 files of your favorite act (legal action by said artists permitting...)

 **From America to Zappa**

101cd.com

www.101cd.com

This UK site boasts over 1.6m titles and while it's easy to be cynical about such claims (who's going to count them?), there's enough on display to suggest that they're not exaggerating. Purchase prices are in UK pounds so it's best to buy by credit card as personal checks must be in sterling or euros. Our only criticism is that although you can browse the music by price and search by artist, it's not easy to browse by category. Good rarities section.

800.com

www.800.com

"Buyer be happy" is the motto of this well-organised entertainment site, which has a huge collection of CDs (42 pages) for under $10. Okay, so Julio Iglesias' *1100 Bel Air Place* isn't the most encouraging start but it gets better, with the likes of Morrissey, Kiss and Nine Inch Nails all making an appearance in the bargain basement. There's also an entire section dedicated to cruising music (Cruisin' Tunes), where you can buy the *Easy Rider* soundtrack for $9.95.

Alpha Craze

www.alphacraze.com

Not the place for a rare piece of vinyl or some leftfield indie, but a good mainstream site with a bargain or two if you're looking for top-sellers (plenty of 30 and 20 per cent off deals). The annoying thing is that you have to go to a second page for the prices of the homepage offers. On the up side, there's the Alpha Craze Shopping Wizard. Download this and, if you're about to buy an item from another site, it'll pop up if Alpha Craze can offer a better price.

Amazon
www.amazon.com
With 30 per cent off top-sellers and upcoming releases that you can pre-order for shipping on the day of release, there are lots of compelling reasons to give Amazon a try when it comes to music. Friday is a good day to visit because of its "insane" one-day bargains in the Music Outlet, and you can also take advantage of third parties selling used goods in good order. There were eight copies of Britney's *Oops* going begging when we dropped in. Strange, that…

THE FAQs

How can I post my band's MP3 files?
Try www.music4free.com or www.mp3-shack.com

Can I see bands online? There's usually lots going on at www.virtuetv.com or you can find an online gig guide at www.liveconcerts.com

---

Which is the best news group for musicians? A good general one is alt.music.makers.dj but www.topica.com/channels/music/ leads you to more

---

Where can I buy tickets? www.ticket-finders.com/rock_concert_tickets.htm is a great ticket resource. If an act's on the road, they should be here

---

Where is the best place to search for a band site? Try www.musicsearch.com or www.artistdirect.com

Barnes and Noble
www.barnesandnoble.com
Good to see it takes music as seriously as it does books. Keen prices, free downloads, articles to read and featured "Boutiques" on particular artists and genres. The Listening Wall is a highlight, featuring 140 different channels or stations from Dream Pop to Baroque. It's also one of the easiest-to-use audio facilities on the Internet and, as you select a track or artist, a pop-up page appears to tell you more about them. If only all Internet audio was this user-friendly.

Best Buy
www.bestbuy.com
Irritatingly, not all products here are priced until you put them in your shopping cart. Okay, you can take them out again, and prices are keen, but this policy is more likely to alienate shoppers than woo them. A shame, because there are lots of good things about this site, and its explanation of MP3 and digital downloading is excellent. It has some good free tracks available and it's one of the few sites that actually tells you how long a track may take to download in two modem speeds.

Borders
www.borders.com
Well organised site, though showing just 5 titles per browsing section barely hints at the vast stock actually available, which you have to find via an impressively well-informed search engine (typing in Kirsty MacColl yielded even albums where she'd sung backing vocals). More features and additional information would help.

Artists direct
Home is where the artist is

When Aimee Mann's third album was shelved in the 1998 label mergers, she decided to release it herself – through the Internet. You can find her site via Artist Direct (www.artistdirect.com), a directory of artists and sites (major label acts included) that also offers news, message boards, MP3 files, videos and even radio. It also sells CDs, but search by artist to find their own site, where you can often buy said CDs cheaper, sign up for newsletters and find exclusive deals (Tori Amos' Venus Envy necklace reduced to $5.59, anyone?). You also get the huge satisfaction of seeing your money go right to the artist.

Alternatively you can use your search engine to find a host of authorized sites which may also offer merchandise. Here are are just a few of the big ones:

www.aerosmith.com	Aerosmith
www.thebeatles.com	The Beatles
www.davidbowie.com	David Bowie
www.depechemode.com.	Depeche Mode
www.bobdylan.com	Bob Dylan
www.elvis.com	Elvis Presley
www.macygray.com	Macy Gray
www.r-kelly.com	R Kelly
www.bbking.com	BB King
www.bobmarley.com	Bob Marley
www.davematthewsband.com	Dave Matthews Band
www.remhq.com	REM

Buy.com
www.buy.com
Fairly predictable music section but it does feature some of the best prices around for the big-sellers. Plenty of bundles and boxsets, and there's a gift suggestion service where you rank CDs in appropriateness for that certain someone and it builds a profile for when you're shopping for them next time.

CDConnection
www.cdconnection.com
The only site we found to open its home page with a Roy Orbison album, but then this is the only music site with the Golden Ears Society presiding over it. They'd awarded the Big O's *Lonely and Blue* album 9.5 points, hence its showcase position. This seemingly secret society is actually not secret at all, since it comprises CDConnections' customer base who have contributed over a quarter of a million ratings and reviews to date. You can see how they've voted under categorised headings, which, for rock and pop, starts with A-Ha's *Hunting High And Low* (8.1) and finishes off with ZZTop's *Eliminator* (8.3).

Records, CDs etc

CDNow

www.cdnow.com

If you like to liven up your shopping with a bit of muso gossip, the occasional interview and the latest on who's releasing what and when, CD Now is your kind of place. The site's magazine approach means the homepage is taken up with articles and features rather than in-your-face discounts and offers. But those wanting more than the latest chart CD at a discount will appreciate it, and the search facility will quickly take you to the CD or record of your choice. It was offering 30 per cent off top-sellers when we visited.

CD Quest

www.cdquest.com

This is a great, well-organized site to head for if you know the song but can't quite place the artist. You can search by song, album or artist, and each title comes with a track listing. Those who prefer to browse are catered for, too. The Quest section leads you to works you may not have known by favorite artists, and there are links from albums to entire back catalogs. Prices are good, less than $10 in some cases, with delivery starting at $2.95.

CD Universe

www.cduniverse.com

An excellent search engine and competitive pricing on top-sellers gets this site bookmarked by many shoppers. The homepage sports a nice clean design that separates offers and discounts from the feature areas. One of our favourite areas is the CD University where you can swot up on a particular genre of music. So far they've covered classical, jazz, blues and country, with the promise of more to come. We eagerly await the easy guide to psychedelic garage. Free downloads span screensavers from Britney to Limp Bizkit.

If your hard disk is in dire need of a Limp Bizkit screensaver, CD Universe is the online store for you

CDWow

www.cdwow.com

A firm favorite in the UK where it offers some of the lowest prices on the market and delivery is free. Shipping is still reasonable enough to make it worth a look for US shoppers and it gets a good rating from the consumer site Bizrate, so there are plenty of happy US purchasers out there. The homepage, divided up into new releases, top-sellers and pre-orders, smacks of low overheads but who cares about aesthetics if it keeps the prices down?

Cheap CDs

www.cheap-cds.com

"Over 91 per cent of new CDs under $11.99", says the homepage and this site is as good as its word. If you're wondering how it does it, go straight to the "How we do it" section which explains that their only profit is a $1.43 handling charge. They also keep costs down by doing all their own programming. There are a million MP3 files to try out and the online catalog is big. There are no frills and it's low on features – although it does give the VH1 and *Billboard* top 100s, as well as the last 100 customer searches for guidance – but it's the price that counts here.

Eil/Esprit

www.eil.com

Fancy that Japanese limited edition picture disc by your favorite artist which came out 10 years ago and was only sent to DJs? This is the place to begin your quest. Ignore the flannel about this being "the world's biggest and best online store". This site, which is updated "many times a day" is far better than such macho posturing might suggest. It's excellent for imports, with a Japanese and even a Thai remix of Madonna's *Don't Tell Me* among the top-sellers when we visited. There's also a good currency converter and an area dedicated to concerts and events.

Express.com

www.express.com

Certainly lives up to its name as the high-speed entertainment site (it also sells DVDs, games and players), with one of the quickest search facilities. The lively homepage invited us to get funkdafied with a selection of funk and soul specials, and best-sellers were up to 30 per cent off. Search by category or

TOP 10

This top 10 of online CD sales during a random week in the production of this book suggests surfers have no better taste than offline fans

1 Original Soundtrack: *Crouching Tiger, Hidden Dragon*

2 Dave Matthews Band: *Everyday*

3 Eric Clapton: *Reptile*

4 Original Soundtrack: *O Brother, Where Art Thou?*

5 Original Soundtrack: *Almost Famous*

6 Shaggy: *Hotshot*

7 Train: *Drops of Jupiter*

8 Enya: *A Day Without Rain*

9 Lenny Kravitz: *Greatest Hits*

10 Moby: *Play*

by artist – keying in Tony Orlando gave us the chance to buy Dawn's 1970s "classic" *Knock Three Times*. Quite a leap from being funkdafied, we'd say.

HMV
www.hmv.com

This site does everything you'd expect a major music store to do. The search mechanism isn't the fastest we came across but the site makes up for it with the number of free downloads and HMV-organised webcasts (click the link to Virtuecast.com). The bargain basement is worth checking, although the Adam Ant compendium and the Charles Aznavour Live six-CD set had a rather desperate "please buy me" look to them. The site was also doing a wedding music promotion which, curiously, included Boney M's *Greatest Hits* as a recommendation. Any takers for Ma Baker as an alternative to Lady Linda?

How bad is it, doc? Pretty bad, I'm afraid...

Cyberspace can be just another name for a universe where truly bad records never go away. Purely for research purposes you understand, we set out to buy online five of the worst records in the history of unpopular music.

If **David Bowie**'s *The Laughing Gnome* – a 1960s British "novelty" hit which includes the immortal chorus "Ha, ha, ha, hee, hee, hee/I am the laughing gnome said he" – has passed you by, don't worry, you can find it on an album called *Deram Anthology 1966-1968* (at www.cdnow.com and other good cyber record stores). Even better news, it's available on Real Audio, Windows Media and MPEG, which is probably 3 formats too many.

Napoleon XIV's *They're Coming To Take Me Away Ha Ha* sold 2 million singles as a US number 1 in 1966, thanks to weird sound effects and lyrics about basket weavers and men in white coats. Thanks to the magic of the Internet and www.rhino.com in particular, you can buy an entire album by Napoleon XIV, including the hit played backwards and its ill-advised sequel, *They're Coming To Take Me Away Again*, for just $16.98.

After this the news that two albums by **Jerry Lewis** (the alleged comedian) are available via http://album.yahoo.com/shop?d=ha&id=1800645749&cf=10&intl=us doesn't even come as a surprise. And *The Best Of Robert Goulet* (the warbler whose appearance on TV usually had Elvis reaching for his .357 magnum) is all too available on www.jpc.de/index_en.shtml

Sadly, the nearest we got to a copy of **Randy Hanzlick**'s *When I Wanted A Bottle In Front Of Me All I Got Was A Frontal Lobotomy* was a postal address on www.drdemento.com. Hanzlick now works at the Center for Disease Control in Atlanta. Hmmm…

The Top 5

www.thetop5.com

A natty premise on which to base a music site: give people the top 5 of each genre. Certainly a good idea for the musically indecisive or those who are getting to know a genre. The homepage opens with the top 5 general albums, and most were priced at just over $13. And yes, there are a lot more than 5 albums or singles in each genre, and most of the categories are fairly well populated.

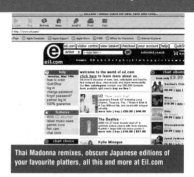

Thai Madonna remixes, obscure Japanese editions of your favourite platters, all this and more at Eil.com

Tower Records

www.towerrecords.com

Does everything you'd expect a big name to do, and a good clean homepage lets you move swiftly to your area of interest. Tower Outlet is the place to go for bargains and bundles. *Shoebox Full of Blues*, aimed at the blues novice and featuring the likes of Howlin' Wolf, John Lee Hooker and Otis Spann, can be yours for $69.99, down from $189.99. If you just want to check out some music, visit the Listening Station, which features 8 channels of 12 featured albums (you'll need Real Audio). Shipping is free on orders over $40.

Virgin Mega

www.virginmega.com

Strangely, Virgin's revamped site doesn't actually sell CDs (or anything else, come to that) any more. Instead it states that it has "temporarily pulled our full catalog offering" (temporary having extended for several months) and that in future "our product offering will focus primarily on Virgin private label products and Megastore gift certificates". While editorial coverage has been expanded, it's still a long way from comprehensive and the few titles that are promoted can only be ordered by toll-free telephone. You'd expect better from Virgin.

Waterloo Records

www.waterloorecords.com

A rare music lovers' haven amidst the hypermarkets. It may use the London subway logo (a tribute to The Kinks?), but Waterloo is based in Austin, Texas. You can find anyone from Aaron Neville to Joe Cocker to Limp Bizkit among the 250,000 titles and downloads, but check out its huge stock of Texan and rootsy music. If Papa Mali & The Instigators' *Thunder Chicken* does it for you, then you'll find it here. If you're not au fait with this kind of stuff, you might have trouble telling the name of the artist from the title of the album.

Specialist For connoisseurs, experts and posers

BLUES
Midnight Records
www.midnightrecords.com
Not exclusively blues but jazz fans won't be disappointed – these people have been serving music buyers for 23 years, and imports and hard-to-find titles are a specialty. The site looks and reads like a fanzine, but the catalog is exhaustive, spanning blues, r&b, jazz, pop, rock and rock 'n' roll, and including such obscure acts as The Ferrets, Dwarves, Suburban Nightmare and the Woofing Cookies, some of whom are on Midnight's own label.

CLASSICAL
All Classical Music
www.allclassicalmusic.com
This friendly site recognises that self-service websites aren't for everyone and urges you to e-mail them for recommendations and help. There's an expansive online . but if you find yourself floundering around, cut straight to "Our picks" where staff tell you what they've been listening to recently. Once you've earned your classical spurs, dip into the Academy for a little light reading, such as an essay on the Origins of the Brandenburg Concerto.

Classical Digest
www.classicaldigest.com
This site describes itself as an information and shopping portal for classical music, and it's a very useful one at that. It's great for reading reviews (it claims to have 50,000 opinions on 14,000 albums) but we found navigating our way out to the shops wasn't always as smooth as it could have been.

COUNTRY
County Sales
www.countysales.com
This Virginia-based site specialises in old-time, bluegrass and "authentic rural music", an outlook that shapes its small country & western section too. Their extensive catalog includes both popular and rare recordings, from the new bluegrass sounds of Bob Amos to obscure German issues of Flatt & Scruggs.

The Music Barn
www.themusicbarn.com
"Bringing back musical memories" is the slogan at this unashamedly nostalgic site. There are some surprising inclusions for an old-time country site (Benny

Hill appears under humor, and Scottish piping music in the British Isles section), but if it's Vernon Dalhart or Lulu Belle & Scotty you're after, you can find them here, along with religious, polka and popular music from the 1930s to the 1960s. The selection is relatively small, but shipping is included in the prices.

DANCE

Trance and techno

www.tweekin.com

How d'you like your house? Dub, hand, jazzy, Latin, tricky, tribal... it's all here. Even though Tweekin is a record label in its own right, it shows its community spirit with a massive catalog of dance music. It also has a set of charts, predominantly from San Francisco-based DJs, and a lively forum.

INDIE/ALTERNATIVE

Imusic

www.imusic.com

Apart from all the usual releases and reviews, this site offers a bargain box, the opportunity to sell and buy secondhand CDs, and the chance to air your view on the latest releases. The news section is huge, and an alphabetised board lets you go straight to your favorite band. You also get a chance to post an epistle on something you feel strongly about: Kittie was being described as an unholy union of Britney and Korn when we dropped by.

CDNow

www.cdnow.com

It's been mentioned earlier, but the indie/alternative pages here are tops and worth singling out for commendation. They have truthful reviews, new releases, interviews and really good staff picks if you fancy chancing something new.

CDStreet

www.cdstreet.com

Undoubtedly one of the best resources for indie music on the Web, covering everything from acid jazz to world beat, with more than 70 pages of news. Pricing is competitive and there are bags of MP3 samples to download. If you're a struggling artist you can sign up for free to sell your goods here, while under Indie Resources you can download a very useful e-book called *Increase Your Fanbase* from A&R Online.

Jazz gems saved from extinction – all yours for $17 from Jazzorade.com with free delivery thrown in

Unsigned

www.unsigned-indie.com

This professional-looking site boasts "the best unsigned and independent artists you've never heard". Hopefuls can post their music here and hope that someone picks up on it. The catch? The submission statement beginning: "As a Christian Organization we have minimal standards our artists must meet…"

JAZZ

Counterpoint Music

www.counterpoint-music.com

Search for all kinds of jazz and blues, from big bands to solo artists, at great prices. There's lots of stuff you won't find on the mainstream sites and they'll even try to hunt down a special order for you if you can't find what you want.

Jazz Oracle

www.jazzoracle.com

A CD label which issues jazz and hot dance sounds from the '20s and '30s, thanks to a bunch of skilled and dedicated people transferring the music to CD from the best copies of an original recording. If you're into jazz you'll recognise the gems they've brought back from the brink of extinction and you can monitor their work in progress in the upcoming releases section. All the CDs are priced at $17 and shipping is free to anywhere in the world.

The Jazz Store

www.jazzstore.com

When they say "everything for the jazz enthusiast" these people aren't kidding. If you're struggling over what to give the jazz lover in your life, how about a trumpet tie, or a sax pillow? If it's music you're after, you won't find any such lapses in taste. The site offers a massive online catalog and, if you join the members' club, you save 10 per cent on each order. There's also a wealth of books, framed prints, cards, clothing and other jazz accessories on sale.

ROCK AND POP

Abbey Records

www.abbeyrecords.co.uk

If you're having trouble tracking down British sounds, this Liverpool-based site has everything from contemporary dance and hip-hop to '70s punk, as well as a huge amount of pure pop. It even caters for fans of vinyl – there's a 30-day no-quibble returns guarantee, and you can sign up for a fortnightly information magazine sent by e-mail. US orders should arrive within 7 days.

Hole in the Wall

www.holeinthewall.com

Started as a bedroom venture and has grown into a thriving mail order and used CDs business. The emphasis is heavily on metal but there's some underground too, and you can sign up for the metal "parody zine" *Internal Combustion*. Well-designed if a tad dark, but then what do you expect?

Freak Emporium

www.freakemporium.com/shop/index_ie.html
Specializing in "the best in mind-altering music from the '60s, '70s, '80s, '90s and beyond", this is the place for psychedelia and progressive rock, as well as garage and space rock. If you're not in the inner circle this will seem like another world but if you're a fellow freak, you too will be excited about names like the Electric Prunes and major works like *Chocolate Soup for Diabetics*.

Pop Records

www.poprecords.com
If you're into the sound of surf, this one-man operation is your online hang-out. Okay, so it has a homegrown, text-heavy look, but this is a truly dedicated site with lots of detail. Read the FAQs for unashamedly subjective stock policy ("I only carry stuff that I really like and can personally recommend") but here's where you finally find that copy of *Absurdistan* by Laika & The Cosmonauts.

Siren

www.sirendisc.com
Established source of imports and great for pop from around the world. Not the easiest site to find what you want, but half the fun is browsing and the bargain section can throw up all sorts of oddities, such as a 99 cent CD single from Aussie "pop sensation" Bachelor Girl with the bonus enhanced version of *Buses And Trains*. Better to save your money for real finds like Marc Bolan's *Futuristic Dragon* 1976 reissue for $7.99, complete with three bonus tracks.

Word up! Music magazines and more online

The Web is also a great place for intelligent comment about music. Here are a few of the best:
www.blaze.com and www.vibe.com Two fine hip-hop publications
www.channel1.com/users/obscure is for the musical obscurantist, rock historians and trivia champs
www.laritmo.com Online magazine site for fans of Latin American rhythms
www.launch.com offers new music with lots of exclamation marks!!!
www.mtv.com and www.vh1.com 'Nuff said
www.nme.com is the world-famous (notorious?) UK music paper, online
www.rollingstone.com is authoritative, occasionally worthy, comprehensive
www.spin.com Online offshoot of the magazine, with polls, downloads etc
www.webnoize.com is technical stuff for insiders and professionals

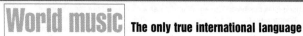 **The only true international language**

ARAE International Inc
www.musichaven.com
This somewhat basic site divides its extensive catalog by country. Scroll through one long list of titles with music from artists in Kenya, the Congo, Madagascar, Nigeria and more, though Ghana and the Congo dominate and music from southern Africa is disappointingly thin. For those with an untrained ear, reviews are on hand to help guide you, and you can listen to a number of tracks online. All CDs are priced at $15, but you do need to order via e-mail.

Descarga
www.descarga.com
Brooklyn-based Latin specialist with a vast catalog on a superbly designed site. It has a great search engine (187 CDs featuring Celia Cruz), extensive track listings, reliable reviews and a journal with features and interviews.

Digelius Music
www.digelius.com
Helsinki-based ethnic music shop, specialising in Baltic and Nordic music.

Mostly Music
www.jewish-music.com
All aspects of Jewish music from the great cantors to klezmer.

Putumayo
www.putumayo.com
Record label with online store featuring reggae, Afro pop, folk, Celtic, and world beat artists, and compilations plus educational material and links.

Real World: the most beautifully designed CD store in the world? Good for fans of Russian peasant songs too

Real World

www.realworld.co.uk/trading

Possibly the most beautifully designed CD store in the world, this is the trading arm of Peter Gabriel's Real World operation. It helps if you know a bit about a genre before you start as there isn't a lot of guidance. That said, we opted for *The Wild Field* by Dmitri Pokrovsky's Ensemble and it did tell us it was a set of Russian peasant songs, apparently written before the 1917 revolution. Our only real criticism is that information like shipping isn't immediately accessible.

World Workout

www.worldworkout.com

Forget Jane Fonda and Cindy Crawford. What you need to shed those pounds is some world music. The World Rhythm Workout CD is the work of a certified fitness instructor who, fed up with the "same sounding" songs to work out to, wrote some herself. Two tracks (*It's Cool To Warm Up* and *Iron Man*) have even won awards at the Nashville City Song Festival. Not cheap at over $20 once you've added shipping, but then a good body doesn't come cheap.

 For some uneasy listening

Gregorian Chants

198.62.75.1/www2/cantgreg/index_eng.htm

We've nothing against a bit of Gregorian chanting – in its place. However, downloading MP3 files of alleluias – even if they are from the St Benedict's Monastery in Sao Paulo, Brazil—is one of the stranger uses of the Internet. Good to see this wing of the music business making use of leading-edge technology though, and it's another source of free music. So, the *Assumpta Est* at 761kb or the more weighty *Confitemini Domino* at 10992kb, then?

Interspecies

www.interspecies.com

Fancy a jam session with Orca? Interspecies is a 25-year-old project in which music is used to communicate with free-swimming ceteceans to help ecology, and they've uploaded some of their labors as MP3 files for sampling here. Other hot downloads include a Tibetan llama chanting with whales, or you can find out how a slight shift in perception can transform a mountain stream into a musical instrument. And you thought Marilyn Manson was weird.

Self Abuse

www.selfabuserecords.com/home.html

Not for the squeamish music fan or, indeed, the music fan. Self Abuse records and releases noise (the sound of a 1khz test zone) and experimental stuff with titles like *Skin Crimes*. Yes, you can buy them online, but do you want to?

Sleep Machines

www.sleepmachines.com

First there was Miami Sound Machine, then Tin Machine, now here's Sleep Machines – a Californian company which sells (along with pillows and scented candles) CDs with a single sound and which are guaranteed to help you nod off. The titles are equally stupefying – *Dryer* is a good example – but they guarantee there are no subliminal messages involved. Serious insomniacs might be better advised to buy Michael Nyman's soundtrack to *The Piano*.

 But hopefully not abused by their previous owner...

Djangos

www.djangos.com

Not just used stuff (save 20 per cent on new releases) but for cut-price CDs, this is a name you can trust. All CDs carry a quality guarantee and have been inspected by Djangos staff. Unlike some online used stores, Djangos takes you where you want to go quickly, with everything – new or used, music or movies – well categorised. Head for Bargain Blowouts for the $4.99 wonders.

Half.com

www.half.com

As with an auction site, the goods offered here (there are books, cameras, computers etc too) are sent direct by the individual seller. The state of the CD is described, and when we dropped by there were "opened but in perfect condition" and "still shrink-wrapped" copies of Dido's *No Angel* up for grabs. A good, fun site, which also has a tribute band and one-hit wonders section (somehow we resisted Kajagoogoo's *Too Shy, The Singles and More* for $7.50). The site is reputable but both buyers and sellers should read the terms and conditions first so they know exactly how the system works.

Rockaway

www.rockaway.com

Some real gems here at one of America's – and the world's – biggest and most popular, used music and memorabilia sites. How about a green vinyl version of Elvis' *Moody Blue* for $900? And there's plenty more where that came from, with objects of desire from all the major world artists. Even an unused Bon Jovi ticket fetches $3 around these parts. All goods are guaranteed for authenticity.

Vinyl Vendors

www.vinylvendors.com

The vinyl comes in any colour, and there are 7 and 12 inchers from around the world. We believe them when they say the database of memorabilia is one of the biggest on the planet, let alone on the Web.

MP3 files Lawyers and other rich folk permitting

As this book went to press, Napster (www.napster.com) was still under siege while MP3.com, having settled with record labels, was entangled in new lawsuits from songwriters. Some sanitised licensing set-up seems likely to emerge, though peer-to-peer file-swapping will be hard to stamp out (try www.imesh.com or www.gnutella.com). Some of the biggest labels were also uniting to launch their own Napster rival on www.musicnet.com.

2look4com
http://en.sonico.com
Fancy downloading a few seconds of Uruguayan grindcore? Or maybe a quick sample of Ecuadorean death-metal? If the answer is yes, you will be sadly disappointed on this occasion, but the beauty of this site is that it lets you search for any combination of type of music and nationality. Perhaps sadly, you're most likely to succeed with traditional Latin American genres.

E.Music
www.emusic.com
Describing itself as "the premier source for legitimate MP3s", this subscription site offers unlimited access to 170,000 songs from 8,000 artists for a monthly fee. The files are professionally encoded and the artists get paid for every download. Multi-platinum artists like Limp Bizkit or Britney are conspicuously absent on this indie-label licensing set-up, but with artists still ranging from Green Day to Elvis Costello to Duke Ellington, they may not be missed.

Lycos MP3 search
http://music.lycos.com/downloads
This site offers one of the simplest and fastest ways to find out what MP3 files are available for downloading and for which artist. Lycos obviously know a thing or two about search engines and theirs fairly zips through your request. Worth bookmarking, especially if you're just starting out in MP3.

MP3.com
www.mp3.com
If you're going to download music from the Net, you are almost obliged to come here. It offers more than 500,000 songs from over 80,000 artists (to say nothing of 3,500 classical recordings), and there's an excellent FAQ if you can't yet tell MP3 from Fun Boy 3. There's a payola section with shameless plugs for new songs (*Why Men Cheat On Their Wives* by Reverend L Rubber Chicken was featured when we visited) and a Top 40 containing relative unknowns like Analogue Pussy alongside big names like REM and Faith Hill.

Shoes and boots

Whether you want tap shoes
for kiddies or ostrich-skin
cowboy boots, or you're into
high fashion or low prices,
the range of footwear online
is simply staggering (ho ho)

Anello & Davide
www.handmadeshoes.co.uk
About to be launched when we looked, this
British site promises a service where you'll be able to choose the style, colour,
and heel height of your shoes, after which they will be handmade for you in
Italy. They specialize in party and bridal shoes, and you can request a
brochure and measuring kit so you know you will get an exact fit (beware: UK
and US sizes are slightly different). International shipping has to be arranged
directly with the store.

Birkenstock Express
www.footwise.com
No longer just the footwear of choice for superannuated hippies, Birkies have
become positively hip in the past few years, and this site offers every style of
shoes, sandals, clogs and boots you can imagine. Work out your precise size
in the fitting room (Birkenstock is a German company so you need to translate
the sizes) and the site will remember it for future purchases. Prices are average,
but there are some deals to be had in the Bargain section. Second-day air
delivery starts at $7.75 depending on your order.

Cloud Walkers
www.cloudwalkers.com
This site promises supreme comfort rather than high fashion, so your feet will
thank you if you take them shopping here. There's a wide range of women's
shoes on offer, from winter boots to summer sandals, and the prices are
reasonable given the care and design that goes into them. Standard shipping
starts at $3.95 and takes up to 8 days, though there are speedier options.

Nordstrom Shoes
http://shoes.nordstrom.com
Imelda Marcos herself would be overjoyed at the range of shoes on offer here:

more than 20,000 pairs, all with the flair and quality you would expect from Nordstrom. Whether you're after classy or casual, you can check out the newest looks in the Trend section, or just shop by brand from Aerosoles to Wolverine. Most orders are sent via priority mail, and you can return any items unused for a full refund, or exchange them at your nearest Nordstrom store.

Off The Bottom
www.handmadeshoes.com
A small but tough range of rubber-soled, leather-upper sandals and flip-flop thongs made in Hawaii, perfect for long lazy days on the beach. Various groovy styles for both men and women are available, and every pair comes with a lifetime guarantee. US priority mail shipping costs $5.45.

Payless Shoe Source
www.payless.com
Online version of the familiar "pile 'em high, sell 'em cheap" shoe store. Prices are excellent, with regular sales and deals making this a mecca for bargain hunters. Select by size then style, and then have your order delivered to your door (shipping costs start at a very reasonable $1.85) or pick it up yourself at your nearest Payless store for no extra charge.

Steve Madden
www.stevemadden.com
Great choice of hip and happening footwear for groovers of all ages and foot sizes (there's a special Size 11+ section for girls blessed with big feet). This fun and easy site allows you to browse by size, price or category, and there's a clear and helpful FAQ section if you need further information before you buy. Prices are good and it's well worth checking the Outlet section for further bargains. Shipping costs are calculated at the checkout and you should receive your order within 7-10 days.

Team Shoe
www.teamshoe.com
Get a pair of high quality classic canvas sneakers featuring the logo and colors of your favorite NCAA school, whether it's the Florida Gators or the Kentucky Wildcats. The shoes are machine-washable, and cost $29.95 per pair plus $5.50 shipping. Your order should reach you within 10 days.

Zappos
www.zappos.com
This is the site to come to if you

Hawaii, fabled home of Five-O, rock-a-hula babies and this online emporium selling handsome shoes

know what you're looking for and have had trouble finding it elsewhere. Every style from solid comfort to high fashion is catered for and prices are competitive. If you're lucky, you might even win some free shoes in the site's weekly competition. Delivery is free on orders over $99 and there's a 60-day money-

 **For cyclists, cops, cowboys...**

If you're looking for something really specific, try one of the sites below:

Boots for Less
www.bootsforless.com
Discount prices on Western, work and motorcycle boots.

Bootstop Southwest
www.bootstop.com
If lizard, ostrich or even stingray skin cowboy boots are on your wishlist, this is the place to come. Fancy inlay or overlay work by individual quotation.

Bowling Shoe Depot
www.bowlingshoedepot.com
Great prices on name-brand bowling shoes like Dexter and Linds. Free shipping.

California Daze
www.californiadaze.com
Skateboarding shoes with terrific names like Tryst, Riot and Stealth.

Five ten
www.fiveten.com
Technical information and prices for specialist rock-climbing shoes.

Golf Shoes Plus
www.golfshoesplus.com
Golf shoes and accessories (including clubs) for the Tiger Woods in you.

If The Shoe Fits, Etc.
www.iftheshoefitsetc.com
Children's shoes with an emphasis on style and correct fitting. Dancewear too.

In Style Shoes
www.instyleshoes.com
Discount prices on a big range of athletic shoes, including hard-to-find Nikes.

North Wave
www.northwave.com
Flashy site with great selection of cycling shoes and snowboarding boots.

Spot Bilt
www.spotbilt.com
Robust but comfortable shoes (as approved by the Chicago Police Dept).

Webbed Foot
www.webbedfoot.com
Dance shoes are their speciality, but they also carry hiking boots, athletic shoes and everyday sneakers. Dance and sports gear are also carried.

Snow sports

All the essential gear
for the slopes, from the hippest
clothing to the coolest equipment.
Even beginners can look the part
on their way downhill, and of course
keep up with the in crowd back at the
ski lodge. Plaster casts not supplied.

 Skiing Who said it's downhill all the way?

Akers Ski, Inc.
www.akers-ski.com
Fairly basic, but easy-to-navigate site specializing in cross-country skis and
equipment, although there's also plenty in their accessories and clothing
departments to interest downhill skiers too. The search facility is speedy and
comprehensive if you know what you're looking for, or you can just browse
through what's on offer. There's a 30-day refund policy on all purchases,
and shipping charges will be calculated at the checkout.

Extreme Comfort
www.extremecomfort.com
No matter how hard you ski, a day on the slopes will always involve waiting to
let the ski school go past, sitting on chairlifts and generally freezing your ass
off. Combat those frozen extremities with Extreme Comfort's range of hand
and feet warmers, and glove and boot heaters which will easily see off the
worst of the weather. Groovy ski accessories, too. Shipping is free within the
mainland US (Alaska and Hawaii residents should phone to arrange delivery).

Finish Line Sports
www.svst.com
Top dollar equipment needs a lot of looking after, and this is the place to come
for tools and products to keep those expensive skis and boots in great shape.
It's all here, from resins to file to edge bevellers, with a sprinkling of technical
tips too. There's no shopping cart on the site, but there's an 800 number you
can call to place an order and they'll tell you shipping charges before you buy.

FOR THE DASHING BLADES

Resorts around the world are filling up with kids whizzing around on what look like two skis that have met with a terrible accident. Even Britain's Prince Harry was seen sporting a natty pair of snowblades on a recent royal ski trip. Since they are still pretty new, blades are harder to find online, but the following sites are worth checking out:

Blades In Action
www.bladinaction.com

Ski and Skate
www.skiskate.com

Lazer Blades
www.lazerblades.com

If just going downhill is starting to get a trifle dull, you can always try the freer telemark bindings to enable you to embark on a bit of cross-country. Learn more about telemarking and the equipment required at:

TSS
www.tss-online.com

The Back Country
www.thebackcountry.net

Telemarkski.com
www.telemarkski.com

Gear Direct

www.geardirect.com

All the gear you need for great skiing at outstanding prices. Check out the featured product section for some stunning bargains, such as V-Matic Easy Carve skis for only $139.99 (usually $380) and if you register, you can knock a further 5 per cent off your purchases. The site also stocks equipment for other outdoor sports such as biking and skateboarding. Standard shipping is FedEx 2-day and starts at $12, or you can arrange an express delivery for a further charge.

Rei

www.rei.com

Despite the hectic home pages, a wade through this vast outdoor site will turn up a fabulous selection of ski gear at terrific prices. As well as bargains on skis and boots themselves, there are particular savings to be made on hi-tech clothing such as Polartec fleeces and thermal underwear, plus a useful gift finder if you're shopping for someone else. Shipping costs depend on the size of your order (a pair of skis being somewhat more hassle than a pair of goggles), but there's an online Delivery Date finder so you can work out when your shipment will arrive.

Ski Net

www.skinet.com

When you're looking to buy skis or boots for the first time, how do you find out which ones are the best for you? This vast ski resource site has nothing to sell, but its Gear section is packed with up-to-date product reviews and has a Gear Finder tool which can match your skill level against a database of different skis. There are also plenty of lively message boards where snow dudes argue about the relative merits of Atomic Beta V8.20s versus the Salomon X-Scream Series.

Snow Country

www.snowcountrysports.com

This impressively designed outdoor sports store offers a wide selection of skis, boots, accessories and clothing for both adults and kids, so you're likely to find everything you need in one place. It also offers you tips, a question-and-answer page, and a calendar of events, and it can keep you up to date about the snowfall in Colorado or wherever you're headed. Prices are reasonable, and there are good bargains to be found in the Last Run outlet. Shipping is by UPS (2-day, 3-day or ground) and costs are posted before you buy.

Keep bang up to date with the snowfall in Colorado, buy some gear and get (most of) your basic questions answered

Snow Shack
www.snowshack.com

Search by manufacturer or equipment type for good deals on many top brand skiing products. There are also a few enterprising accessories that you'll be thankful for on bad weather days – frequent snow sitters should consider the thermal Butt Muff for extra comfort on their next ski trip. There's a choice of shipping options depending on how quickly you need to hit the slopes, and most items are sent via UPS.

Sno-Ski
www.sno-ski.net

No actual skis or boots for sale, but a huge range of skiing accessories such as goggles and ski carriers. The novelties section (watches, CD Roms) was disappointingly practical, but the porcelain Ski Bum statue in the close-out section (a bargain at $49.98) was beyond kitsch. The site also offers a gift wrapping service so it's a great place to look for presents for snow bunnies. How about a Hot Loc Ski Rack ($39.98) to protect an expensive pair of skis? You can return any item unused within 30 days for a full refund, and shipping costs between $4.95 and $24.95 depending on which service you use.

TECHNICAL INFORMATION

You can get further technical information on any skis you're considering at these manufacturers' websites:

Elan	www.elanskis.com
Dynastar	www.dynastar.com
Goode	www.goode.com
K2	www.k2skis.com
Rossignol	www.skisrossignol.com
Salomon	www.salomonsports.fr
Telemarkski	www.telemarkski.com
Volkl	www.volkl.com

Snowboarding

Be the dude who says "Eat my snow"

A Snowboards

www.a-snowboards.com

A Snowboards don't actually sell their products (or those of their partners, Northwave and Kana Beach) online, but deserve a mention for the imagination used in putting their site together. Downloading first time around takes time, but once in, you can travel around the cartoon snow village visiting the bar for a bit of snowboarding chat and the shop to see what's hot this season. Each snowboard description includes a freestyle or freeride rating. Jackets, boots and bindings are also available for window shopping. Worth a look for a bit of research if you take your hobby seriously.

Big Deal

www.bigdeal.com

Big Deal is divided into separate snow, skate and wakeboard shops, but browsing remains quite difficult due to the sheer number of items stocked. Select boards, for example, and you get to see the first 12 in a range of 194. You can opt to search by brand if you know what you want – top names include Salomon, Gnu and Morrow. Prices are for the serious boarder, whether you're looking to buy the works or just a pair of thermal gloves – boards begin at $400. Each item comes with a full spec sheet and enlarged images. Our advice is to head straight for the specials section, where deals help to lessen the financial pain of the whole experience.

Bond Snow

www.bondsnow.com

Okay, so there are only 3 designs to choose from, but we're talking handcrafted boards here – special specifications, a wood core between 2 pieces of unidirectional fiberglass, and 3-D state-of-the-art cosmetics – all priced neatly between $100 and $200. If you don't need options but do want a special board to impress your buddies, Bond has the Lizard, Junior and Performance to meet your needs.

Chaos Sports Inc

www.chaossnowboards.com

For custom-built boards you can either contact California-based Chaos direct to discuss details and prices (they promise "sensible customer-driven solutions") or use their site to select a board and then add the graphics (any Chaos graphic can be put on any board). You can even design your own graphics for your choice of board, and each board is made to order with your choice of flex size. Details and prices are clearly displayed. You'll probably end up paying around $350 including delivery – quite expensive, but you will come out with a unique board that will be the envy of your friends.

Fusion
www.fusion.com

Either browse through the usual categories of gear (boots, boards, clothing, accessories) or search by your favorite brand. The tiny pictures are hard to view and the tiny condensed type difficult to read, but clicking on the desired item brings an enlarged image and (usually) extended information. Videos and watches (well, 1, when we visited) are among the extras, and there are sections for surfers and skaters. Shipping is by FedEx ground and reasonably cheap costs (which are displayed) vary according to the amount of your order.

Jester
www.jester.com

The Jester's site (which also caters for skaters) is stylish but hasn't gone overboard on the "we're so cool factor" evident with some competitors. Search by product (boards, boots, accessories and bindings all included) or, for those in the know, by brand (top names include Vans, Avalanche, Heelside and Betty Rides, although we're not too sure about this last one). Music, games, electronics and a women's section (including a thoughtful Girls' View feature) complete what's on offer. There are no discounts, but prices vary from moderate (around $200) to pricey ($450), so you should be able to find something to suit. Ordering is simple, and shipping (by a choice of UPS services) is competitive, at the most $30.

Snowtraders
www.snowtraders.com

This site sells boards, boots, and almost every accessory imaginable, but the shine begins to disappear when you start shopping. Many items are discounted but prices are still high compared to their competitors. Boards remain around the $400 level. If you do find something you can afford, you can't move any further until you register all your details with the site. There's a choice of shipping prices, from $5 (standard ground) to $35 (overnight). On the upside, the information about each item and choice of colors and sizes is unrivalled, so at least you do get good customer service for parting with all that money.

TDC Snowboards
www.tdcsnowboards.com

The TDC site is simple in layout, but can be confusing. You can select a board (own brand or from a large range of others) and choose the size and color, but

MEANWHILE IN MONTANA
Resort Ski Network
www.rsn.com

If you measure out your life in ski holidays, you might want to log onto Resort Ski Network. The site has won loads of awards but what really makes it stand out is an idea so simple it's pure genius. RSN has put webcams on the slopes of 110 ski resorts.

When you do your planning you can check the weather via webcam, then buy your gear and even order your holiday (often at low prices) through this site. And even if you can't go skiing, you can console yourself with the thought that there's no snow in Big Sky, Montana – not today anyway.

The only problem with this French snowboarding site is that its cartoon snow village is so charming that after a few minutes' browsing you find yourself wanting to live there

then you can only order by phone. (Ask about shipping costs, because no info is provided here.) Clicking on a board will bring up an enlarged image, but no amount of feverish clicking will get you any of the information you get with the other items (boots, bindings, accessories). Confused? You will be. TDC is a useful site, but if you already own the very latest fiberglass board technology, you won't find the next level here. What you will find are plain, inexpensive boards, ideal for those just starting to snowboard and who aren't willing to pay over $150, or who haven't yet grasped that it's all in the design.

Ten 80
www.ten80.com
Ten 80 sells a limited selection of men's, women's and kids' ski and snowboard clothing but these are no ordinary jackets and pants. Every detail of the design and production has been carefully thought through, even down to where the lift-pass pocket will be located, and whether underarm ventilation is needed. Obviously such technical precision-detailing doesn't come cheap: jackets are around the $275 price range. There's plenty of detail on each item (except, oddly, the competition wear) but, annoyingly, you can only buy the caps and bucket hats featured online; you have to contact one of the listed dealers if you want one of those stylish jackets or zip pants. www.telemarkski.com

Sports

Whether you're into basketball or bodybuilding, the Net can kit you out so at least you look the part. It can also act as your online personal trainer. Now if only it could just go to the gym for you...

 General Outdoors, indoors, in the gym, on the field

A Workout
www.aworkout.com
Billed as "your virtual personal trainer", this site offers (for $10 a month) a food plan and exercise routine that is constantly revised as you e-mail in your experience after each workout. Sadly you have to get to the gym on your own. A small online store sells such things as supplements and protein drinks, but there seemed no easily accessed information on shipping rates and the return policy. A useful discussion page allows you to get advice from other members. A unique idea that relies on you to keep in touch for best results.

Fogdog
www.fogdog.com
If you're a complete sports nut, Fogdog might just prove *too* exciting. You're unlikely to find another store with as many sporting categories and double that in sub-categories. For each sport you can learn, shop and even share your opinions with other like-minded fans. You seldom find this much comprehensive additional information with detailed views, comparison charts, customer ratings and reviews anywhere. Prices are good and they offer excellent customer service. One of the best and may, hopefully, get better as the site was being revamped as this book went to press.

Jack La Lanne BeFit Enterprises
www.jacklalanne.com
Yes, Jack and Elaine are still around, taking advantage of the latest technology to keep spreading their own special brand of fitness. You can

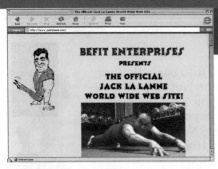

view clips from Jack's old fitness show and TV specials about the couple. If you are sufficiently inspired, you can order video tapes and books to put it all into practice. Now catering to the over-fifties, this is a nostalgic look into an icon's career that just keeps on going, and going, and going.

Sports Authority
www.thesportsauthority.com
A cocky name you might think, but fortunately the content lives up to it. This straightforward site excels itself in terms of information overload, with descriptions, spec sheets and in-depth benefit reports. With such an extensive catalog, even those on the most meager budget should find something to buy. Delivery charges start at $4.99.

Sports Terminal
www.sportsterminal.com
Sadly, this isn't a site which warns you that sports can be fatal. It's not quite that much fun, but it isn't bad. If you didn't quite make it to the majors but you're still the kind of sports nut who keeps tabs on high school wonders of the future, Sports Terminal is a frantic but comprehensive sporting directory. Every sport from the obvious (baseball to boxing) to the more idiosyncratic (lacrosse) are covered, with news, player stats, fixtures, league tables and links to buy those ever-stylish caps and acrylic shirts. One for crazed rooters.

Yoga Zone
www.yogazone.com
Yoga has never been so popular, and if you think there isn't much by way of products related to the practice, you are wrong. This site has not just mats and leotards, but videos, books, CDs, incense burners… there's even such a thing as a Cosmic Cushion on sale. And with a cable television show by the same people, you can put all that gear into practical use.

Team kits and a whole lot more

Athletic Team Uniforms Direct
www.ateamuniformsdirect.com
This site offers direct from the manufacturer quality team kits. The selection
is vast with a wide color choice. Lettering is not offered, thus keeping costs
down. The minimum order is $100; the more you order, the lower prices go.

Backcountré
www.backcountre.com
This well-organized site concentrates on outerwear for rugged sports like
mountain biking, mountaineering, adventure sailing and skiing. Specialty
items include hydration kits, navigation equipment and portable stoves.
A sensible "Tip" page will ensure a safe day out. Custom design available.

Complete Sportswear
www.sportsteam.com
Primarily for the high school or university team (and lovers of lurid typography)
this site has everything from uniforms and cheerleading gear to mascots.
There is a good selection in each category with many color options. Some
items are only represented by a drawing but we all know what a track uniform
looks like, don't we? Minimum order is $100, with no discounts on shipping.

Jacques Morét
www.moret.com
A small, specific selection of exercise apparel for women and kids. The outfits
are geared for general gym workouts, with good illustrations and descriptions.
An added bonus is the Travel Workout section, with addresses of gyms all
over the US, plus recommended jogging paths and a profile of each city.

We Play Sports
www.weplay.com
Good to see a site that has its policies and shipping details on the homepage.
This site caters to the serious athlete, with a good selection of general gear
plus brand names and links to team pro shops.

 **No more excuses**

Big Fitness
www.bigfitness.com
A good selection of new and reconditioned equipment, and again the
shipping is free. The navigation bar leads you to all necessary info, so there's

no having to hunt around for the return policy. The only complaint with this site is the type size – squinting at the screen can't really be good for you.

Body Trends

www.bodytrends.com

This site wants to do more than sell you exercise equipment. It wants you to adopt a healthy lifestyle and to that end has articles about dieting, injury prevention and pregnancy. A monthly newsletter carries fitness tips and seasonal recipes. The fitness equipment for sale is divided into men, women, athletes and new moms, with a separate section for fitness professionals. A clear, easy site that's more than just product. Ground shipping is free.

Coast Fitness

www.coastfitness.com

This site ships for free in the continental US and its selection of equipment is solid. Good specifications and a highly descriptive paragraph takes some of the doubt out of ordering equipment without being able to try it out. No advice or articles, just a clear, simple online catalog.

Fit2Fit

www.fitauthority.com

This site also has a personalized exercise program plus a freely available newsletter with tips and specials. Essentially, though, it's an online store full of all the equipment, videos and accessories you might need. There's also a good fitness forum, well used by members. The return policy is clear, but brace yourself for some serious shipping costs.

Just Balls

www.justballs.com

Just Balls should really be called All Balls, as everything from sport and fitness to toy and even engraved balls can be ordered online here. Unless you have a

If you're serious about shedding those pounds then Fit2Fit has plenty of gear and advice to offer

passion for balls you won't necessarily be familiar with those of the Koosh, Swiss and Body therapy varieties, but a vast range of foot-, base- and basketballs are also included. There's not much more you can say about balls and, to its credit, the site doesn't really try: there's none of that science of balls nonsense. The navigation is sub-Amazonian. Delivery charges start at $2.95 for UPS ground shipping.

Topaz Medical
www.topazusa.com
This site sells equipment used in rehabilitation exercise. The selection is small: simply Mediballs and sleds. The description of exercises is disappointing – it tells you what they are for, but not how to perform them. The price list is on a separate page for no obvious good reason, and there's an annoying form that you have to fill in rather than "add to cart" options. No help in calculating the shipping charges either.

 **If the shoe fits**

Brown's Enterprises
www.nbstl.com
A New Balance retailer who also provides plenty of information on foot care and pedorthics (that's manufacturer-speak for the science, design and manufacture of shoes). Prices are discounted and shipping free for orders over $100.

California Daze
www.californiadaze.com
Skateboarding shoes is a niche market for sure, but one that has been around for 20 years. This site is simple in the extreme. There is no info about the brands or the advantage of one style over another, just pictures and prices. But the shipping and return policies are clear, and if you can't see what you want, you can e-mail them and they may be able to find it.

Classic Sports Shoes
www.classicsportsshoes.com
An online store stocking the big names from Adidas to Tretorn. More than just a catalog listing of shoes and

prices; as you select each shoe, there is a paragraph of information about the style's design and function. Shipping gets cheaper the more you order.

New Balance

mall.miamicity.net/cgi-bin/newbalance.storefront

An easy-to-navigate site with clear info on the hows, whys and wherefores of ordering online. There's also a section on shoe construction, so you can see the R&D your bucks are being spent on (or so you hope). There's also an "Ask the Pro" section for expert answers by e-mail.

 **From fishing to martial arts to nostalgia**

1-800-Paintball

store.yahoo.com/800paintball/index.html

Paintball is no longer just for executives trying to promote "team building", it must be one of the fastest growing sports and this is a good place to find the necessary gear. Costs will add up – face goggle, CO_2 bottle, hopper and elbow, not to mention the gun and paint! Packages and sale items ease the pain, but beware the 20 per cent restocking fee on all returns.

1st Choice Bowling Supply

www.1stchoicebowlingsupply.com

This site carries a great selection of products, but you have to re-enter item numbers into an order form rather than clicking a simple "add to cart" button. A "call for latest prices" instruction doesn't make the process any easier if you are on the opposite coast, and seems almost to defeat the idea of being able to order online conveniently.

Altrec

www.altrec.com

If you're going camping, hiking, snowboarding, trail-running or even fly-fishing you'll find everything you could possibly need under one roof, even down to a thermos flask. Narrow your search down to a specific sport or select a product and particular brand to speed up your shopping. Top brands include Salomon, Marmot, Eagle Creek plus many more, with discounts galore. Once you're all kitted out, Altrec also offers a comprehensive travel and adventure directory. A good general site.

Bingham Projects

www.binghamprojects.com

Everything you'll need to buy a traditional longbow and to recurve it if that should prove necessary. The very simple homepage has a prominent and very beautiful picture of a deer at sunset on it; the implied message being, presumably, "This is your target".

Weird and wacky Sepak Takraw, anyone?

Too skinny to be a football player? Too short to get near the NBA? Then why not start a new trend in your neighborhood by having a go at one of these?

Boomerangs
www.concentric.net/~Davisks/catalog/
Prepare for a boomerang boom as a wealth of portals open up with tips on throwing technique and handcrafted boomers to buy. Check out the link for tailored advice for beginners upwards.

Carpet Discs
www.carpetdisc.com
Who needs balls when you have the carpet disc, which can be used in golf, basketball, bowls, even track and field. This $5.95 wonder can also be used as a handy seat cover, presumably for when you're watching a real sport.

Disc Golfer
www.discgolfer.com
Based on the swish design of this disc golf site, we'd say this could be one to watch for in future Olympics. Bags, discs and clothing, recommended by the best touring disc golf players including Al "Sugar" Schack.

Sandboarding
www.venomousboards.com
Do you live near the desert plains but want to be a surfer dude? No worries. Sandboarding is about to take off, and boards, clothing and accessories can be bought online; board prices start around $160.

Sepak Takraw
www.gajahmas.com
Sepak Takraw is Malaysia's premier sport and if you're not put off by the high kicks in the photo gallery, why not place an order? Shipping is free.

Street Luge
www.landluge.com
As if luge wasn't mad enough, now you can throw yourself down a concrete track in the name of street luge. Butt boards, bushings and bumpers for sale.

Twirling
www.fultonstrim.com
A serious business for many adolescent girls. Just count the rhinestones here. Could batons be the female equivalent of the light saber?

Bicycle Mall
www.bicyclemall.com
A directory of bicycle shops and classifieds. You find the product you want, type in your zip code, and the site will produce all participating stores which carry that item within a certain radius of your location. Links to these stores are, however, a bit hit and miss, and you can't always order online.

Boaters World
www.boatersworld.com
Unimaginative design, but the same can never be said about the products. Obviously you'll find a fishing rod or 20, but they also sell items slightly more high-tech than a piece of string attached to a twig, with fish finders, depth sounders and GPS systems to find your nearest Moby Dick. Ordering is simple with useful descriptions and images. Prices are competitive.

Chicks Discount Saddlery
www.chicksaddlery.com
Scroll down the list of items here and you should find what you need from the lists of English and Western saddlery, tack and apparel, and lots more horse equipment. Grooming supplies and medication are also available at discounted prices. There's online ordering from the printed catalog but the order form annoyingly requires you to insert the model number and description.

Chuckie Jones Extreme
store.yahoo.com/chuckiejonesextreme/index.html
While not the biggest online skateboarding store, this was blissfully easy to

Tell Bicycle Mall the bike you want and they'll provide links to all the nearest stockists; then you just have to hope those links work...

use, with terms and conditions up front. A simple click and the item is in your cart. A bit more product info would be useful, but otherwise no complaints.

Classic Jerseys

www.classicjerseys.com

Hockey and baseball jerseys from long-gone but not forgotten teams, reproduced and for sale. The hockey selection is extensive and the newer baseball section is promised to expand. Orders are custom made so delivery can take 6-8 weeks, but they do allow refunds on customized jerseys.

Cyclone Taylor Sports

www.cyclonetaylor.com

Get your sticks, helmets, skates and jerseys here – and if you're not sure of your size, send in your measurements and it will be sorted out. Don't see what you want? Give the company a call as they probably stock it in the offline shop. A nifty facts section tells you such things as the importance of flex and lie when buying a stick. Yet again an annoying order form that you have to fill in with product descriptions, but no moans apart from that.

Fitness Etc

www.fitnessetc.com

Aimed at the body-building market, Fitness Etc has a range of clothing to showcase your hard-earned muscles to the best advantage. Posing suits, tights and string vests are just a few items available. You can even get digital fat calipers to keep track of your progress towards that body beautiful.

Football

www.football.com

This site is an Aladdin's cave of information, headline news, stats, reviews, games, and schedules. The shop has general football equipment as well as

NIKE GETS PERSONAL

The Nike iD store makes a big noise about its interactivity and it does give you the chance to customize your Nike gear. Up to a point. It allows you to take a step away from off-the-shelf footwear, and bring a little originality to your fashion style, but your newly designed trainers are a one-off solely because you've branded it with your name of choice.

If your name is John or your preferred nickname is the Fonz, however, you'll probably discover you've wasted your time and there'll be plenty of others wearing footwear identical to yours. The Nike iD process works by letting you select one of three basic shoe styles, choose your base and accent colors, and add your own ID. They then assemble it and send it to you within 3 weeks.

www.nike.com

team specific gear, accessories, videos, games, posters and novelty items. A one-stop shop.

Hoop Heaven
www.hoop-heaven.com
This site has a wide variety of basketball-related merchandise including cards, videos and novelty items. The downside is there are no photos for many products, and you have to write down the items you want and then insert the information into the order form. Better design and illustrations would help make this site a little more user-friendly.

Pacific Rim
www.iloveracing.com
Featuring branded clothing (Honda, HKS) as well as original designs, this site sells T-shirts, posters, stickers, frames, software – in other words, anything to do with racing other than the actual cars.The instructions are clear, and the site is reassuringly large and professional.

Sakura Martial Arts Supply
www.sakura-0.com
Martial Arts practitioners are no longer just male teenagers who dream of becoming Kwai Chang Caine. This site sells all the equipment you need: uniforms, mats, belts, books, protection gear and a frightening selection of swords and weapons. There's also an online auction.

Soccer Shop USA
www.soccershopusa.com
This shop has a good selection of equipment and apparel for soccer players, and promises to beat any advertised price in the world. There are clear illustrations and pictures, and an order form that shows the various shipping charges already calculated each time you add to your cart. There's a 24-hour shipping guarantee too.

Tennis Company
www.tenniscompany.com
Another site that has the professionalism and clarity that gives confidence to the first time Net shopper. A large selection of products, an easy-to-use navigation bar and clear policy and contact page. The people behind this site seem knowledgeable and keen to offer the best service. How refreshing.

Television & video

The only place TV and the Web are really merging is in commercial hyperspace, where you can get bargain deals or spend a fortune on a plasma display

General For those who want to merge with their sofa

800
www.800.com
Not all the categories at this general electrical store offer more than a few products to choose from, but if you're shopping for a new TV set or DVD player you could end up complaining about too much choice. Search by brand or price to view feature lists, reviews and enlarged pictures. With such a selection you should easily be able to find something in your price range; otherwise check out the sale items, reduced by as much as $100.

Abes of Maine
www.abesofmaine.com
Despite specializing in photography equipment, Abe's also sells a limited selection of video recorders and DVD players, from top names including Sony, Pioneer and Panasonic. Information is extensive – though jargon heavy – and there are prices to match all pockets: DVD players from $250 to $1,000.

Best Buy
www.bestbuy.com
A comprehensive site, with everything from the sets and players to the furniture from which you can build your entertainment center. The information is detailed with additional facts and recommendations. Where they fail is in catering for those who simply want to buy at the best price and aren't too interested in whether their plasma display is state of the art or not. Admittedly

Best Buy sells below the RRP, but prices are often kept under wraps until you get to the checkout, giving those with budget concerns a major headache.

Cheetah Deals
www.cdeals.com

We were expecting a few animated big cats and groovy black-and-orange designs, but the Cheetah website blends in with the hundreds of other electrical retailers out there. Still, it's not all about image. You can select from portable to projection-size screens and portable to recording DVD players. But Cheetah does catch the eye with its prices. Names are top of the range – Toshiba, Panasonic, Sony – but you'll be able to pick up a DVD player for less than $200. Orders are processed within 2 business days and shipping is free on some items.

Circuit City
www.circuitcity.com

Considering how long the television has been around you'd think buying one would be a simple process. What else is there to consider other than if it has a remote? It's not so simple, however, if you're faced with decisions on 7in, 14in and up to 31in models, tube, digital and projection, coded and uncoded DVD. They might as well give us the parts and let us construct our own.

Circuit City is ideal for those who like to have such choices and enjoy learning about the intricate workings of a set before they take the plunge. Read the articles, browse the spec sheets complete with jargon explanation and scroll through the list of 82-tube television sets alone. Prices from $250 to $3,500.

DTV City
www.dtvcity.com

If size does matter to you, DTV City sells only widescreen televisions and when we say widescreen, these models are up to 63in and beyond. Obviously big sizes mean big prices: from $2,000 to $20,000 for branded plasma and projection systems. Ordering comes complete with order tracker, but you generally have to call DTV direct if you want one of the pricier items.

Great and unique spherical space age television in excellent and restored electronic condition!

Simply perfect for watching *Lost in Space* or the original *Flash Gordon* in glorious black and white?

Egghead
www.egghead.com

Egghead sells retail and wholesale goods via its online store, so prices are good, but you have to get in quick. The homepage is busy yet well-organized; head for the "After Work" category for visual products. Prices are worth the time it takes to find something to suit – the initial one-line descriptions certainly aren't much help – with Panasonic TV and DVD combos going for $600 on our last visit. You will, however, have to register to use the service.

Good Guys
www.goodguys.com
Standard but comprehensive site offering good deals on TV sets, VCRs and DVD players. The information on the general product page will allow you to make a confident purchase; if it's a dissertation about the latest dual-deck VCR you're after, that's there too. And if it's got the features you want but doesn't match the other chrome items in your entertainment center, there are direct links to similar products.

Harvey Online
www.harveyonline.com
Harvey's dreary design doesn't do justice to all the useful tools featured. It doesn't allow you beyond the homepage until you have first checked whether they deliver goods in your area. From here you can simply search, by brand or price, the mammoth selection of plasma and projection display screens, DVD players and VCRs. They'll also help you create your perfect home entertainment area – though at these prices most of you will simply be talking TV rather than watching it. eBay bargains to be found at the Swap & Shop stop.

New Era Antiques
neweraantiques.com/overview.cgi?televisions
Hard to believe but TV is now so old that you can buy retro models. And they don't come much more retro than this. For around $200 you can get portable TV sets from the likes of JVC, Hotpoint, General Electric and Admiral. The *Happy Days* 1950s designs range from two-tone color models to what look like astronaut helmets. No online buying sadly but you can e-mail to ask how to buy. You might also want to drop in on www.retrostuff.com which has an *I Love Lucy* toy TV set for less than $20. It sounds horrendous, looks charming and may well be sold on eBay for a small fortune in the year 2025.

Remote Control Finder
Fox.NSTN.Ca/~gfong
If the only time your television is off is when you can't find the remote, here is the solution. The site should win an award for amateur appearance but the producers have definitely cornered a niche market. The match-boxed sized

device can be attached to any remote, then just clap your hands and it will betray its hiding place by beeping. The perfect gift for your favorite couch potato. E-mail orders are accepted at $5.95 plus postage and packaging.

Vanns.com
www.vanns.com
Good prices on top-name DVD players, replay television systems and VCRs, but no actual TV sets. Browse, search by brand, or get the shopping assistant to get back to you with what you need rather than what manufacturers want you to buy. Delivery is free via UPS ground, and although you must register, membership is free and you get exclusive offers and 30 per cent discounts.

Advice Put yourself in the picture

Active Buyers Guide
www.activebuyersguide.com
This ingenious idea is perfect for the clueless among us. And it's still worth a look even if you think you're pretty savvy with the entertainment game. The instructions displayed on the navigation bar make it all sound easy and (for once) it is. Select any category of product (not just televisions but everything from baby strollers to rowing machines), add a few specifications and Active will come up with an expert's selection of products best suited to your individual needs. You can make your search as detailed as you choose with price, brand and feature specifications, and if you're just looking for a nudge in the right direction, the general advice details the kind of prices you should be looking to pay and what additional features are actually worth the money. Once you've made your choice, they'll gently lead you to where you can put that money down.

JUNK TV

Not as in Jerry *"I married a horse"* Springer (the working title of one of his banned shows) but as in "$4.95 for a 4in model TV set that plays *Frosty the Snowman* and *Rudolf the Rednosed Reindeer* by people you're too young to remember". This can only be bought on Yahoo Shopping as the shop's own URL (*www.sterling. store.com*) links to a page about domains. However, if you're more intrigued by TV's future, be amazed at *www.flat-tv.com*.

ETown
www.etown.com
Professional site with consumer-friendly advice on buying everything from a tiny portable television to a complete home theatre. Whether you're more concerned about value and performance, or you're after the very best, eTown can lead you to specific machines, and the best doesn't always work out as the most expensive. If you like what you see, there are direct links to buy at the best possible prices, with hundreds of dollars in discounts on all items.

If your roof seems naked without a dish

Blue Sky Satellite
www.satellitedeals.com
Nothing to buy online, but if you're a complete satellite novice, Blue Sky is a useful starting point. Read up on installation requirements, check out the free installation and dish offers and choose from the vast channel packages from DirecTV and the Dish Network. If you find anything you like, call to buy.

Bulverde Home Theatre
www.satellitezone.com
Bulverde has enhanced its satellite boxes and dishes by adding color to the site. The site also neatly guides you to the 500 channels. Use the scroll down menu to view complete systems, accessories and channels available to buy online, with just enough technical information to inform but not confuse.

You might also find these sites of some use:

Audio Excellence
www.audioexcellence.com
Search by brand for a limited selection of visual products at knockdown prices. Good value but you need to know exactly what model you want.

Outpost
www.outpost.com
Comprehensive, with products supplied by Tweeters. Standard prices with free delivery on some items.

Roxy
www.roxy.com
Limited range of satellite and wireless goods from a reputable store.

Simply Cheap
www.simplycheap.com
Well-organized discount store. Pick up a VCR for only $75.

Sound City
www.soundcity.com
Jam-packed site with useful info, excellent images, and discount prices.

Total Mart
www.totalmart.com
Well-organized one-stop shop for VCRs and DVD players, but no additional information. One for those who already know what they want.

Tickets

Not the kind you need before you hop on a bus, but the kind which will see you taking in some top sporting action, an evening at the opera or getting into Anger Management on tour

General Book tickets and receive "personalized" info

Go Tickets
www.gotickets.com
A wide selection of sporting tickets are currently on sale but Go Tickets is now also expanding into theater and music. The site is easy to navigate with facilities to search by type of event or scroll through the monthly calendar. As you would expect baseball, basketball and football are all covered. There's also the option of rodeo in Las Vegas, college sports and WWF. It's annoying, however, that only members can buy online, and joining involves more than a simple password registration.

Ticket City
www.ticketcity.com
Ticket City sells all the usual sporting and entertainment tickets – Tina Turner, the Indy 500 and so on – but it also sells gateways into worlds you probably haven't considered exploring. For example you could introduce yourself to the wonders of figure skating, rodeo championships or theater shows… in London. Each new experience comes with additional information, venue details and a useful customer service section. Online ordering comes with free shipping, but note the service charges. Sadly, none of the awards events listed (the Oscars etc) had any tickets available on our visit.

Ticket Master
www.ticketmaster.com
As you would expect, Ticket Master's online offering is a slick enterprise covering all the best entertainment events, from top sporting games to Norman Rockwell exhibitions. All the information you're likely to need is featured on one helpful page; additional highlights include venue details

complete with directions, any restrictions and seating plans. Best of all, in many cases you can print out your own tickets complete with a unique barcode, so there's no hassle with delivery times and charges.

Ticket Office
www.ticketoffice.com
Ticket Office specializes in tickets to "sold out" events, so it's got to be the place to go when those must-see events sell out within minutes of the tickets going on sale. Possible options to while away your vacation time include Stomp for $125, the Cincinnati Bengals for $85, or Bon Jovi for $65. You'll probably end up paying more than slightly over the odds, but then these are hard-to-come by tickets. The site itself is a bit of a headache to navigate, with scroll-down menus and tiny script. There's also little to nothing in the way of additional information, making it hard for the casual browser. Tuna Christmas, for example, really ought to be formally introduced.

Ticket Trader
www.tickettrader.com
This one-stop shop is a quick and easy link to standard events and more unusual past times, including Anger Management on tour, Matt Groening with advice on the 21st century family, and Mickey Rooney (on how to marry, presumably). Simply scroll through the alphabetical menu, click to buy, and fill in your details. One key problem, however, is that you have to be a part of a pair or group of 4 to buy. No singletons here, thank you.

Ticket Vision
www.ticketvision.com
If you're only interested in getting to see the top class performers such as Ms Streisand or the Backstreet Boys, Ticket Vision is a good place to start. It sells theater, concert and sports tickets only for the most popular events. Search according to the venue closest to you, or your own entertainment selection from a range including NBA, NFL, NHL and MLB games, theater hits such as *Lord of the Dance* and *Fosse*, and whatever happens to be playing in Las Vegas. You can buy online but in some instances the must-buy-in-pairs rule applies.

Web Tickets
www.webtickets.com
Great selection covering every event in America, from

GROOVE TICKETS
www.groovetickets.com
Despite currently only covering California and Utah, Groove Tickets is a great site to look at if you are thinking of grooving and clubbing in the sun. Stylewise the site is bright and cheerful, but the logo of a wilting flower does make us suspect you won't feel that fresh after clubbing with De La Soul, Frankie Bones, and British DJ supremo Danny Rampling. Tickets are cheap at around $15 and if you're worried you've got nothing to wear, or you need to practice your moves before you head out into public, the site sells suitable fashion and music.

Tickets

Lakers tickets to admission to Knotts Berry Farm and those hard-to-come-by tickets for N-SYNC. On the downside you couldn't find a more confusing site. It's hard to see whether you should search by artist, tour schedule or just link to their official website. If you do persevere, their catalog is extensive and they'll even buy any of your unwanted tickets – if, for example, you realize at 55 you're just a little too old for Britney Spears…

 For the more highbrow among you...

Culture Finder

www.culturefinder.com

Leave your partner glued to the television set with sports coming out of his ears, and access the Culture Finder for all your classical, opera, dance and art needs. Search by area or event to find out the when, where, what and whos of everything that's happening. If you're looking to make an informed purchase read the selection of reviews first or send the Answer Wizards your theatrical query, and then either buy online or use the information to book in your usual way. In most cases booking online is possible.

GOING TO THE MOVIES?

www.movie-tickets.com

Movie theaters over here are starting to see the light where waiting in line is concerned. Not everyone likes to be stuck out in the cold trying to get in to see the latest Spielberg offering only to find when they reach the ticket booth that it's sold out and Jim Carrey is the next best thing. Currently only one cinema, in Santa Rosa, California has stepped forward as a guinea pig for online ticket sales, but Movie Tickets promises more in the future. To buy, simply click on your film choice and send your details. You can read reviews for a more informed choice. One to watch.

High 5 Tix

www.high5tix.org

Don't click on music and assume you're heading straight for the usual array of pop hopefuls and their arena tours. Music here means the Minnesota Orchestra or a Schubert festival. If it's theater, it's not a Broadway musical but *Hamlet* and *Julius Caesar*. Add to this a whole host of museums and opera and you have an impressive array of cultural activities. You can find out all the details on each simple page, before you buy online.

Keith Prowse

www.keithprowse.com

Dining in the Big Apple, sightseeing in New Orleans, or just enjoying the high life at Caesar's Palace, Keith Prowse has something to celebrate any occasion and the ticket prices won't always break the bank. The Jazz Brunch on the 107th floor of the World Trade Center is available most days for less than $50, and the tour of New Orleans' French quarter is cheap at $15. Simply make your selection and in most cases you can book there and then.

Ticket Vision deals strictly in A-list entertainment; this is a site devoted to those acts that expect (and get) top billing

Sports events For jocks without a ticket

AAA Tennis Tickets

www.aaatennistickets.com

You can't buy directly from the website, but AAA is a useful starting point for hard-to-come-by tickets to the US Open and the Davis Cup. For the serious tennis fanatics out there, they also hold tickets for Wimbledon and the Australian and French Opens. US Open finals tickets can currently be bought for anywhere between $225 and $2,995, depending on your seats. Seating plans are available and you can call or e-mail your request.

Daytona Race Tours

www.daytonaracetours.com

Join Daytona Race Tours' VIP mailing list and they'll send you exclusive information about future events. Otherwise the site itself is comprehensive with details of ticket prices, ranging from $175 to $600, seating charts (so that you know if your tickets are really worth the money), and hotel information right down to the en-suite facilities and mini-bar. Online ordering is available and you can track your ticket via Federal Express. It's just a pity they haven't expanded beyond Daytona.

Ticket Max

www.ticketmax.com

This site deals exclusively in sports tickets. You should be able to find access to all the top events here, the Rose, Sugar, Super and Orange Bowls included. It's not immediately obvious that you can buy online, but you can. Click on ticket prices, find the area of the particular stadium that you would like (and can afford) to sit in and click to buy. Helpfully, the site also provides additional information including package holidays, where to stay, recommended restaurants, and other snippets of info about the host city.

Toys

With more cuddly
toys than you'd find in
your local Disney store
and enough games to fill
an infinite number of rainy
days, the Net means you have
absolutely no excuse for buying
gift certificates for your niece

 Save money, time and family relationships

American Toys

www.american-toys.com

You can buy almost any toy the child in your life (and that includes your inner child) could possibly want here, as long as what you want is what this site defines as "a 19th or 20th century antique". Not really for the budget conscious but if you have $895 to invest in an art nouveau chrome robot lamp made in Turin in the 1970s, then go ahead. (Bear in mind that one of these very self-same lamps recently sold at Sotheby's for 4 times that amount.) Our favorite was the Superman record player, a steal at $165.

FAO Schwarz

www.faoschwarz.com

FAO lets you search by category, brand, boutique or character so you won't show your age buying Sindy rather than Gene. With bright colors and the occasional well-known character, the site is obviously geared towards the kids but don't let them get carried away as there are no discounts and shipping (7-10 days) can work out quite pricey, $7 for under $30 of goods.

Moomin Shop

www.moominshop.com

This Hawaii-based store has pretty much every object you could create in the image of Moomintroll and Tove Jansson's other classic characters: music boxes, stickers, fine ceramic mugs, a full wardrobe for adults and children.

Oh, and the full range of books and videos (not easily available elsewhere).

Toys R Us

www.toysrus.com

You expect a comprehensive and professional service from any outfit affiliated with Amazon, and that's what you get here. You're unlikely to find any unique, "see your child's eyes light up in amazement" kind of toys, but there are benefits to shopping here, the biggest being the range of

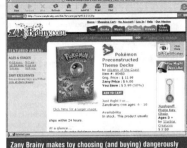

Zany Brainy makes toy choosing (and buying) dangerously easy. And with hefty discounts, it's dangerously cheap too

toys and discount prices. Customer service is excellent, with no ambiguity in shipping policies or returns. Delivery takes 3-7 days, and starts at $2.99.

Turn Off the TV

www.turnoffthetv.com

Bright and vibrant, the site is well organized and easy-to-use, being based on what you know about the child. Search the games, toys, puzzles and activity categories or age groups, or use the personal shopper or Gameologist to find the perfect present. The shopping guides and staff picks feature comprehensive reviews of a number of items, but generally the information is limited to a star rating. Not always enough if you're faced with the Orbitron game.

Zany Brainy

www.zanybrainy.com

A novice toy-buyer's dream. Not only can you search by age, brand, character, category, learning skills and even skill level, but everything is discounted, some toys by 50 per cent. There are standard and extended descriptions and enlarged images to view, and they'll keep you informed when out-of-stock items become available. You don't have to do a thing, except pay.

 From Elvis to the ancient Egyptians

Board Games

www.boardgames.com

Looking for something to brighten up a dreary Sunday? Or maybe something to drive your grandparents out of the house at Thanksgiving? Board Games holds a catalog of entertaining distractions larger than anything you're likely to

ROBOTS TO PLAY WITH

Robotoys
www.robotoys.com

Robotic pets is the latest craze to almost burn itself out. But almost every child still wants its very own Poo-Chi or Meow-Chi, and now you can even get a robotic moth, obviously not quite as cute an option.

If pets are just a little too cutesy, cutesy for your tearaway child, Robot Toys also holds a vast catalog of OWI construction kits for beginners or advanced creators, robot transformers, and standard K'NEX kits. Each robot has their own special skill, be it avoiding obstacles or solving crosswords (not), and prices range from $10 to $500, depending on just how adept your choice of model is.

find offline. The handy navigation bar on the left will lead you to games to suit parties, kids and adults, and the sub-categories ensure that you keep world domination games clear of the Elvis trivia (the 1700 Elvis trivia facts, to be precise).

Board Games Express
www.boardgamesexpress.com
All the old favorites are here: Monopoly, Hangman, Jenga and Risk. Search through the usual categories, adult, trivia, strategy, through manufacturers, or via a keyword. Every game is described in full, discount prices apply and alternatives can be suggested.

Discount Games
www.discountgames.com
Good for the unusual at outstanding prices. Discount Games displays a vast catalog of games, from the traditional to computer at bargain prices. The 28 different kinds of Monopoly, from Las Vegas to golf and Harley Davidson, should keep any competitor quiet, though the site would be improved if it featured more pictures of the games.

Timbukii
www.timbukii.com
Imagine yourself as an explorer in 1920s Cairo, or searching the depths of the Palace of Knossos with three rival archaeologists hot on your heals. Wadget, Palenque and Labyrinth of King Minos are designed to harness the Indiana Jones side of your personality. They're slightly pricier than your average board game at $60, but they are all museum quality, educational, and definitely different. Ordering is simple and there's plenty of information available about each game.

Modern toys   Bleeding potatoes explained

Cool Kids Toys
www.coolkidstoys.com
It resembles many other toy stores and has the same search facilities (by category or age group), but the toys and activities here are straight out of Bali. While you browse through pages of Little Boy Bali dolls and Indonesian magic puppets, you can read snippets of information both about the toys on display

and about Bali itself. Fun, and educational with it. The prices aren't expensive and you'll probably come away with something pretty unusual.

ExploraStore

www.explorastore.com

For those of you sick of your precious 8-year-old blowing up anything they can lay their tiny hands on, ExploraStore has suitable toys for the budding chemistry, physics and biology professor. Brief descriptions are available to explain the purpose of Putty Buddies, Crystal Farms and Bleeding Potatoes, including the vital details of whether adult supervision is necessary. Prices are affordable and ordering is, well, child's play. Almost.

Traditional toys "For kids of all ages!"

Action Man

www.actionman.com

Be warned – if you're visiting this site in the office you will become horribly conspicuous in a cybersecond as the arrival of the homepage coincides with the kind of alert siren you used to hear on the good old *USS Enterprise*. When you've chosen the country you're browsing from, you'll be called to action stations. You can't buy direct from the site but once you've reminded yourself that the Polar Mission Action Man outclasses Skateboard Extreme no problem, you can link to a variety of stores to buy. Well worth a visit – especially for thirtysomething men who can't believe the soldier of their youth is still kicking ass (and has kept all of his realistic hair).

Construction Toys

www.constructiontoys.com

Whether you're looking for something for the big kid or little kid in your life, you can't go wrong with building blocks, and Construction has them all. All the obvious names are included – Lego, Duplo and K'NEX – alongside more of your hand-crafted items: alphabet bricks for the toddlers, ImagiBricks for life-size constructions of a more disruptive nature, and Anchor Storm products that, judging by the "elegant stone building blocks" description, are suitable for your next house extension. Such simple toys don't come cheap but shipping is reasonable, there's a free gift for every $25 you spend, and if they fail to deliver in time they'll knock 10 per cent off the order.

Dolls House

www.dollshouse.co.uk/us/acatalog/index.html

If you're going to be a serious doll house collector you will need quite a hefty allowance. Prices here range from $200 to over $1,000 for a small bijou summerhouse. A large Tudor number comes in at the wrong side of $3,000.

The prices aside, the houses are beautiful, external and internal views are available, and there are hundreds of accessories allowing you to keep collecting for years to come.

E-Farm Toys

www.e-farmtoys.com/toys.htm

You can't get a more traditional, "when I was a child" type toy than good old-fashioned construction kits and farmyards. Those less ambitious in their agricultural exploits can opt for standard toy tractors and combine harvesters, with the choice of numerous accessories to customize your model. You can, however, always opt for the deluxe options, which are pedal-operated models so you can really get stuck in. Prices are anywhere between $10 and $200.

Up to toddlers — To keep the little darlings happy

Amazing Toystore

www.amazingtoystore.com

Despite a vast catalog of toys for those up to teenage years, the Amazing Toystore specializes in those at a tender age, with maternity and baby sections alongside toddlers. Search by age range or your child's budding talent – music maker, painter and so on. Top toys include hula dress-ups for the big kids, festival sound orchestras and Rolly the Cow. Prices are standard, descriptions are useful and shipping is free on orders over $25.

Babies R Us

www.babiesrus.com

The baby version of Toys R Us offers diapers, a range of gadgets and larger items such as strollers, car seats and high chairs as well as a decent selection of baby toys, Mr Potato Head, discovery centers and activity farms.

Toys by Step 2 Company

www.toysbystep2company.com

Take the little ones outside for a stint on the dolphin swing or just put them in the garden playhouse – two lovely durable plastic contraptions from the Step 2 company. Prices from $20 (carousel ponies and angel fish rockets) to $300 for kitchen sets. Shiny, plastic and just good fun.

Whimsicality

www.whimsicality.com

Link to Baby Lane through the site to find toys for those at the younger end of the scale. You won't find many synthetic materials on this site, so you do end up paying for the privilege of hand-painted wooden building blocks, and one-of-a-kind Bear and Blankie toys. Useful if you're after something special.

Single product sites Straight to the point

If you know exactly what the kid in your life wants, big or small, cut to the chase and head straight to the websites that cater for the decisive shopper.

Barbie
www.barbie.com
Flowery, plastic and pink all over, it can only be Barbie. The ultimate little girls' doll in her full glory and multiple guises, including celebrity variation Brandy, and Generation Girl, Blaine. You can't buy, but you get the full catwalk show.

Boinks
www.boinks.com
Boinks, the original pocket rockets. Shoot 'em, boink 'em or just plain rocket 'em. Terrorize your enemies without finding your name on a lawsuit.

Burp Gun
www.burpgun.com
The ultimate combat weapon that makes funny noises and shoots harmless but effective items. Go straight to the style of your choice. Shipping is even included in the price for those looking for minimum effort.

Dream Kitty
www.dreamkitty.com
A marketing dream with hundreds of items solely dedicated to the supreme plush kitty, Miss Kitty and friends, Tare Panda, Kogepan and Buru Buru Dog.

Harry's Trunk
www.harrystrunk.com
This amateur site sells merchandise solely associated with the latest craze to hit both kids and adults: Harry Potter. Products include figurines of Harry, Ron and Hermione and collectors' stones.

Waterballoon Launchers
www.waterballoonlaunchers.com
Gone are the days of water balloons simply being dropped from 10th-storey windows. Now we have the water balloon launcher (1, 2 and 3-person versions), plus video clips and advice on technique. Thank you so much…

Also worth a look:

Embryonics	www.em-bry-on-ics.com
Kid Direct	www.kiddirect.com
TX 40	toys.tx40.com/index.asp

Travel

Whether you think it's
better to travel or to arrive,
the Internet offers such a vast
choice of destinations and ways
to get there that browsing can
induce a virtual state of analysis
paralysis in the weak-willed…

 Where to go and how to get there

Airlines of the Web

www.flyaow.com

We're taking their word for it that flight and accommodation reservations can
be made online, as on our last visit the system was a little shaky. Otherwise
fill in the usual details, dates, price range and so on, and they should manage
to find a selection to suit your needs. What makes this plain, straightforward
site stand out is the additional information that could make your 16-hour flight
that little bit more bearable. Useful tips include disability-friendly airlines and
hotels, how to save on airfares and long-distance phone calls, and links to
Business Traveler magazine. The site supposedly checks all airlines for your
specified trip but we found cheaper flights elsewhere.

Atevo

www.atevo.com

If you're a planner rather than a spontaneous traveler, Atevo could be
a godsend to you. If it's destination guides you're after, select a country, state
or city to read everything from historical notes to bank holiday calendars and
tipping rules. If you like what you read, book that flight, reserve that B&B from
a choice of 20,000, and heed the wise words in the advice section: "Be nice
to ticket and gate agents as they enforce rules and can make exceptions."

Cheap Tickets

www.cheaptickets.com

Cheap Tickets prides itself on having been around for 15 years and its site
has (in the nicest possible way) a bargain-basement ambience. All your basic

requirements are catered for: flight, accommodation and car rental bookings. Yet, self-defeatingly, they insist that (unless you're booking hotels) you register before you even see what flights are on offer. On the plus side, the comparison prices and the hotel info on the power searches are excellent.

Expedia
www.expedia.com
Arguably the biggest brand in online travel, Expedia is an easy-to-navigate complete travel resource, with online booking for flights, accommodation,

Car rental The open road, a set of wheels, no gas...

Advantage Rent-a-Car
www.arac.com
Advantage, covering western America and Mexico, are so confident about prices that they'll display their own quotes alongside those of their closest competitors. Online reservations can be made, but we advise you to check the location list before you begin.

Alamo
www.alamo.com
If time rather than money is your prime consideration, simply click on "quick reservation" to avoid the sales spiel; otherwise online quotes can be obtained just as easily with the option to specify child safety features and even ski racks. Each request offers multiple car choices, with prices starting at less than $100.

Hertz
www.hertz.com
If you're looking for a bit of adventure and exploring the countryside of Cyprus, Morocco or Costa Rica is an idea, Hertz can help in all these locations. Choose your destination, dates of travel and sporty 2-door or 4-wheel drive.

Rent-A-Wreck
www.rent-a-wreck.com
If you're looking to blend in on your travels, Rent-a-Wreck specializes in used cars. Select a destination and submit your rental enquiry.

Speciality Rentals
www.specialityrentals.com
If you don't want to be seen in any old auto when you drive up to your Hollywood audition, you can pick up a BMW Z3 for the week for a little over $600 or a flashy little Corvette for $1325. Pricey, but look at it as an investment.

package holidays, car rentals, resort and even airport guides. When booking a hotel room, you can make as many specifications as you want: non-smoker, wheelchair access etc. Flights generally aren't that cheap, but it's certainly worth a look if price isn't your main concern.

My Travel Guide
www.mytravelguide.com

If you've got the time and energy to explore this site with the care and patience it requires, you will be rewarded. If you're simply after a quick fix of information, you may find all the navigation too taxing. The busy homepage directs you to continent, country and city guides, currency converters, ATM locations, driving instructions, street maps and guides to the subway systems in 60 cities around the world. You will be singularly well-prepared for your trip, but so exhaustive is all the information that your brain might need to switch to parallel processing to take it all in.

Travelocity
www.travelocity.com

As with Expedia, you can book flights, package deals, hotels and car rentals online, but the tedious registration process gets in the way of any immediate vacation gratification. Where Travelocity beats their competitors is with destination reviews from the experts and bargain flight deals. The "any date" option for those with flexible schedules is a neat idea. Stick with it if you're looking for a good deal and plenty of information.

Travelscape
www.travelscape.com

Yet another online travel agency hoping to tackle all your vacation needs, except, alas, looking after pesky youngsters while you enjoy your well earned rest. Package trips are available alongside standard flights, car rentals and accommodation bookings for the obvious destinations (Acapulco) to the not-so-obvious (New Jersey, a state which, so the local joke goes, has two seasons: winter and construction). If you're looking for a bargain, the Hot Deals section offers tons of offers, free accommodation and other discounts.

Uniglobe
www.uniglobe.com

The site design is from a genre that should be known as sub-Amazonian but that shouldn't obscure the fact that this site gets the job done. Covering everything from internal flights to European cruises, the simple system ensures that you can be on your way with little fuss. Although Uniglobe itself doesn't go in for the resort information angle, it does hold a useful directory of agents from which you can book everything from restaurants to limousines and even movie listings in the area. It also specializes in e-discounts, and when searching for flights will display your original choice alongside similar but more competitively priced possibilities.

All-in-ones — One-stop shops

Club Med
www.clubmed.com

If you're not familiar with the Club Med experience it's all about kicking back and relaxing, with perhaps a few bouts of sport in between sips of your pina colada. The bright, breezy and swimsuit-clad site is set up clearly to draw you closer into the spirit of Club Med. You can search for your perfect destination by location, create your own sublime resting spot or pick a profile that is most like you and let the site take the strain. There's not much extra info but they probably assume you know what you're letting yourself in for.

Great Hawaii Vacations
www.greathawaiivacations.com

If the islands of the South Pacific are your idea of heaven, click here for immediate gratification. For the discerning traveler the vacation planner allows you to specify certain criteria so the site can help you select the right accommodation. Failing that, you can simply choose the island with the most unusual name and browse. All the necessary info is here, down to jacuzzi sizes. Paradise, Hawaiian-style beckons.

Lowest Fare
www.lowestfare.com

Patriotic site design and patriotic prices wherever you want to fly. No need to fill in annoying fields with preferred travelling dates – a simple table format does the comparing up front. Some flights can be booked online, but you will need to call the company after you have found your dream package.

South of the Border
www.southofthebordertravel.com

Part of the fun of planning a vacation is envisaging the white sandy beach, dazzling water, the hotel's unusual definition of a kingsize bed etc. This site hides its resorts under a bushel, offering few clues as to what its wide selection actually look like. But it's still a decent online brochure if you want an idea of how much your holiday in Mexico will cost. You have to call (or e-mail Elena; be patient – she must be very busy) for details of holidays in the rest of Central and Latin America.

 **Taking it slow and easy**

Greyhound

www.greyhound.com

Practically a national institution, the company's air-conditioned tin cans are the most popular way to see your country. Fortunately Greyhound has developed a practical and stylish website where you can buy tickets online or simply plan your route. There are 3,700 terminals in America, Canada and Alaska, so you shouldn't have too much hassle busing your way around all of North America, and there are few cheaper and easier ways to do it. For the serious explorer opt for the Ameripass and bus your way round the globe.

Trailways

www.trailways.com

Comprising a host of independent operators, the company offers charter services and tours as well as scheduled services covering the greater part of North America. You can check out prices, pore over route maps, and get tips on how to charter your own coach. Not a bad site for a company which says it plans to be a "worldwide, multimodal, transportation organization".

 **A floating resort**

All Cruise

www.allcruise.com

All Cruise's site is all function. You almost pine for the deeply shallow glossy sites which just set out to seduce you with sumptuous photography. Some of the blurb falls in love with itself: "You awaken to cappuccino and gourmet scones. Luxuriate in a seaweed and mineral bath. Roam around an exotic island, a bustling market or an Alaskan cove. Propose a toast with a martini made perfectly to your liking. Feast on cuisine prepared to the standards of Master Chef Michel Roux. Only here, do you awaken to do it all over again." As a certain King of Siam once said, etcetera, etcetera, etcetera. All that said, it's hard to fault the variety of destinations, liners and prices you'll find here.

123 Cruise

www.123cruise.com

Select a liner and date of vacation and browse the long list of offerings. You can e-mail requests for additional info but you can't book online.

1-800 Cruise Now

www.1800cruisenow.com

Lists weekly cruise specials for around the world.

"Oxygen masks will be provided"

Aloha Airlines
www.alohaair.com
Not one of the big boys but there aren't many options if Hawaiia is your destination. Flights leave only from Las Vegas, Orange County and Oakland, so you may have to make complex arrangements to get to one of those first. The Spirit of Aloha section will get you in the holiday mood with local recipes. Added bonus: a feature oddly entitled "Dressing up island women."

American Airlines
www.aa.com
Like many of its rivals, American Airlines offers vacation packages as well as flights online. Each hotel has been given an "Eagle" rating, with detailed lists of amenities. You don't get much feel for the vacation spots, but this is easy to use and offered an online-only 10 per cent discount when we visited.

British Airways
www.british-airways.com
Britain's most famous airline's site. Prices vary and the quality is assured, but apart from the odd special offer, it's hardly the cheapest option.

Cheap Airline Tickets
www.cheap-airline-tickets-online.com
A straightforward name for a straightforward site. Fill in the usual details with no need to consult that dictionary of airport codes (that dictionary you don't have) and in seconds you're presented with eight of the cheapest flights. At these prices the flights may not be direct, but worth a look if you're not in a rush. The city guides aren't bad either.

Continental Airlines
http://cooltravel
assistant.com
Some good deals, and some helpful tips and

Say aloha to Hawaii with this site which has decent prices, and good-to-know tips on "dressing up island women"

money-saving advice. If you're flying transatlantic, you would do well to consider Continental's award-winning partner, Virgin Atlantic. You can book online by logging on to www.virginatlantic.com/main.asp?page=5.0.

Delta Airlines
www.delta.com
Respectable name, standard prices, and lots of choice.

Northwest Airlines
www.nwa.com/
A decent site with decent prices, and decent travelers' tips. Booking tickets online is pretty straightforward too.

South West Airlines
www.southwest.com
The low-fare, no-frills specialist has a site devoid of trappings (give or take the odd bit of puffery for a corporate webcast) but full of seriously low fares.

United Airlines
www.ual.com
When last visited, this site's homepage was full of invitations to browse the bargains in "E-Fares". It was a slight disappointment, then, to click on the appropriate buttons only to find the bald statement: "At the present time we are not offering E-Fares for any destinations." Otherwise, worth a look. United has recently merged with US Airways (www.usairways.com).

Independents For something completely different

Arthur Frommer's Budget Travel
www.frommers.com
The name that launched a thousand travel guides (it's not actually quite that many – it just seems like that) has one of the deepest sources of travel information online. There are so many invitations to "click here" on the homepage that your mouse would probably expire if you did attempt to click 'em all. The site's "Spot of the Month" feature once memorably chose as its top spot… Europe. That's right, the entire continent. Flights, rooms and cruises can be booked through Frommer's affiliates.

Away.com
http://away.com/index.adp
If recently you've hardly ventured out of the suburbs, never mind the country, Away.com is a fantastic source of ideas and info. Destination and activity guides cover every country and adventure imaginable, from watching the Hopi pray for rain in Arizona in springtime to the best jazz festival in South

Africa. There's a good Trip Finder for those who might feel out of their depth. No online bookings but you can e-mail for more info. The only downside: the pop-up windows can, on occasion, be only slightly narrower than the screen.

Council Travel
www.counciltravel.com
If you're a student and you just want to shove those books and escape to someplace better, warmer, or at the very least homework-free, Council

Of moose and men   Yes, it's Alaska calling

The 49th state of this fair land hasn't had enough publicity since it was bought in 1867 for the knockdown price of $7.2m. Right now it's back in the news because of fears that the oil companies want to buy the entire state for several times that amount.

Fancy some northern exposure? This bed and breakfast directory is not a bad place to start

That and the odd TV show apart, Alaska hasn't had too much northern exposure. But if you want to see the US's true final frontier, check out United Airlines' website (www.united.com) for low cost but comfortable direct non-stop tickets. If using other airlines, be sure to check that the flight is direct, as Boston to Anchorage worked out as 5 different stages through one other carrier. Prices vary according to departure date, but an April flight from Boston booked in February came to around $400. Don't forget to look out for the world's biggest stuffed bear, currently loitering in Anchorage airport terminal.

For the complete Alaskan experience book into the Ultima Thule Lodge (www.alaskan.com/ultimathule), whose owners see Alaska as the land "remote beyond reckoning". For $900 a night, the company offers luxury lodging in which to recover from your tussles with huskies, moose and glaciers.

For those travelers for whom $900 a night is indeed remote beyond reckoning, the state's biggest city, Anchorage (aka the City of Lights), has its very own bed and breakfast directory (www.anchorage-BnB.com) where you can search and book rooms.

If you'd like a sneak preview of the city, Anchorage boasts its own website (www.ci.anchorage.ak.us) complete with visitors' guides and a virtual tour. The state capital Juneau has a neat guide on http://juneaualaska.com which, among other things, reveals that 26in of snow falls there in a typical January.

Travel has all the information you're likely to need to travel to a host of exotic locations. Whether you want a simple vacation, a year's tour of the globe, or to study abroad, you should find prices to suit. Easy to navigate, this cheery site uses more exclamation marks on its homepage than most junk e-mails.

Gorp Travel
http://gorptravel.gorp.com
If you like to do nothing more during your vacation than top up your tan, this is not the site for you. Gorp is all about getting active, flexing those muscles and scaling the Himalayas – they're only mountains, for heaven's sake. Mountaineering isn't the only adventure you'll find here – there's everything from safaris to downhill skiing and dude ranches (a la *City Slickers*). Search by destination, interest or activity and Gorp produces dozens of suggestions, which you can then book online. The detailed itineraries and fact sheets are accompanied by reviews from those who have been there, done that.

Deli Llama Wilderness Adventures
www.delillama.com
Not to be confused with the Dalai Lama (who'll take you on a completely different kind of journey), this family-run company will take you on a trek through Washington state, with the "silent brothers" (as Bob and Mariam Shapiro charmingly call their llamas) carrying some of your luggage. Poor beasts. Treks are available from May till September for $145 per person per day. That price includes such exotic dishes as Moroccan lamb tajine for lunch.

High Mountain
www.nepalmountain.com
Don't be put off if the text overlaps on the homepage: this is a better-than-average site for anyone who fancies a short walk in the Himalayas. Be

Students have their own site to fit their particular needs: a year going around the world, an ordinary vacation or the overwhelming urge to look at a site displaying loads of exclamation marks

warned, many of these trips are described as "strenuous". As one of their destinations is Everest base camp, this may well be a serious understatement.

Rough Guide
www.roughguides.com
This is what is technically known in the high-powered world of book publishing as a "shameless plug" – although you would, of course, be ill-advised to go anywhere without consulting Rough Guides. Here you can find basic info on cities from Acapulco to Zurich and countries from Antigua to Wales. You can also link to online partners like the Internet Travel Network.

Rail travel — Some old-time romance

American Orient Express
www.americanorientexpress.com
You can't actually book online here, but you can do everything else. This simple site offers a choice of 7 tours of America aboard a luxury train taking in the sights of the Pacific coast, the Rockies and Yellowstone or the glaciers of the northwest. You can browse day-by-day itineraries, or you can order a brochure to make your reservation. Prices range from $3,000 to $6,000 depending on the level of extravagance, and there are discounts on advance bookings. Sadly, however, the American Orient Express doesn't offer the chance to solve a murder mystery.

Amtrak
www.amtrak.com
America's biggest train operator is worth visiting if only to check the long list of discount fares available. The online booking system has been upgraded.

Cape Cod Central Railroad
www.capetrain.com
If the Orient Express is a little out of your budget, you could try the Cape Cod Railroad for a scenic day excursion with or without dinner. There's no online booking, although faxes are accepted, but you can read brief descriptions, sample menus, rates and get directions to their station in Hyannis.

Rocky Mountaineer Railtours
www.rkymtnrail.com
Take in the sights of the Canadian Rockies, care of Rocky Mountaineer Railtours. Itineraries, rates and schedules are available, but there's no online booking for what the site calls "the most spectacular train trip in the world".

Resting places | A room with a view

4 Hotels
www.4hotels.com
There were a couple of glitches with their hotel reservation service but no problems requesting information on accommodation deals from Hawaii to the Caribbean. You can also book flights.

All-Hotels
www.all-hotels.com
An easy to use database of 60,000 top hotels and bed & breakfasts throughout the world, up to and including the Arctic. Discounts are available if you're heading for the more popular destinations such as Paris, London and New York but you can also find rates for more obscure destinations, like the Kazakhstan capital, Alma Ata. Descriptions and images are available, and where you have the option, booking online is quick and simple.

American Accommodation Network
www.americanhotelnetwork.com
Whether you're traveling for business or pleasure, this hotel network claims to be able to fix you up with accommodation in all the main US cities with big chain hotels such as Holiday Inn, the Sheraton, and a few less familiar names. That said, our spot check on Massachusetts came up with only one hotel in Boston – pretty remarkable considering it's a major convention destination. Descriptions, pictures and rates are listed. Booking is through a separate area of the site so it's best to do your research first.

Bed & Breakfast
www.bedandbreakfast.com
The best advice is to look at all the B&Bs in your area, as the information provided varies from simple descriptions right up to a list of amenities, photo galleries, and even guidelines on what type of person is best suited to stay at that particular establishment. The listings of more than 27,000 B&Bs cover most of the world's major cities. You can book online and e-mail for a reservation. Added bonus: a homepage which gets straight down to business.

Vacation Homes
www.vacationhomes.com
A useful online directory of privately-owned vacation homes everywhere from Ireland and Switzerland to Antigua and South Africa. Most of the listings display interior and exterior images and a thorough list of amenities (although on some the info is a bit scanty). Bookings can be made online. You can also register your own property for rent for $199 a year. Rates vary from $465 a week for a cottage in Transylvania to $4,000 a week for villa in Palm Beach.

Korea move
See the Stalinist Las Vegas

In the capital Pyongyang stands a rare realistic statue of North Korea's great late leader Kim Il Sung suffering from backache

For the genuinely independent traveler, there is only one part of the world that now counts as seriously unexplored: North Korea. The People's Democratic Republic (or the weirdest place on Earth, as it is semi-officially described) may seem like the most closed society on this planet but it has not been slow to embrace the Net. Indeed, leader Kim Jong-Il has now got his very own e-mail address (and no, he didn't choose AOL).

If you fancy a different type of package holiday you can do some research on www.stat.ualberta.ca/people/schmu/kitc.html, the official site for the Korea International Travel Company, the brainchild of Kim Il Sung, the late, lamented (in Pyongyang) leader. This site says that 30-40,000 tourists arrive annually in a republic that takes pride in calling itself "the eastern country of courtesy". The 5 packages on offer all start in the capital Pyongyang, the Stalinist Las Vegas. You can't book online, only by telex, mail or fax. Conveniently the postal address, telex number and fax number are among three of the items missing from this site, jettisoned, presumably, to make room for the statue of the first Kim returning from the local chiropractor.

You won't be going to North Korea for the climate, but if you want to check out the weather forecast for last week in Pyongyang, then log on to www.lightingandelectricals.globalsources.com/TNTLIST/TRAVEL/ACCU/NKOREA.HTM If you've still not given up hope, you can book your package tour of North Korea by e-mail through the Dutch travel agent VNC on www.vnc.nl/korea where you'll also find such essential information as the fact that the word for bee is "maekchu".

Want to check the news before you go? There's no better place than the official Korean news agency site www.kcna.co.jp to find out which ambassador is presenting his credentials. You may have heard some fuss about North Korea and its nuclear missiles, which are often in trouble for being pointed at the wrong people (ie everybody). You can check out their nuclear arsenal on www.fas.org/nuke/guide/dprk/nuke/index.html. A final thought before your Korea move – you would be well-advised to check your holiday destination with that nice Colin Powell.

Winter Somewhere to chill out

Canadian Mountain Experience
www.canadianmountain.com
Strictly for those who don't stress about such
incidentals as how their vacation will turn out. Select
a destination such as Banff, Lake Louise or Panorama,
send in your booking request indicating the type of
accommodation you want, transport requirements and so
on. The pictures of where you'll be staying are on a par
with an artist's impression, but then snow looks the same
wherever you go. On the plus side, prices are good – a week
in Banff could set you back as little as $475.

Jackson Hole Snowmobile Tours
www.jacksonholesnowmobile.com
Skiing and snowboarding are old news. At least, according to companies
like this one which promote snowmobiling. Some go just for the thrill of
skimming across the snow in their own high-speed buggy, others are there to
take in the wildlife. Through this site you can experience both. With tours of
Yellowstone Park, the Grand Canyon and Togwotee Pass on offer, you should
be able to catch a glimpse of a bald eagle, bison or a coyote or 3. Prices vary
depending on the length of your tour but the figure includes transport, guide,
gas and food. Easy to use with online booking.

Moguls
www.skimoguls.com
Moguls is as comprehensive a site as you're likely to find, but be aware that
if you're researching resorts, book flights, accommodation, car rentals,
insurance and lift passes (phew!), you may well end up surfing here for some
time. But all you need is a rough idea where you'd like to go – be it Canada,
within the US, Europe or even the southern hemisphere – and roughly when,
and Moguls can line you up with a weekend, week or by-the-day options.
Prices are listed according to what city you'll be flying from. Despite its URL,
Moguls caters for the non-skiing vacationer too, but all packages revolve
around outdoor sports and activities. The descriptions of accommodation
vary from adequate to downright sparse but resort cams and snow condition
reports are on hand if you're a complete and utter snow bunny and skiing
is the be all and end all of your vacation.

Ski Vacation Planners
www.skivacationplanners.com
You can tell from the start that the Vacation Planners strap-line "for skiers
by skiers" is true. Select your destination from a choice of Canada, South

America, New Zealand and the US, and then read up on country and resort details right down to summit elevation, the number of lifts and package holidays available. There's no immediate booking available, but you can request a quote which is at least vaguely related to your budget and will helpfully include all the additional extras such as lift tickets.

Steamboat Snowmobile Tours
www.stmbtsnowmobiletours.com
Bookings taken for riding and dining in the Rocky Mountains, with tours ranging in length from a couple of hours to a day. We only hope the gourmet food comes after the high-speed buggy chase.

Trailblazer
www.columbine.com
No online booking but plenty of pictures of elk and top of the range Arctic Cat mobiles to get you in the mood. Not to mention the Internet discounts. You may have to be patient: this site can sometimes to be slow to download.

Sound advice Weather, bugs, ATMs...

United State Department of State
http://travel.state.gov/foreignentryreqs.html
You gotta have the right visa and this site has the foreign entry requirements for every country, principality and state. As policies change frequently, it provides the contact numbers of each embassy and the fees involved.

Road News
www.roadnews.com
The Road News team will help ensure your laptop need never stay home again. They can give you advice on what hardware you'll need and how to make sure you find your friendly local ISP.

Tips 4 Trips
www.tips4trips.com
Tips tried and tested by independent travelers, including how to pack, what to pack and handy tips from storing money in your bra to taking bubble wrap and masking tape with you for those must-have breakables.

Visa
www.visa.com/cgi-bin/vee/main.html
The location of every Visa ATM in the world. Trivia buffs (and bank robbers) are bound to have this one bookmarked.

Watersports

Offline surfing is now so mega that someone will soon decide it's the new rock 'n' roll. Meantime, feast your browsers on this lot...

Bart's Watersports
www.bartswatersports.com
Bart's appears to have decided that trying to design an inspirational site would just be too bothersome. Instead they opt for lists of categories (and little else) but the catalog itself is impressive enough to compensate. Listed alphabetically, every watersport product imaginable is covered, from bimini tops to knee boards and snorkel gear. Whether you have cash to spare or are saving the odd dollar here and there, you should be able to afford something.

Caribe Catalog
www.caribecatalog.com
Let's cut to the chase. If you're any kind of boarder, you shop by brand name. Caribe realize this, so all you have to do is select the cool manufacturer of the moment and buy away. Bitchin' names include Rip Curl, No Fear, Bad Ass, O'Neill and many more. On a sensible note, shipping is economical, searching is simple and the descriptions are kept to a bare minimum.

Hang 10
www.hang10.com
Hard to know what to make of this wetsuit specialist site. There's a pleasing outer homepage on which you click to proceed to a page promoting the wetsuits. This is wonderfully uncluttered (there are just 6 buttons on the nav bar down the left of the screen), but the lack of options also applies to the range on offer. Women have a choice of two styles, but at least they're better off than kids, who can have any style they want as long as it's the HT J850. For all that, the sizing chart is useful. and prices are pretty good.

Marine Products
www.marine-products.com
This Salt Lake City-based store sells everything from boats to wakeboard and waterski accessories. Descriptions are sparse, as are the images. Shipping costs are calculated once you've ordered, but nothing is charged to you unless you agree. More unusual items include water trampolines for $700.

Orca

www.orca.co.nz

Orca is a New Zealand-based company, but you too can get your eager hands on the world's fastest wetsuit. These are triathlon wetsuits, so they're strictly for the professional (and the richer ones at that). The site itself is suitably stylish, with just enough information so that you too can become a wetsuit bore. Learn all about the speed, flexibility, materials and even the design of the hyper-stretch gusset. There are only a few designs on offer, along with a range of bodywear, modelled by some very serious-looking models. Prices are in US$ but shipping costs can add more than 10 per cent to your order if you're ordering 1 or 2 suits.

Overton

www.overton.com

Overton's isn't really a site for the casual browser, but if you know exactly what you want you can be in and out in minutes. The lengthy list of categories includes apparel, boats and big boats, with each then divided into various sub-sections. The catalog is extensive, larger images are available and the product info is adequate. Pricewise, you should be able to find something to suit your budget: wakeboards, for example, range from $100 to $500. Not really a site for the surfer who worries constantly about his or her street cred.

Steamerlane

www.steamerlane.com

Aimed at the professional surfer dude, Steamerlane can kit you out with wetsuits, rash guards, boots, and even Doc Plug's, said to be the ultimate earplugs on the market, although you have to take their word on that. To compensate for the high prices, generally around $400 per suit, they are practically made to measure. You can specify colors – conservative, non-conservative and all black – and sizes, down to your shoulders, waist and chest measurements. The images of each product are pretty clear, which only serves to prove how few people look good in head-to-toe neoprene.

SurfTrader

www.surftrader.com

No coverage of watersport on the Web would be complete without mentioning this free marketplace, where buyers and sellers of surfing collectibles like a 1947 Ford Woody can meet online. This is financially backed by (among others) the fantastically named Phat Cock Clothing.

Tommy's Slalom Shop

www.tommysslalomshop.com

With funky graphics and equally funky products, Tommy's may look and sound like a site strictly for professionals, but it's also the perfect place for the novice as the descriptions of its wakeboards, wetsuits and waterskis are jargon-free. Top names include Liquid Force, O'Brien and Blindside.

Weddings & Bar Mitzvahs

Big day approaching? There are loads of sites with cool goods like "honey dust" to make it truly special. None of them, though, can do anything about your partner's parents

 Stag/hen nights and biodegradable confetti

Just Married
www.justmarriedkit.com/honey.html
Here are presents in kit form – fun in a box! Ranging from the Kama Sutra Weekender Kit (Oil of Love, Pleasure Balm and Honey Dust) to that all important Car Decorating Kit to truly embarrass the newlyweds.

The Knot
www.theknot.com
Ever wanted to know how the Quakers say their wedding vows? No, nor us. This site is full of such info, tips on writing your own vows and which poems to recite. (Oddly the list doesn't include TS Eliot's *The Waste Land*.) You can view dozens of real weddings to get inspiration, of a positive or negative kind.

Martha Stewart
www.marthastewart.com
Martha is the uncrowned US queen of the upmarket wedding. Her website has a whole section devoted to wedding ideas (think discreet luxury rather than raucous knees-up). In the Martha by Mail section, you can buy things like her signature wedding favor boxes, glass cake stands and other items of all-round unique loveliness for the stylish wedding.

Ultimate Wedding
www.ultimatewedding.com
Essentially a gateway to other sites with some relatively brief informative articles, this site is useful but never quite achieves "ultimate" status. Worth checking out.

US Bride

www.usbride.com/

This site's value lies in allowing you to find vendors in your area, from gowns to caterers to where to book dance lessons (for your partner, of course). The bad news is that it covers only 11 states, but our search of Massachusetts was helpfully broken down to 7 smaller regions. It will link you to online vendors as well as give the addresses of offline stores. A decent directory.

Wed Guide

www.wedguide.com

Fantastic prices on wedding accessories such as bubble-blowers or car and cake decorations. There are lots of things here that will add an individual touch to your big day. An excellent help section will guide the novice online shopper. Added bonus: only two heart-shaped graphics on the homepage.

Wedding Bells

www.weddingbells.com

Brought to you by the good folks at *Wedding Bells* magazine, this site has all the usual dresses, etiquette answers and planning advice, as well as good city-specific sources. One of the more interesting features is the "entertaining calculations" option, which helps you figure out how big a tent you'll need for your guests (it's best to allow 12 square feet per person apparently). Pretty to look at and easy to navigate: nothing on this site will offend your maiden aunt. It just lacks a bit of inspiration. The only other flaw is the complete absence of useful ideas on how to stop dad strutting his funky stuff on the dance floor.

 A different kind of tradition

Jewish Celebrations

www.mazornet.com/jewishcl/weddingr.htm

This very busy site is a must for Jewish brides. It has advice, resources, explanations of traditions, and even updated info on Jewish genetic diseases. There is also a Jewish dating service for those still looking for their dream mate. Also offers planning help and advice for other Jewish celebrations such as bar mitzvahs.

Melanet

http://melanet.com

African-Americans should check out this site which covers planning, advice and fashions specifically for an Afro-centric wedding. This site has recently been improved with appropriate links and instructions. The fashion section is a must with information on the fabrics and styles. History and traditions are explained and good books recommended.

Make sure you only get what you want

After I Do
www.afterido.com/
Got enough toasters to toast the local baker's annual bread production? Then check this site out – it lets you register your honeymoon. Not only can guests contribute to getting you there, but their gifts can be as specific as buying you a cappuccino in the Piazza San Marco or a gondola ride. There is also a monthly newsletter with informative articles. A good idea.

The Wedding List
www.theweddinglist.com
Not for the budget-conscious, this gorgeous site is from those famous women who run The Wedding List Shops in London, New York and Boston.They have now taken their mission – to take the pain out of registering – online with this selection of luxury goods that would top anyone's wish list. The design is simple but elegant, the photography exquisite and clearly illustrates each product. Almost worth getting married for.

 You've fixed the time but not the place

Vegas Weddings
www.vegas.com/weddings/index.html
Sometimes you want to skip the fuss and just do it. This site guides you through the process with lists and links to Las Vegas chapels and venues, DJs etc, plus lots of ideas to make it a unique experience – like getting married on the starship USS Enterprise, in a helicopter, or even submersed in a tank. Makes getting married at the local church something of an anti-climax.

 **"Mr and Mrs request the pleasure…"**

ABC Publishers
www.shadicards.com
Your wedding invitation is the first indication of the style and focus of your wedding. Couples of all cultures can chose from dozens of stationery styles that reflect their beliefs and traditions. Simple and straightforward to use.

Big Leap Designs
www.bigleapdesigns.com
A very impressive, bright and modern wedding invitation and thank-you card

site. There are plenty of designs and they do orders of service, candles, place cards, evening invitations and reply cards. The order form is incredibly thorough and there's a dog named Bruce. No, we don't really know why either..

Princess Wedding Invitations
www.princessweddinginvitations.com/
Lots of designs to satisfy the majority of tastes, all at 25-35 per cent off retail prices. All the advice for wording the invitations and reply cards, plus a selection of verses. Saccharine webpage color but very easy to use.

We Are Paper
www.werpaper.com
For green-conscious brides, this company specializes in handmade 100 per cent recycled paper, with flower petals and leaf impressions. The selection for wedding invitations is small, but the other paper styles can be adapted.

Musicians "And now for *It Should Have Been Me*"

Wedding Musicians List
www.nuwebny.com/wedmusic/usa.htm
This is a paid-for listing, but the number of entries should provide a selection of bands in your area. One of them should be able to fulfil your dreams of that Big Band sound getting people on to the dance floor at your reception. Some bands have their own websites; most have at least e-mail.

Bar/Bat Mitzvahs Make it a kosher event

Bar Mitzvah Find It
www.BarMitzvahFindit.com
This will help you find all the sources for catering, gifts, entertainment and more. Choose the state, click on one of 17 categories, and up pops a list of vendors with a brief description and contact number. What could be easier?

Rosenblums World of Judaica
www.alljudaica.com
Original Bar and Bat Mitzvah gifts as well as supplies for the ceremony.

Talit.com
www.jewisheart.com
Online mall of Jewish products are shipped directly from Israel. As the site is based in Israel, you are responsible for any import duty.

Weird stuff

Fear not – not every Internet novelty has to do with flatulence or Bill and Monica. Surf and ye shall find, from a redneck doll to a combined telephone and blender…

A noble title

www.elitetitles.co.uk

This British site should probably be rechristened Fantasists R Us. For as little as $325 you can buy a deed entitling you to call yourself a duke/duchess (heck, it's only $1,600 for a title complete with a parcel of land in old England). Sounds too good to be true, but the site says that according to international law it isn't. (Titles for Continental Europe are also available.) Your reign as baron(ess) will not necessarily entitle you to the right to pass this honour on to your offspring, nor will it give you a seat in the House of Lords (the British Parliament's upper chamber) but think what it will look like on your driving license or credit card. An off-the-shelf title could be yours in 14 days, though a title with land could take 8 weeks. A small price to pay for ersatz nobility.

Cattle mutilation T-shirts

www.ufoshirts.com

T-shirts featuring a drawing of a cow with a bullet hole where part of its midriff should be are just some of the highlights on this site. The designs may be naff and at $15 a throw these bad taste T-shirts don't come cheap either. If you need extra protection from "government truth beams and cosmic rays", the manufacturers advise you to line the shirts with aluminium foil.

Demotivational calendars

www.despair.com/index2.html

For those who, like English poet Philip Larkin, don't want to let the toad called work squat on their life, this is the ultimate site. The online catalog contains an array of demotivational posters and calendars, containing such perversely inspiring slogans as "If at first you don't succeed, failure may be your style", and "This mug really makes everything taste bitter." Not to be missed.

Diving maps for the Red Sea
www.venus.co.uk/diveplan/intro.htm
Fancy diving in the Red Sea but scared that your lack of local knowledge will let you down? Well, shed those fears and get ready to scuba because for a meager $45 you can buy a dive plan pack which includes a 16-page guide describing each site and incredibly detailed maps packed with such useful information as "much small life".

E-mail the rest of the universe
www.messagetospace.com/index2.html
Sending a message into space could, the people at the Message to Space company politely suggest, release your inner self and enhance your creativity. Whether it does either, both or none of the above probably depends on the sender, but one thing's for certain: it will cost you $10.95 for a one-page message and $4.95 for each subsequent page.

Flightless fruit flies
http://drosophila.herpetology.com
Inspecting the shipping and returns policies of a site is usually the dullest part of online shopping but not here. To the FAQ "What is our liability?" the Drosophila Company (snappy motto: "Flightless fruitflies for reptiles and amphibians") replies, "We only guarantee live delivery and you must notify us within 24 hours of any DOA vials." A vial contains 25 to 50 adult insects, so if they are Dead On Arrival that's probably the fruitfly equivalent of genocide. Inviting genetically impaired (and biologically grounded) fruitflies into your home doesn't sound that drastic. After all, they only live for 25 to 30 days. But they do spend most of those days breeding. So if you fancy having your pad taken over by sex-crazed, rotten-fruit gorging fruitflies which can't fly, this is definitely the site for you.

Food-blender and telephone
www.cycoactive.com/blender/
It's a telephone and a food-blender all in one! It comes with a testimonial from Bill Jenkins who bought it for a friend's wedding and says: "It was incredible… the groom kept ringing it on his mobile all night… it was the only gift they carried home with them". If you think it's a tasteless wedding present, recall the Blendmaster's wise words: "It's their fault for getting married." It's only when you e-mail for info that you're convinced it isn't a spoof.

Funeral.com
www.funeral.com
Death may be the ultimate inevitability, but we have our whole lives to arrange for it. This site helps you to plan everything from your theme song to your memorial table and headstone engravings. Browse each, equally sickly theme, make your selection, then register and pay now or in instalments up to the big day. Caskets emblazoned with trophy animals we had a passion

for shooting during our lifetime, and the theme from the Andy Griffith show, *The Fishin' Hole*, playing whilst we're cremated, is probably not quite the gracious exit that most of us hope we'll eventually make, but at least this way you can prevent your granddaughter with a passion for melodrama from insisting on *My Heart Will Go On*. Hey, it's your funeral.

Grateful Dead ceramic train cookie jar

www.rof.com/giftswithstyle/GD_locomotive.htm

"An excellent addition to any cookie jar collection" and an "unforgettable gift for a Grateful Dead enthusiast," this souvenir limited edition jar (only 4,800 of 'em in existence, folks!) can be yours for just $150. (Shipping is free.) Probably the most pointless piece of celebrity merchandising since Richard Nixon's brother Donald decided to launch the Nixonburger.

Humorous underwear

www.cautionunderwear.com

If men's boxer shorts decorated with a road sign which says "Slippery when wet" tickles your funny bone, this site is for you.

Inflatable big bottom chair

www.opane.com/index.html

Go on, you know you want one. At the time of review, this indispensable item was on special offer at $19.95, a price only slightly heavier than the chair itself. Simply a must for every person who's not ashamed to admit that they too have an inflatable big bottom.

Musical Coca-Cola carousel

www.franklinmint.com

"A musical masterpiece of carousel artistry that moves round and round, up and down" is how the Franklin Mint Company describes this musical carousel, decorated with authentic vintage Coca-Cola signage, which costs only $245. Soon, a university near you will be offering courses in the history and theory of carousel artistry.

Racoon penis bone

www.jtleroy.com/raccoon.html

The unkindest cut of all, certainly as far as the racoon is concerned. San Franciscan JT Leroy has shown the true entrepreneurial spirit by collecting the corpses of roadkilled racoons (and photographic evidence that they are hit-and-run victims), removing their penis bones and selling them at 13 bucks a throw to be worn as necklaces by people with absolutely no fashion sense or taste. People like Leroy's friend Mike Pitt, shown wearing this unusual item of jewelry, who looks like a slightly less sane version of Christopher Walken's Bond villain. But remember, as the site says, no racoons were harmed in the making of this jewelry! Well, actually, that's not quite true: they were killed, albeit not by Leroy, and killing, insist the experts, can be quite harmful.

Redneck doll

http://www.spumco.com

From those terribly amusing people who brought you *Ren and Stimpy* comes the subversively named *Spumco*, probably the Web's finest cartoon show. Buy a George Liquor doll for just $34.95 plus shipping and, the blurb promises: "He'll teach you to be a God-fearing American, no matter what foreign country you're from. Girls! Give one of these to your boyfriend. George will make a man out of him for you!" But don't order in July because everyone in the studio store goes on holiday. All month.

Samurai-style helmet

www.majestic-n.com

The place to go if you're willing to fork out more than $235 on "an authentic style samurai helmet". (Note the careful interjection of the word "style" in that description.) If that doesn't tempt you, why not treat yourself to a fairy, gargoyle or a skull-shaped piggy-bank? The generous people from Majestic Novelties have also been known to give away stuff like a miniature barbarian axe, promoted with the (undeniably catchy) slogan: "Get them while they're hot!" Sadly, you need an ID and password to visit the sister site Swords-R-Us. And no, we are not making this up.

Urine For Sale

http://UrineForSale.com

Worried that over-indulgence during the weekend may show up in your company's random drug-testing on Monday morning? Well, worry no more. You can buy this "pre-tested" urine, fresh on day of shipping, for use for, well, whatever you fancy really. The site (which insists the urine is shipped using a "high-tech delivery system") claims you can refrigerate it for up to 6 months, or freeze it. Apparently popular with actors, who may be the only ones who can afford the extortionate $67 plus shipping for just 5 liquid ounces.

Woolly mammoth teeth

www.twoguysfossils.com

Elton John need look no further for his next hair transplant. For $60 he can buy some 2 million year-old hair with one careless owner: a Siberian woolly mammoth. But hurry, Elton, there are only a few samples left. Among the other prehistoric artefacts on this site are 1/10 scale models of tyrannosaurus rex, a sabre-toothed tiger's skull and what's left of a 36 million year-old wolf spider. As the homepage so wisely says: "Fossils are the oldest antiques on Earth."

SOUND EFFECTS

If you harbor a secret desire to be Shari Lewis (and your doctor cannot suggest a cure) log on to *www.axtell.com/vent. html.* All you really need is a Net-friendly computer, a cuddly toy to stick your hand up and a willingness to ignore the baffled looks from your workmates as you practice throwing your voice in the office.

After 10 minutes you should feel qualified to join the International Ventriloquist's Association on *www.inquisite.com.*

And remember, to paraphrase an old cliché, on the Internet no one can see your lips move.

Wines, beer and spirits

Facing the rather grim prospect of a cocktail hour without any cocktails? Don't know which wine goes with which cheese and which guest goes with either? Is Bud Light your idea of an exotic beer? Worry ye not: the Internet is ready, willing and able to come to your rescue

 From old Belgium to old Bastard

Beer on the Wall

www.beeronthewall.com

Not the greatest design job in the world, but this is a good straightforward website offering you the chance to sample some rare microbrews – a change from the Buds and Coors on offer at the supermarket. Wouldn't you just feel hipper downing a bottle of Old Bastard Ale? You can join their Bunch of the Month club which entitles you to 6 or 12 bottles of selected brews and you can even get a few cases of beer made up with customized labels for a special occasion. The usual restrictions about ordering alcohol online apply, so check your delivery charges and times before you buy.

Belgian Shop

www.belgianshop.com

Belgium is famous for the quality of its plain and flavored beers, so if you fancy yourself an expert in the field of beer appreciation, this is the place to come. Whether it's raspberry flavor beer or a serious dark brew, there's plenty here to whet your appetite for the real thing. Many of these beers have a higher alcohol content than your regular brew. Shipping to the US is pricey (starting at $28) so it's only really worth it if you're going to place a large order.

Vanberg & DeWulf
http://belgianexperts.com

This New-York-based site specializes in importing some serious ales, to judge by its selection of traditionally brewed Belgian beers. A handy map shows you where in your state you can get your mitts on the stuff, but those living in New York have the advantage of seemingly being able to buy this beer on practically every street corner. There's also information on Belgium, the brewery and recipes from starters to dessert.

Beer on the Wall offers a Bunch of the Month club giving you a steady supply of Old Bastard Ale

World of Beer
www.realbeer.com

Beautifully laid out site with lots to look at and read about top quality beers and ales, plus tips on home brewing, beer appreciation and traditional brewing methods. There are also plenty of links to brewers who sell direct, and other great sites for getting your hands on a case or two, or you can join their own Beer of the Month Club and receive a regular selection of interesting brews chosen by the site's founder, Michael Jackson. Added bonus: the site's suggestion that beer is the perfect Mother's Day gift.

 Make mine a double

800 Spirits
www.800spirits.com

If you can get drunk on it, it's here. Premium brands of brandy, vodka, tequila – you name it, it's available to buy online as a gift for yourself or someone else (go on, you deserve it). Prices include gift wrap and delivery, so they are not the cheapest you'll find, but the selection is outstanding and the site is easy to use and hassle-free. Added bonus: the selection of fine cigars for the complete après experience.

Alcohol Reviews
www.alcoholreviews.com

Some people subscribe to the theory that you can tell a lot about a person by what they drink, so you don't want to be seen drinking Tia Maria and Coke at any cost. Using Alcohol Reviews you'll know your premium tequilas from your gasoline substitutes, and exactly what drinks such as calvados and grappa are made of, and indeed whether you want to be seen in public sipping them. The reviews are interesting yet fun, with links to online stores.

Bacchus Cellars

www.bacchuscellars.com

Great site for stocking up your bar, with good prices on a variety of spirits and liquors. Tequila gets a special mention with more than 50 different types to choose from, starting at $12 per bottle.The customer service section has a good guide to which states will accept alcohol deliveries and what it will cost.

Internet Wines & Spirits

www.internetwines.com

You can't help but marvel at the fabulous selection of spirits on offer here, particularly if you're a fan of vodka, tequila or scotch. Yes, prices are good with delivery charges starting at $9, and yes, ordering is simple, but making a final selection could be a nightmare. If you're a vodka drinker how do you decide on the brand, never mind the flavor, from a list that includes orange, lemon, pepper, chilli, current, raspberry and (definitely one for the women) chocolate? Take your time.

Mixology

www.mixologys.com

You might think your bar is complete with a couple of hi-ball glasses and an ice-pick, but, oh no. Mixology is here to help transform even the most modest home bar into a professional cocktail station with a selection of exactly the right glasses for all your drinking needs, whether it's a vodka martini or a Shirley Temple.

Planet Liquor

www.planetliquor.com

This is more of a reference site, though it does offer links to online liquor stores. Click on the spirit of your choice, and this site gives a long list of brands with a description of each. Great if you don't know your Chivas Regal from your Suntory Square.

The Whisky Shop

www.whiskyshop.com

From familiar blends to rare single malts (how about a bottle of 40-year-old Bowmore single malt for around $6,000?), this site will keep any whiskey-drinker more than happy. Although direct delivery to the US is not available, there is a San Francisco store attached to this site and the number is available online for you to order through them. Delivery costs depend on your address and the shipping method you choose.

ABSINTHE FRIENDS

Absinthe is enjoying a new dose of popularity at the moment and there are websites devoted to the scary green stuff popping up all over the Internet. You can find out why there's so much fuss about this unbelievably strong, wormwood-infused spirit and even buy yourself the odd bottle at the following sites, although be warned, it has been known to induce hallucinations.

Of course, this could be exactly what you're after... One site even suggests an absinthe and Red Bull cocktail for people who really don't care if they get to see their next birthday.

Eabsinthe.Com

www.eabsinthe.com

La Boheme
www.laboheme.uk.com

From Japan, France and Federal Express

1-800 4 Champagne, Etc.

www.18004champagne.com

More a gift site than a source for party champagne, but nevertheless this site is worth checking out if you want to send someone a bottle of domestic or French champagne, or a bottle of good wine. Prices are pretty standard, but include taxes and gift wrapping. Delivery costs $8.95 per address, and same day service is available for certain orders.

Arthur's Wine Shop

http://arthurs-wine.com

Long-established North Carolina wine shop specializing in finding rare and quality wines from around the world. The site is pretty plain in its approach, so don't expect to learn a lot about the wine you're ordering, but there are some interesting selections to try if you're in the mood to experiment. Delivery details are equally sketchy, but costs are calculated at the checkout.

Berry Bros & Rudd

www.bbr.co.uk

Can you serve red wine with salmon? Well, yes, as long as it's dry and fruity like the selection recommended here in the hugely useful food and wine matching section. This top class British wine merchant has been going since 1698, so they should know a thing or two about what they're selling. You can find delicious vintages, or simply outstanding everyday wines. Learn about your choices and the site's own recommendations before you buy. A great place for people who would like to drink better. Once you have placed your order, the company will contact you to arrange delivery (remember to factor in any import duties you might be liable for).

eSake

www.esake.com

Learn the history and etiquette of Japanese rice wine and then order a bottle or two for home consumption from this Japan-based site. There's a good selection here, spanning a huge range of prices (all shown in yen), and also gift sets if you need to impress someone. When we checked, overseas ordering was not fully up and running (you have to ship to an address in Japan first), but the site assured visitors it is coming soon.

Finest Wine

www.finestwine.com

Upmarket wine site for folk interested in getting French wine imported direct, or tasting the best that California has to offer. There's a wide range of excellent wines at prices that are not as terrifying as you might expect

Wine and spirits

Find out which wine goes with which cheese at the online arm of Sam Rosen's Chicago-based liquor store

(although fans of Mad Dog 20/20 might not feel the extra cost is worth it). The best rated wines, for example, come down in price to around $40 a bottle. You can search by Chateau, Domaine or simply by price per bottle. There is also a selection of champagnes, including kosher ones, and wine-related gifts on offer. Shipping from France will typically take 8-10 days and the cost is calculated for you at the checkout (if you spend more than $400 your plonk is delivered free).

Mad About Wine
www.madaboutwine.com
Great selection of worldwide wines with a range of prices from a Cuvee de Vignerons Blanc at around $6 to a bottle of 1905 Sauternes for around $8,300. Their mixed cases, along the lines of Party Solutions, are good value and since this is a UK-based site (prices are shown in £ so get your calculator out), some of the wines are bottles you're not likely to come across at your local liquor store. There's a useful freight calculator for you to check charges before you put anything in your cart. They do their darnedest to get orders delivered to the US within 5-10 working days.

Rozi's Wine House
www.rozis.com
Well-designed and easy-to-use wine and wine gifts site. There's a good value Wine of the Month Club to introduce you to new flavors from around the world, or to give as a terrific gift, or you can order some of Rozi's selections to try. Each week the site features a wine tasting, so you can sample opinions on varieties before you buy. Standard shipping is calculated for you at the checkout, or you can contact the site if you want prices on a Next Day or 2nd Day Air service. Added bonus: sells winemaking sets and beer barrels.

Sam's Wine and Spirits
www.sams-wine.com
Sam Rosen owns a 33,000 square-foot liquor store in Chicago, and this is the online arm of his empire. Possibly as a result, this site is less stuffy than some others, making it more than worthwhile shopping for alcohol here. You can browse Sam's suggestions about which wine to serve with certain dishes or just buy a recommended selection of everyday wines. Party planning is made easy as you can e-mail the site about cocktail recipes, microbrews and how

much wine to order for your guests (although, as always, that depends on the guests). Shipping costs depend on your order and the type of FedEx delivery. The warehouse sale is worth a peek with discounts of up to 50 per cent.

Wine.com
www.wine.com
Panic-stricken last-minute gift shoppers could save their hide with an e-mail gift certificate from this outstanding wine site which features an excellent range of wines from all over the world. If you're shopping for yourself, Peter's Picks is a good place to start with a variety of moderately-priced discoveries from the site's founder. Shipping costs depend on your state. As this book went to press, this site had just joined eVineyards (www.evineyard.com) so things may have changed somewhat by the time you pay a visit.

Wine Today
www.winetoday.com
This is probably the wine site that Niles and Frasier Crane would visit. News, truckloads of reviews and advice on becoming a connoisseur from this appreciation site brought to you by the *New York Times*. There's no online shop but you get plenty of links to individual vineyards around the world and merchants selling wine and wine accessories online.

And for the morning after "Aaarghhh!"

Ever since man first woke up with a mouth that felt (as Elvis once said) as if Bob Dylan had slept in it, he's been searching for the ultimate answer to the morning after. Try these for expert advice.

Beer Geer
www.beergeer.com
Hangover cures listed and rated by a website that should know.

Estronaut
www.estronaut.com/a/hangovers.htm
Advice for women who can't remember how they got home.

Sobir-K
www.hangoverstopper.com
Miracle pills said to cure even the hairiest of hangovers. You have to remember to take them while you're still drinking though...

Wrecked
www.wrecked.co.uk
Prevention being better than cure, one look at this drinking information site will put you off the sauce for life.

Part three

Stuff that doesn't fit anywhere
else, like the glossary and index

REFERENCE

What (most of) the boring technical words really mean

GLOSSARY

Access Provider
Company which sells Internet connections, more usually known as an Internet Service Provider (hence the initials ISP)

Acrobat Reader
Stand-alone program or web browser plug-in from Adobe that lets you view a PDF file in its original format and appearance. The Acrobat Reader is free and some online stores will allow you to download their catalogs as PDF files.

Address
The identifier to access a site: http://www.roughguides.com (see URL).

AltaVista
Search engine at http://www.altavista.com

Applet
Small (Java) program embedded in an HTML page. When you open that web page, the browser downloads the applet and runs it on your computer. Don't worry – applets cannot read or write data on to your computer. Applets only work if the browser you're using supports Java.

AUP – Acceptable Use Policy
AUP is a policy for the use of the Internet laid down by an organization. Some companies (including your own) may use a AUP filter to exclude some Internet services for staff. Parents can also set AUP limits to block certain sites.

Attachment
A file included with e-mail. If, for example, you bought insurance online you would probably get a file confirming the policy attached to the return e-mail.

Autoresponder
A software program running on a computer server. If someone sends an e-mail to an autoresponder's e-mail address, the autoresponder automatically e-mails this person an answer (for example: "Thank you for your message. I will reply shortly"), and sends the incoming message on.

Banner

An advertisement, in the form of a graphic image on the Web, usually found at the top of a web page. Most banner ads are animated GIFs.

Bookmark

Netscape browser feature which lets you save a link to a web page in a list so you can revisit it easily. In Explorer, the same feature is called a Favorite.

Bot

Virtual robots which behave like search engines, only instead of finding the best web pages they find products you have told them you want to buy.

Bps – Bits Per Second

A measure of how fast data is moved from one place to another, normally in thousands of bits per second (Kbps) or millions of bits per second (Mbps). A 56K modem can transport 56,600 bits per second.

Broadband

Rapid Internet access.

Browser – Web Browser

The software program which allows you to surf the Web. At this moment in cyberhistory, almost everyone uses Internet Explorer or Netscape Navigator.

Browsing

What you do when you visit the Internet, aka surfing.

Cache

Computer memory or directory on your hard disk where your browser stores the web pages you have most recently visited.

Clicks 'n' mortar

Any store which sells products online and offline.

Client/Server

A client is a computer system that requests a service of another computer system (a server) on a network.

Compression

Technology that reduces the size of a file in order to transfer it rapidly.

Cookie

The small text file that a web server sends to your computer hard disk via your browser. Cookies contain information such as log-in and registration information, shopping cart information and preferences etc.

Cyberspace

The term first coined by the science-fiction writer William Gibson to describe the virtual world which exists within the marriage of computers, telecommunication networks and digital media.

Data encryption key
String of characters used to encode a message. This encoded message can only be read by someone with another related key.

DNS – Domain Name Server or Domain Name System
A Domain Name Server maps IP numbers to a more easily remembered name. When you type http://www.roughguides.com into your browser, the DNS searches for a matching IP address. If the DNS doesn't find an entry in its database, it will ask other DNSes until the entry is found, and you will see the Rough Guides site. Otherwise, you'll get an error message.

Domain name
A unique name which identifies an Internet site. A domain name points to one specific server, while this server may host many domain names. If you look at the URL for this page, you'll see www.roughguides.com at the beginning – "roughguides.com" is our domain name.

Download
What happens when a web page comes up on your screen. You can use your browser or File Transfer Protocol program to download files to your computer.

E-commerce
Selling goods or services over the Internet. Customers choose what they want to buy (often using a virtual shopping cart) and then type their credit card details into a secure payment form on the site.

E-mail
Electronic mail which is sent and received via the Internet.

Encryption
Technology which scrambles the contents of a file before sending it over the Internet. The recipient must have software to decrypt this file. If you want to transmit "hot stuff" like credit card information, you have to use some form of encryption. PGP (Pretty Good Privacy) is one such encryption program.

Enonymous
Download for the PC which reads a site's request for personal information and sends an immediate enquiry to their database to check the site's privacy policy rating. Information is then sent back to your terminal in real time.

Excite
Search engine at http://www.excite.com

FAQ – Frequently Asked Questions
You will find one of these on most shopping websites you visit. An FAQ is simply a file which is supposed to contain answers to the most commonly asked questions on a particular subject.

Favorite
The Explorer equivalent to a Netscape Communicator Bookmark.

File
Anything stored on a computer, like an image, text or a program.

Firewall
Internet security which defends a Local Area Network against hackers. Hardware and software combine to act as a firewall to divide the LAN into 2 parts. Normal data is available outside the firewall, while secret squirrel stuff is kept inside the firewall. A firewall can also be designed by a company to make sure that, for example, you cannot buy products from your computer at work.

Flash
Software plug-in which adds interactivity and brings animation to web pages.

Frame
Technology which allows web designers to break the browser window into several smaller windows, each of which can load different HTML pages.

GIF – Graphics Interchange Format
A compressed graphic format used widely on the Net. Mostly used to show clip-art images (photographic images are usually in a format called JPEG). The GIF 89a standard permits the use of multiple images in a single file, and many online shops will use a GIF file to show some animation on their website.

Hacker
Someone who breaks through computer security strictly for the fun of doing so. If someone does it with criminal intent they are called a cracker.

Hit
A single request from a browser to a server. Some servers also count each graphic on that page as a hit. This is why the boast that X site has Y million hits a month is now a devalued way of measuring a website's popularity.

Homepage
The main page of a website. The term is also applied to any website, typically created by a private individual, which only has one page.

Host
The server on which a website is stored. Hosting companies store websites of their customers on powerful web servers (with fast, permanent connections to the Internet) so, theoretically, you should always be able to access the page you want, providing the owner has not taken it down (off the Web).

HTML
Hyper Text Mark-Up Language. In simple terms, this is the language used to create web documents.

Hyperlink

A highlighted word (or graphic) within a web page (technically, these pages are described as hypertext documents). When you click a hyperlink, it will take you to another place within that page, or to another page on the Net.

Hypermedia

Pictures, videos, and audio on a web page that act as hyperlinks.

Hyperspace

Less commonly used variant of cyberspace.

Hypertext

Text that includes links to other web pages. By clicking on a link, the reader can jump straight from one web page to another related page.

Internet Explorer

Web browser from Microsoft.

IP – Internet Protocol

The rules that provide basic Internet functions. Without IP, computers would not be able to find each other.

IP address

A unique 32-bit Internet address consisting of 4 numbers, separated by dots and sometimes called a "dotted quad". Every server – connected to the Internet – has an IP number. The Domain Name Server converts this number into the domain name.

iPrivacy

Software download which brings anonymity to online shoppers. Personal information is stored, allowing you to surf privately. When buying it generates unique information for each purchase, keeping your actual details hidden.

ISP – Internet Service Provider

Most common usage is the same as Access Provider. But it also means any company that provides Internet services such as website development.

Java

A platform-independent programming language invented by Sun Microsystems, used by web developers to create applets. Java-enabled web pages can include animations, calculators, scrolling text, sound effects and even games. Although many web designers like Java, many people using the Web surf with a Java-disabled browser because they don't want to wait until some applet is entirely loaded into their browser. It's not uncommon when accessing a website to get a pop-up box full of numbers and code headlined "Java error messages". Don't worry – this doesn't mean your terminal is crashing. Just click on the box to shut it and keep on browsing.

JPEG – Joint Photographic Experts Group

Image compression standard, optimized for full-color (millions of colors) digital images. You can choose the amount of compression, but the higher the compression rate, the lower quality the image. Virtually every full-color photograph you see on the Web is a JPEG file.

Link

Marked text (usually underlined) or picture within a web page. With one click of your mouse, a link takes you to another web page (or to another place on the same page). Depending on the type of file, when you click on a link it will be retrieved and displayed, played or downloaded.

Log in

Entering into a computer system. Also the account name (or user ID) you must enter before you can access some computer systems. Many websites ask you to log in before viewing their pages. Before you do, it's worth checking what the site's policy on privacy is. You don't want to give your e-mail address to a company which is going to pass it on.

MBNA Wallet

Shopping service from the MBNA Bank designed to ease shopping online by taking care of form filling, password management and privacy protection.

Mirror or mirror site

More or less an exact copy of another site. Mirror sites are created when too many people want to access the original site. If buying goods from a global company you may be pointed to the mirror site nearest to you to make it quicker for you to access the pages.

Modem

Abbreviation of MOdulator-DEModulator. A modem allows computers to send information to each other on ordinary telephone lines.

MP3 or MPEG 3

A compressed musical format (see www.mp3.com) which enables you to download music to your computer from the Internet.

My Points

Online shopping incentive program which allows you to collect cyber points while you shop which can used to buy goods from participating stores. Others include Beenz (www.beenz.com) and Netflip (www.netflip.com).

Navigator

Netscape's web browser.

Page

One single document on the Internet.

Patch

A temporary or interim add-on which fixes or upgrades software. Often available from the suppliers for free. For example, iMac users can download a free patch designed to manage modem communications somewhat better.

PDF – Portable Document Format

A file format created by Adobe (see Acrobat Reader) designed to make sure the file can be read on different computer platforms. Created for offline reading of brochures, reports and documents with complex graphic design. When you download a PDF file, you get the whole document in a single file.

PGP – Pretty Good Privacy

Program, developed by Phil Zimmerman, which protects files from being read by others. You can also use PGP to attach a digital signature to a file to prove you are the sender.

Plug-in

Small piece of software, usually from a third-party developer, which adds new features to another (larger) software application. When visiting sites, you may often be asked to plug in programs like Flash or RealAudioPlayer. Downloading these packages can be time-consuming so decide whether it's worth it. There is also a risk that a plug-in may carry a virus.

Portal

A website which attracts visitors by offering free information, or free services. When you are on a portal site, you can use this site as a base from which to explore the Web. The most famous portals are the major search engines.

Protocol

A set of rules and conventions that describes the behavior which computers must follow in order to understand each other.

Search engine

Website which allows you to search for keywords to find relevant web pages, rather than having to know the specific web address. Every search engine has its own strategy for collecting data, which is why one particular search produces different results on different search engines.

Secure-It-e

Credit card protection service which, for a base price of $4.99, will handle all disputes with online merchants, banks and legal authorities to recover money after any fraudulent online purchases.

Server

A (powerful) computer that has a permanent connection to the Internet. Websites are stored on a web server.

Site

A place on the Web. Refers to a homepage or to a collection of web pages.

Snail mail

Mail delivered to your door by the mailman instead of being delivered to your computer by a network.

Spam

Junk e-mail, considered a serious breach of netiquette.

SSL – Secure Sockets Layer

Protocol that allows encrypted messages to pass across the Internet. SSL uses public key encryption to pass data between your browser and a given server (for example, to submit credit card information). A URL that begins with "https" indicates that an SSL connection will be used. In Netscape, you can also check if a site you are using is secure – look for a gold padlock at the bottom of your window of the site to which you are sending your details.

Surfer

Slightly passé version of browser.

Time out

When you request a web page and the server that hosts the web page doesn't respond within a certain amount of time, you may get the message "connection timed out". Try again immediately if it's urgent. If not, leave it 5 minutes. If it persists, the site may be down temporarily or permanently.

URL – Uniform Resource Locator

Web address. Our home page's URL is: http://www.roughguides.com

User ID

Unique identifier that you must enter every time you want to access a particular service on the Internet. The user ID is always accompanied by a password.

Webmaster

The person responsible for the web server (usually the system administrator).

World Wide Web

Hence the WWW bit. Graphic and and text documents published on the Internet interconnected through clickable "hypertext" links.

XML

eXtensible Mark-up Language, to give it its full name, is a new language for writing web pages. It's more flexible than HTML, is already running alongside it and may eventually replace it.

Yahoo!

Search engine at http://www.yahoo.com

The Rough Guide to Internet Shopping Offline Browser

INDEX

Index

Index

From boxing nuns to emu oil and a tour of Old Plovdiv

57 THINGS TO BUY ONLINE

Okay, you want to buy something. And by "something" we don't mean anything as dull as groceries. Here are 57 varieties of stuff you can buy at the click of your mouse. The goods listed on auction may have been sold but if you follow the web address you should find other equally ludicrous bargains

1 An 1978 official Gene Simmons pencil, $15
www.skyblues.com/kissrocks.htm

2 Skoal and beech-nut chewing tobacco patches, $1.50
http://auctions.yahoo.com

3 A complete medical history of potential sperm donors, $15
www.thespermbankofca.org

4 A Millennium earth flag, $85
www.earthflag.net

5 A 1950s Davy Crockett coonskin cap, $75
www.deco-echoes.com/futures/items.htm

6 Snoopy and Woodstock telephone and coin bank, $20
www.nisa.net/~rherman/TelephoneA.html

7 Dancing Elvis telephone (his hips swivel when the phone rings), $84.95
www.elvis-presley.com

8 White Trash cookbook $19.95
www.babette.com/white.html

9 Bubble machine with free bubble juice, $79.99
www.coolstuffcheap.com

10 A New Orleans "cookin' with jazz" snowdome, $8.50
www.snowdomes.com/gscatalog.html

11 Teacup-size poodle (live), $700-800
www.cabinpoodles.com

12 A Furby dalmatian inflatable chair, $11.96
www.amazon.com/exec/obidos/ASIN/B0000205Z3/craigbrown/103-
4793666-1314210

13 An ostrich clock decorated with paper toile yellow roses and violets, $288
http://freespace.virgin.net/eggsclusive.design

14 A straw stetson, $99
www.metropulse.com/dir_market/dir_classifieds/260.html

15 Hula girl kite, $45
www.molokai.com/kites

16 A hand-held lightning detector, $195
www.scientificsales.com/conligh.htm

17 Shamrock carriage clock, $32.95
www.vstore.com/cgi-bin/pagegen/vstorehome/tattoothis/page.html?
mode=products&file=/page/prodlistv4/productlist.spl&catid=21774

18 Alcohol breath-tester, $89
www.alcoholbeveragecontrol.com

19 A four-bedroom lakeside home in Texas, $625,000
www.possumkingdom.com/properties/s625g.htm

20 A British gas mask bag, $9
www.roundflat.com/shop/enter.html?target=Military_Surplus.html

21 Modern witch's spellbook, $10
gothicauctions.com/viewcat.cgi?a_050

22 A Professor Bones skeleton, $42.50
www.sciplus.com/new.cfm

23 A set of two devil duckies, $8.50
www.mcphee.com/products/wicked/10676.html

24 A B3 "Party On" beer-making kit, $299.90
www.morebeer.com

25 Double yellow-headed parrots (bonded pair), $1,900
members.aol.com/MayaPets/available.htm

26 Wild Maine blueberry pie filling sample, free!
www.fruitfillings.com/samples.html

27 A pound of rattlesnake meat, $34.95
www.exoticmeats.com/cart/product_items.asp?line=21

28 One day rental of a Viper R/T 10, $849
www.exoticcars.com/pri-ind.htm

29 A pound of maitaki mushrooms, $15
members.dca.net/westmj/mushrooms/

30 Minimum bet on sporting event, $1
www.alohacasino.com

31 Chilean rose hair tarantula, $14.99
www.herpeton.com

32 Kryptolight illuminated crystal necklace, $29.95
members.aol.com/alwysglwng/ppglw.html

33 Boss DR770 drum machine, $349.95
www.zzounds.com

34 A quarter pound of Brother O'Jahs knick-knack blend incense, $35
www.ethnobotany.com/herbs/smoke.html

35 Rajasthan & pushkar camel fair tour, $1,790 plus air fare
www.exoticjourneys.com/monthlyspecial.html

36 16-sided dice, $1.49
www.crazyegors.com/CrazyShop/TreasureChest.html

37 A 6-tape James Bond video collection, $33.49
www.reel.com/movie.asp?mid=131255

38 A Varna II hand cycle, undisclosed
remote-ability.com/frame.htm

39 A Civil War .44 caliber bullet, $3.99
www.southern-mart.com/civil_war_bullets.html

40 Gun holster concealment vest, $49.95
www.azl.com/whacky/vest.htm

41 Good time gecko dog toy, $3.99
www.innovet.net/toys.html

42 Angel chime necklace, $15.99
http://spiritwinds.com/ANGEL_CHIME_NECKLACE.html

43 A Tibetan thangka painting, $175
www.exoticindiaart.com

44 75 assorted 4-6" koi, from $112
www.egardenwholesale.com

45 A day-long tour of Old Plovdiv for one, $30 + $15 for restaurant lunch
www.digitaltravel.com

46 An axis deer, from $300
www.exoticdeer.org/blaschke2.htm

47 A certificate to show you have leased 1 acre of the moon, $15.99
www.universeshop.com

48 A kit fox throw with tails, undisclosed
www.lassitersbath.com/Misc.html

49 A full American belly alligator golf bag, $6,800
www.gatormall.com/afford.accessories1.html#Golf%20Bags

50 A magnetic therapy roll massager, $19.95
www.sharperimage.com

51 Cezanne's *Tree Trunk With Flowers*, pencil & water colour, undisclosed
www.EuropeanPaintings.com

52 A yellow, pink and white diamond watch, $407,275
www.bestselections.com

53 An 8oz tin of edible honey dust, $23
www.romantics.net/scandals/kamasutra/honeydust.html

54 Haji Japanese wind-up astronaut robot, $295
www.spacetoys.com

55 Download Chuck Berry's *Johnny B Goode*, $1.42
stage.vitaminic.com/chuck_berry

56 A 6-hour Kenai Fjords national park cruise, $109
www.alaskan.com/kenaifjords/

57 Edible birdseed church, with plywood frame, $65
www.catalogcity.com

Will you have enough stories to tell your grandchildren?

Yahoo! Travel

DO YOU YAHOO!?